AMERICAN

BUDDHIST

REBEL

The Story of Rama - Dr. Frederick Lenz

REVIEWS

"This is definitely a book that changes your perspective on life for the better....The author is present interacting with Rama throughout the book. We as the reader are made to feel that we are part of the journey and that we are in the room with Rama and Liz."

Independent Book Publishers Association (IBPA)
Benjamin Franklin Award Review

"A biography of the spiritual leader, Rama, this book details the life and teachings of a man who not only brought his followers to a keener awareness of mysticism, but also urged them to take an active role in the contemporary world, urging participation in activities such as digital software development and even presidential politics. The book provides varied stories from students, family members and associates. Some recount seeing light flow from his hands, others saw him levitate, and yet others tell of his practical nature. Rama, whose legal name was Frederick Phillip Lenz, cautioned his students not to view him as a teacher, but to see everything in life as a teacher."

U.S. Review of Books

"This fascinating biography captures the wisdom of a genuine, compelling teacher who combined absolute miracles with humor, fun and adventure. When you read this fast-paced book, you feel you are there, learning and transforming. This is an original and exciting read."

Lynn V. Andrews
Author *of The Medicine Woman* series

"Born Frederick P. Lenz, this elusive young man leaps off the pages of Liz Lewinson's book, showing that magic and enlightenment are available to everyone, right here, right now. She shares the twists and turns of his remarkable journey with warmth, detail, and openness. This book sheds new light on an untold chapter of American Buddhism."

Judith Simmer-Brown
Professor of Religious Studies, Naropa University

"This book presents an honest look into one of the most intriguing and controversial spiritual movements of the 80s and 90s. Rama was a very unconventional teacher and his teaching often caused people to rethink their basic assumptions on spirituality. In a way, he reminded me of my other idols of our age—Bruce Lee, Michael Jackson and Steve Jobs. They were all not only filled with crazy passions about their lives, but were so unconventional in their approaches that they caused major disruptions in traditional values. They were people who believed in themselves, walked their own paths and did not compromise."

Francis Wang
CTO, Xtelligent Inc.

"This book is full of heart and wisdom. It is a clearly written, fascinating story of an extraordinary individual, the lives he affected, and the potential he showed the world for waking up. It was a wonderful read."

Yael Shy
Senior Director, Global Spiritual Life at New York University

"*American Buddhist Rebel* will take you back to your first moments of bliss in pursuit of higher consciousness. Remember, and smile. Remember, and renew your passion for the present moment of power."

Rev. Linda Martella-Whitsett
Unity Church of San Antonio

"I was fascinated, moved, and inspired by this clear and compelling biography of Rama. I found myself very drawn to this true Crazy Wisdom guru who offered so much to his students and who, like all great teachers, also suffered at the hands of those who could not recognize the value of his bodhisattva offerings."

Margaret Wheatley
Author of *Leadership and the New Science*

"I enjoyed this book immensely! I read it in one sitting. Just couldn't put it down. My mind went back to the day in an obscure village in Costa Rica (well over a decade ago) when I picked up a dusty copy of *Surfing the Himalayas* while vacationing. Although Rama had already transitioned, I received a direct transmission from him! Shortly afterward, I searched for a teacher and began the Buddhist path, ultimately becoming a monk. Currently at a crossroad, I have again received insight and encouragement. The Dharma, through Rama's biography, spoke clearly to me."

Venerable Dr. Pannavati Bhikkuni
Co-Abbot, Embracing Simplicity Hermitage

"I truly enjoyed this book. My husband and I knew Rama for a long time as a friend, not a teacher. This book was an excellent read and I learned so much more about Rama's physical and spiritual being and more about his Buddhist history. It's very fast reading, moving and so interesting. I truly recommend it!"

Linda Marcus

"It is the blend of Rama's wisdom and his life journey in teaching groups and individuals across the country that makes this biography so unique: part travelogue, part spiritual reader, and part biography, it's a celebration of his life and perspectives as much as it is an account of how American Buddhism spread across the nation....Any interested in accounts of Eastern religious thinking and growth will find the book filled with unique, perceptive insights."

Diane Donovan
Midwest Review of Books

"A fascinating read about the man that Dr. Frederick Lenz turned out to be. Author Liz Lewinson provides an insider's view of the man— the development of his values as well as his personal highs and lows in the transmission of his teachings. There are amazing stories of natural phenomena, his sense of humor and love of music to help transform human consciousness. He spoke a lot about meditation and I loved his description of advanced meditation as 'Having a wonderful sense of humor, particularly about yourself and your own situation, yet not simply laughing but working to change and improve things, even though, at times, it seems impossible.' Well worth reading!"

June Ryushin Tanoue
Co-founder of Zen Life & Meditation Center of Chicago

"This book is an entreé into the early teaching years and heady days of the controversial and fascinating spiritual teacher, Rama, Dr. Frederick

Lenz. It is a well-written and fast-paced work that engages the reader at once. As a latecomer to Rama's path, arriving long after the delightful accounts in this early bio occurred, and four years prior to his death in 1998, I sadly missed many of the magical experiences and encounters revealed in the book, making the retelling of it all the more delicious for me. As the book shows, Rama was a complex individual with incredible talents, skills, powers, and knowledge. He combined these to create entire worlds of experience, just for the purpose of teaching certain spiritual or practical principles. He was one of the world's greatest teachers for beginners."

Rev. Eva Hermogenes
Zen Priest, Hollow Bones/Mondo Zen Rinzai Lineage

"This book has you feel as if you are right there, learning and soaking up the teachings directly from Rama himself. Don't let this spiritual phenomenon pass you by! You learn so much, not only about the path, but also about yourself."

Hui Reccow
Readjustment Counseling Therapist for Combat Vets

"For those of you too young to have experienced the new-age movement, this book will convey to you the zany optimism of the times, the eclectic world-view, and the lust for adventure that your typical spiritual seeker embodied. I envision historians of the future utilizing this book as reference, a guiding star that places us right in the center of new-age America. If you are genuinely interested in Buddhism, Vedanta, or mysticism this book is a treasure of thoughtful quotes by the PhD Guru Dr. Frederick Lenz. If none of that stuff interests you, it is still a great journey through the spiritual self-help renaissance of the late 20th century."

James Forgy
President, Relational Database Consultants, Inc.

"This is not a regular book. This special book has the power to change lives. You will feel the power as you read it and it brings you to all the events that are in the book as if you were there."

Tracy Z.

"Just reading the first few pages of this book was a transformative experience. I loved the compilation of many students' recollections, writings, publications and stories. They weave a tapestry of what the inner journey is really like—challenging, demanding, enlivening, awakening, humorous, liberating and unending."

Chris Fellows
CEO, Incentive Budget

"If a fully self-realized being walked the streets of America today, would anyone take notice? What would such a being undergo to reestablish their Enlightenment in this life? *American Buddhist Rebel* provides a riveting investigation into this complex Koan by chronicling the life of Rama - Dr. Frederick Lenz. The product of hundreds of well-documented interviews of firsthand eyewitnesses, *American Buddhist Rebel* is the most complete written record I have seen describing the research-and-development aspects of Buddhist Vajrayana and Zen. This is a must-read for anyone interested in the living-breathing-evolving dynamics of the Self Discovery process."

Mo Howes
Author of *Three Storms of Tantric Zen*

"Through interviews, quotes, and personal experiences, Liz Lewinson offers a seat as she takes you on an epic journey of an American bodhisattva and his students. It's a hero's adventure of wonder, impossible odds, self-discovery, and like many great tales, full of love. This book recounts Rama's life as a teacher of enlightenment. Through the years, his teachings would take many forms, but the underlying lesson was always about absolute love, not unlike another great teacher's. Rama and Jesus were (are) very different men, in very different times, facing very different circumstances yet they shared a common thread: that Perfect Love, or Divine Grace to be more specific, transforms and transcends all. It is the ultimate power, the ultimate lesson to be learned."

Rev. Mary-Rose Engle
Interfaith Minister

AMERICAN BUDDHIST REBEL

The Story of Rama - Dr. Frederick Lenz

Liz Lewinson

This book is dedicated to Rama - Dr. Frederick Lenz.

Heartfelt thanks to the over 100 people I interviewed, received materials from or generally assisted with the writing of this biography. Everyone I spoke with was tremendously kind and helpful. Kathleen Forge provided invaluable guidance and insight, B.A. Smith provided foundational support, and Rock Rochte was a giant help in taking the book from first draft to finished production.

In addition, thanks for the inspiration, fun and good wishes of the many Kickstarter backers of this bio.

Special thanks to:

Amelie Marchand	Leslie Roberts
Arlene "Sati" Bellairs	Mark Elton
Carol Ornstein	Michael Mill
Cathy Jean Graham	Michael Raboy
Chinjandra	Mo Howes
Daniel Horton	Norman S. Oberstein
Elizabeth Delgado	Rock Rochte
Jeffrey Sutter	Sebastian Wittenkamp
Jordan Ausman	S. Schindler
Lawrence Harding	Steve Diehl

CONTENTS

∞

INTRODUCTION

In this incarnation I am trying an experiment—I am treating all of my students as if they were very advanced.

- Rama

Growing up in the 1960s, 70s and 80s, flaunting a spiritual life was as cool as driving an offbeat car, advocating for social justice or falling frequently in love. Quiet or flamboyant, it was part of who you were, it defined you. "I am a student of XYZ," where XYZ might be a Tibetan, Indian, Japanese or American teacher who offered an amalgam of East and West. Teachers and students reinvented spirituality, just as the times reinvented views of dress, hairstyles, lifestyles, politics and aging.

For me, the harbinger of a spiritual awakening was a book, *Autobiography of a Yogi* by Paramahansa Yogananda. I read it when I was 16. It was a revelation, an entry into a world of teachers, saints and miracles. At age 19, when I had the opportunity to learn to meditate, I seized it and meditation became my world. Travel, study and terms like "cosmic consciousness" held me happily ensconced in a group of like-minded people. We did not take drugs, we meditated and that was our contribution to society.

I and others who joined new spiritual paths followed different strands but were united in one core assumption—it was our right and privilege to freely explore new spiritual opportunities. Teachers had the right to teach their view of transcendent awareness and students had the right to learn.

Into this exuberant metaphysical potpourri came Rama - Dr. Frederick Lenz. He had recently broken away from his own teacher and in March, 1981, embarked on his first lecture series in Los Angeles. I lived in Los Angeles, a hotbed of guru-hopping aspirants. I had been meditating twice a day in the same manner for many years but suddenly, doubts had dislodged my practice. I had become disenchanted with the guru who espoused the meditation technique and had decided to distance myself from the group and not look for another teacher. After all, life itself is a great teacher. One of my friends, however, always cruised for the latest spiritual bubble. In April, 1981, she saw a poster for "Atmananda" (who later became Rama) and rushed to hear him speak. My friend frequently saw auras—the subtle physical body of energy that surrounds a person's physical body. The aura often displays vivid colors that reflect states of mind. After she heard Rama's talk, she phoned me, quivering with excitement. "Honey, you have GOT to see this man. He's young. He's funny. He's American. He has a beautiful golden aura. I've never seen anything like it. Honey, you have GOT to go."

Over the course of my studies, I had read that golden light emanating from the subtle physical body is a sign of enlightenment or at least of a being who has attained an advanced consciousness. My friend was genuinely elated. She was always inviting me to hear different teachers speak and I always said no. This time, I agreed to go.

I drove to the University of California at Los Angeles (UCLA) to hear what turned out to be the last in a series of ten talks that Atmananda/Rama was giving on that campus. Before I went, I decided to simply be open minded—neither cynical nor hopeful.

I sat about ten rows back in the lecture hall. Rama walked in wearing a collegiate, plaid madras shirt and beige corduroy pants. He looked to be about 30 years old. He had sandy-colored, short curly hair. He spoke very easily about meditation, and I enjoyed the talk. When it came time to meditate, he asked us to keep our eyes open and gaze at him with a light focus. I had never meditated with eyes open before, but OK, whatever. He put on some melodious electronic music.

It was a few minutes into the meditation. I gazed at Rama as he sat in a full lotus position on a professor's desk, the soles of his feet facing the ceiling. I wasn't sure what to look at. All of a sudden, he levitated. By this I mean that in total stillness, without moving a muscle, his cross-legged body rose gently several feet into the air and hovered there in space, above the desk. And then gently, in stillness, without bodily motion, he gently floated back down to the desk. His eyes were closed and I saw him do this several times.

I was surprised but not shocked. After all, a) the group I used to study meditation with claimed to teach levitation; and b) the literature of Vedanta speaks of levitation as one of the powers possible in states of advanced meditation. So, fine. I had just seen an advanced teacher levitate. No biggie. A few minutes after seeing Rama levitate, I was still gazing in his direction. Suddenly all I saw was the desk. No Rama. The desk looked kind of old and scratched. Behind the desk—nothing, no Rama. I kept gazing—where was this man?!?—and about 20 seconds later, Rama reappeared—no physical effort, just profound stillness. This was great stuff, and I had a reference for it—"siddhas." In the literature of Buddhism and Hinduism, a siddha is a magical or mystical power attained by an advanced practitioner of meditation. The group I used to study with claimed to teach people to disappear. But no one, including the guru, ever did. I continued to gaze at Rama, my eyes lightly closed. Suddenly, all I saw was his face, no body at all, hanging upside down in the air in front of me and grinning like a Cheshire cat. 'Saucy siddha powers!' I thought to myself, as I formed a mental smile.

When the talk ended, Rama climbed down to the front of the raised teaching platform at the front of the hall. He spoke to people individually. As I watched, a gap opened and no one stood in line to speak with him. I felt kind of sorry for him—he was just standing there. I decided to say hello and thank him for the talk. When I walked up to him, Rama extended his hand and we shook hands. That surprised me, as most spiritual teachers do not like to do that.

We chatted for a few minutes, then I turned around and started up the cement stairs towards the large, beige metal classroom door. As I walked, warm energy began pulsing up my back along the area of the spine. The energy filled my mind with a deep sense of recognition. It was the most powerful and unusual experience I had ever had, as my feet still walked upstairs. I had never experienced love at first sight, but suddenly, I knew what it might be. Not romantic love, but teacher love. I suddenly realized I had found my teacher, even though I wasn't looking for one. I knew, in the core of my being, I had studied with him before.

My hand hit the bar on the classroom's metal doorway. I kept walking. I had planned to meet several people who also attended Rama's talk that night. We gathered in the Good Earth Restaurant in Westwood. It turned out that four out of five of us had seen Rama levitate and disappear.

I did not enroll to study with him that evening and didn't see him again for several months, and when I did, it was to interview him for an article for the *Los Angeles Times* Features Syndicate. We sat on the floor of his La Jolla home and leaned against a wall while I asked questions and took notes. He wore white tennis shorts. At the end of the interview, I asked to become his student. He looked at me closely and said, "OK." It seemed amazing. Out of the swirling snowstorm of travel, boyfriends, work, study, family, colleagues, hobbies, sports, teachers, teachings and groups, I had somehow encountered Frederick Lenz.

As described in this biography, Rama was a teacher of the mystical, the spiritual and the practical, who regained his past life enlightenment (in stages he described to his students) at age 31, soon after I met him, and then went on to go further in realization. From the time I first saw him—the young, boyish-looking college professor in a button-down shirt—to the time I last viewed him on stage at State University of New York in 1998—the stern, sunglasses-wearing, poised man in Armani clothing—he remained engaged and caring, immersed in the teacher's role. His mantra was, "If I can do this, so can you."

The field of light that surrounded him—a visceral force, like creation merging, mind-melting stillness, a dynamic, luminous fission—grew ever stronger. I started out in 1981 sitting in the front row to soak up the rays and ended up in the back row to avoid energy burn.

Rama said he had a mission—to find his past life students and help reawaken them to the higher mind-states they had known in other lives so that they could attain samadhi in this life, or at least achieve such luminous and fluid states of mind that they could go on to higher and happier worlds at the time of their death, whenever that might be. There are many words written about this type of selfless teaching, but one fact is true—the mission is primarily accomplished non-verbally through the transmission of consciousness—in the form of energy and light—from teacher to student.

Rama was tireless and dedicated in this task. He set up precise and grueling teaching schedules to find new students. Once he accepted a student, he worked with them according to their ability to transform and change. To make all this happen, Rama looked constantly for American ways to bring his students' consciousness out of their stuck patterns and into light.

After 1982, at any given time, he had about 400 students who enrolled to study with him. At the same time, a revolving group of closer students received one on one teachings to the extent they could keep up the learning pace—which might range from ten minutes to ten years, depending on the student.

The path turned out to be much more fun, radical and fast than anyone thought. I was in the general student body of Rama's students for many years, and that was fine with me. I helped out with a few things like selling tickets at one of his public talks (which were soon attended by up to 1,000 people in Los Angeles) and in return, along with other helpers, I would be invited to a special desert trip, or dinner, or an additional public lecture at a venue too small for all the students to attend.

One such invitation was to a class he gave at UCLA. Only those who had helped at his public lecture series at the Beverly Theatre in Beverly Hills were to attend. I went, sat towards the back, and absentmindedly watched Rama move his hands gracefully while he spoke. At one point, a number of things happened at once. I became so still that I felt completely out of my body—lodged in a dimension of nonphysical infinity, like a separate, vast universe looking at this one. Simultaneously, I perceived Rama on the stage, moving the palms of his hands together. As he did that, I saw that he was folding time, shaping it like clay, as if it were putty. My awareness was so far beyond the dimension of time, that I could easily perceive this.

As he continued to speak, I began to feel like I was in void-space, something like being seated at the restaurant at the end of the universe. The voidness or absence was so vast and endless that it made my self-awareness very nervous. Where was my "self"? In a panic, I dove back, back, back down into that tiny little speck called my body and FWAM!, I was back, stuffed into a shoe that was suddenly way too small. Habit and fear brought me back. And there was Rama, up on the stage, and I saw that he was performing classic *mudras* (movements that shift energy) and had been doing that all along, for years, but I had just never noticed.

I began interacting more closely with Rama in 1987. In the years of my study with him, and with his encouragement, I had gone from a free-lance writer earning $300 per month to a Hollywood public relations executive, a senior vice president at a television and film studio, earning six figures. So in 1987, when a surprising, false and distorted media article about Rama erupted onto the front page of a major California newspaper, he turned to me for help. I was not well prepared. During the 80s, I had not had a lot of experience with trash and burn journalism. I had been trained in classic ways—present your side of the story with credibility and dignity.

Yet for me, the twisted journalism crafted by a small group of people, every one of whom was affiliated with an organized, criminogenic hate group, was a strange opening. I began to interact more with Rama, and one of the most amazing things I saw was that he turned every opportunity, even the darkest intentions against him, into uplifting learning lessons. His power and light grew as adversity increased.

To stand up for what one knows is true is a privilege; it is the ultimate dignity and surrender. I was afforded that privilege by standing up against the false media coverage that Rama received. I did not bow to the darkness that attempts to destroy light. Hey darkness, get a clue! You can't destroy light. It just changes forms and gets brighter. You can, however, destroy darkness by rooting out its causes.

Rama's life as a teacher was not easy, even without absurdist media. Enlightened ones such as Rama are completely psychic and sensitive—sensitive to toxicity in their surroundings; to the psychic detritus of an overpopulated planet; to their students' unresolved needs, mind-states and jealousies. It all worked together to make it more painful for Rama to simply exist. Because of his sensitivity, Rama was often in excruciating physical pain. He said his samadhi was the way beyond bodily pain. From time to time, he quoted a line from the film, *Lawrence of Arabia*—"You don't mind that it hurts."

In 1998, he came up to me at a small New Year's Eve gathering that he held for people who had helped him on his staff that year. The gathering was at a French restaurant in Pound Ridge, New York. We were all dressed in our New Year's best. I wore a sleek black pants suit. Rama wore a tux. The restaurant had two floors, and I met Rama on the stairway. He looked thin and pale. He leaned his tall frame against the wall, folded his arms, looked me in the eyes and held my attention. "You will be my biographer," he said. He adjusted some knobs in my being.

I sensed his intent—wrapping things up—and responded, "Yes, but it's not time for that yet." Three months later—April 12, 1998—he was gone.

This biography covers Rama's life from his birth in 1950 through his early teaching years (1981 to 1989) when he set down many of the major tracks of his teachings. Remembrances of over 100 students, family members and professional associates are presented, along with his own words from impromptu gatherings, recorded talks, printed literature, videos, etc.

Throughout the biography, many of the students' most vivid recollections involve the siddhas—Rama's playful displays of enlightenment. Not all siddha masters are enlightened, but Rama stated that his teaching of enlightenment for the West would include displaying the siddhas because the times merited it. Witnessing a siddha power— or "miracle" or "Buddhist magic" as Rama termed the manifestation of the higher strata of 10,000 states of mind—created an opening that allowed Western students to believe in the possibility of enlightenment.

Descriptions of siddha powers—such as levitation, disappearance, growing very tall, becoming very small, clairvoyance, clairaudience and more—are found throughout the literature of Hinduism and Buddhism. From Patanjali's *Yoga Sutras* and Yogananda's *Autobiography of a Yogi*, to accounts of the great Tibetan teachers such as Padmasambhava and Milarepa, the ability to perform the siddhas comes with the territory of higher awareness. Siddha powers are never a goal in themselves, they are one expression of higher awareness, and the choice whether or not to display them is left up to the teacher. Whether or not the aspirant actually sees a siddha and what they actually see, is dependent on the teacher, the state of mind of the aspirant and the aspirant's mental conditioning.

Whether meditating with Rama in a lecture hall or in the desert, Rama's advice was to practice beginner's mind. This is a state of openness, no expectations, and ideally no thoughts. Rama never announced a specific action ahead of time. Instead, he manifested a range of bright, unexpected, often humorous displays of higher awareness, gently nudging his audience into other dimensions of being. And then, meditation over, he matter-of-factly asked what people saw. Mirroring Rama's tone, perceptions of profound spiritual phenomena were reported back in a matter-of-fact tone.

"I like miracles," Rama said. "They inspire me. Miracles cause you to believe, to have faith in the unseen, to look further into things, deeper into things. Miracles are the fun of enlightenment. When a teacher does a miracle—an enlightened teacher—and someone sees it, they're astonished. Suddenly they have faith in what the teacher has to say about self-discovery and spirituality and enlightenment."

In addition to giving thousands of talks to the public and his students, writing books and recording audio tapes and videos, Rama produced music. At his encouragement, three student musicians formed the band Zazen (originally called Nirvana) and worked closely with Rama to convey the state of enlightenment through music. Between 1986 and 1989, they released 14 albums. By 1997, a total of 31 albums were created. As the band improved, Rama would sit and meditate while the musicians cut the final tracks in a studio. He said he inserted enlightened energy—timeless luminosity, available to a listener today and forever in the future—in between the notes.

As a music producer, midway through each song, he introduced a transition from something simple—that the students and the band were comfortable with—to something more complex that would challenge both listeners and players. He said that midway through each incarnation, his teaching would go through a similar transition.

Throughout the course of Rama's life, he had several names. His birth name and legal name was Frederick Phillip Lenz III. Friends and family called him Fred or Freddie. The teacher he studied with for many years gave him the name of "Atmananda," which means bliss of the soul. In late 1982, as his past life enlightenment returned, he received an inner bulletin that he had a new name—Rama. This biography calls him Freddie, Fred, Atmananda, or Rama, according to the timeline of his life.

In their own way, in their own cultural setting, enlightened teachers find ways and means to express the ineffable to help their students grasp higher and higher rings of awareness. Rama did this for 21st century seekers and beyond.

1

THE MAGICAL, THE MYSTICAL, THE ENCHANTED TACO

This solidity is not true. The apparent solidity is the delusion of the senses and of the self. Everything is made up of infinite, intelligent light. If you look into anything, you can follow that light back to its source, which is everywhere and nowhere, which is nirvana, which is enlightenment. - Rama

I learned to love the beautiful, still, mysterious desert with its deep silence and vast empty spaces, its wild beauty as the sun set and the stars came out, lighting our path, the gangly shrubs and ocotillos. I learned about the desert because of Rama. He found the desert for us, his students, a particular sacred spot where we gathered, sometimes several times per month in the early days, to meditate and watch him perform those effortless, humble, whimsical and delightfully unimaginable miracles. We went to a place where, Rama said, it would be easiest for us to "see" into other dimensions. It was a place where he could nudge his Western students forward.

We typically spent seven or eight hours at a time there, meeting in the late afternoon, hiking in, meditating in several spots, devouring our respective snacks during breaks. Often we would emerge at dawn. The young college students, lawyers, doctors and people like me, the West L.A. publicist, who comprised his student body, would enter the silent desert world with our fixed ideas of self and reality and emerge brand new, our fixed beings dissolved in light and introduced to new worlds and states of awareness.

He advised us to tighten up our lives before going to the desert. That meant scrubbing the house, filing papers, paying bills, ordering cabinets and tossing excess. The office and tasks at work were to be in the same polished condition. When the physical world is in order, the mind is free to soar. He advised us to exercise, stretch and get enough rest. "You are preparing yourself for a journey into the world of enlightenment. If your body, mind and spirit are happy, your journey will be more fulfilling and successful." I followed these suggestions and they worked.

Leaving Los Angeles, I would drive at first on the main highways then turn off onto the winding mountain roads that led to the Anza Borrego desert. Stopping at a Denny's, I would find other students, new and old, all clad in jeans and hiking sneakers. The excitement level was so high that self-doubt was wiped out. We were en route to the unknown, a wild-eyed band of seekers!

Rama invited all the enrolled students to join him for Christmas 1983 in the Anza Borrego. At the appointed desert location (a mileage marker on the side of the road), lots of other cars were already parked and pulled off to the roadside. I assembled all my gear into my first-ever cloth backpack, a nifty gift from my father. According to the weather service, the temperature would fall into the low 40s during the night. I was armed with layers of clothing, long johns, down jacket, two hats, scarves, and a number of small self-heating packets that you rubbed together and inserted into your gloves and shoes. The packets generated instant heat and took the stress out of cold temperatures.

Then I added food that I'd prepared and made sure everything was placed in perfect order. OK, ready, go. I walked 1/10th mile into the desert and met up with over 300 other people, put my pack down in the sand, and sat to meditate and wait for Rama. It was 5 p.m. and already getting dark.

When Rama, clad in shorts, sneakers and a sweatshirt, arrived, we fell in behind him as he began to hike at a brisk pace several miles up the dirt road leading into the gorge. The line became long and straggly as people hiked at their own pace in the soft sand. No flashlights were used, no conversation. Just the crunching of sand under feet, desert shrubs lining the path.

Eventually the line veered off to the right, towards the base of a mountain. Rama waited quietly at the foot of the mountain. The waning moon began to rise. We sat in a circle around him in the sand. As soon as we had settled down, he stood up, raised his arms toward the sky, then dropped his hands down towards his thighs rapidly with a loud whooshing exhalation. Within moments, a light wind came down the gorge. The wind hummed around my head in tendrils and wisps. It was cold yet soft. I felt it was checking me out and doing some housekeeping, blowing away my hard and tough spots. Rama exhaled a second, powerful, WHOOSH. The wind grew stronger.

I glanced up at the night sky, a vista of stars so packed together they looked solid, sparkling unlike anything you can see in a city or suburb. So many stars, they looked like a mass of glittering, tiny Christmas lights.

"Watch this," Rama said. I looked in his direction and saw two beams of blue light emanating from his raised hands and shooting up into the night sky. Then, as I looked at the sky, that solid panoply of twinkling light began to whirl in dancing patterns—artfully, joyfully twirling in artistic shapes.

I looked at Rama again. He spoke in a deep voice, "Watch this." I saw him grow very tall, half the size of the mountain behind him. Then he disappeared, reappeared, and skated across the semi-circle of open sand that had been formed between our group and him. When I say skating, I mean that within the space of one second, with no visible movement, he zoomed from one edge of the circle to the other, a distance of several hundred feet. No footprints or track marks on the sand. I wanted to laugh aloud but just let joy permeate my being. Complete stillness and ecstasy.

Rama turned to us and asked what we were seeing. I did not speak, but people reported observing the sky fill with light, and Rama dashing across the sand without touching it at all. Someone said she saw him zooming up and down the mountain behind us like a kite on a string.

We stopped for a break and to eat the treats each of us had brought in our backpacks. I knew from previous desert trips what I loved. I ate a tuna sandwich and a small chocolate bar and drank canned apricot juice and bottled water. Some of my friends brought thermoses of hot beverages, but I loved my Kern's apricot juice. It was a feast. No food on the planet could taste better.

After the break, we packed up, carefully picking up every drink can and scrap of paper, and shouldered our packs for another walk deeper into the gorge. Rama explained that the power was greater as we walked further into the gorge. He would only take us as far as we could handle.

The next gathering spot felt different, somehow older, cooler and deeper. Rama asked us to watch him. He became very still, flickering in and out of visibility. Suddenly, I saw him become a tall thunderbird, like the ones in American Indian art. The vision lasted several minutes. "What did you see?" Rama asked. I called out that I saw him become a thunderbird. He nodded. Then another person said they saw him become an ancient Egyptian bird. Rama then asked us to meditate with our eyes closed. I closed my eyes. I became aware of the gentle wind, still playing around my ears, and as my mind settled down, I became aware of a city of pyramids, one after another. They stretched out endlessly. Then my mind merged with stillness.

When we opened our eyes, Rama said that he had shown us a world that was like the ancient pyramids. Someone called out that they saw a wide oval shape behind Rama. "Ah," said Rama in a deep Irish brogue, "the enchanted taco." That got a few giggles.

Rama asked us to lie on our backs and look up at the sky. This time the sky looked different. It had a reddish hue. All the constellations and galaxies were different. I could not recognize any of them. I felt a tug at my solar plexus. I felt not in or of this Earth. It was like looking out the window of a spacecraft and taking in the star map of another galaxy.

After some time, Rama asked us to sit up. "What's happening out there?"

Someone said they saw the stars disappear and reappear like fireflies, with lines of light criss-crossing the stratosphere.

"I think we went to a different world," I called out.

"We did," Rama replied.

As Rama stood before us, I saw him become transparent, then disappear. When he reappeared, all I saw was luminous white fibers in the shape of Rama. I saw him growing shorter and taller. The images flipped quickly, like watching a deck of old movie cards.

After a few more comments, Rama announced it was time to pack up our gear and begin the hike out. A light wind began to blow at our backs, pushing us gently forward. I saw countless bright pinpoints of colored lights in the air around us. We silently walked out of the gorge in a long, scattered line and met again near the blacktop road.

The first light of dawn streaked brightly along the horizon— vivid orange and sunflower yellow sunlight peeking through morning clouds. We spread out and formed a circle. We stood facing Rama, who gazed at each one of us in turn for about 10 seconds. When our eyes met, the magical journey was sealed, and a band of gold light connected us. The sand in the circle looked like a flowing riverbed of golden light. Rama asked us to thank the desert. He said we never knew when we would be back, but that the desert was now a special place for us. He said that whenever we returned we would find him there.

As the circle of 300 people broke apart, Rama reminded us to drive safely. For those heading back to San Diego, he recommended a taco stand. For me, returning to Los Angeles, I knew I would marvel at the luminous person who would soon stare back at me from a Denny's restroom mirror.

Several nights later, at a student meeting during the gap between Christmas and New Year's Eve, Rama commented on the desert journey.

"Here I am, I have all these students of mine out there and I'm trying to make them aware of nonexistence. And to be happy in their lives. I'm trying to help you have a breakthrough, right? So I'm doing all this great stuff, and it's stuff you can't even see, and if you could see a fraction of what I'm doing, you'd all run away and hide! It's true.

"Now we're out there and remember the moon is flashing? Remember I'm bringing up the winds? The world is exploding in color and lights, and there's transformation in your feelings, and all these things. But nobody's believing any of this. It's great! You're all experiencing it, but what I mean by believing it is that none of you are taking it all the way down to your total self. You're experiencing it, but you're separating yourself from the experience.

"What I'm trying to do is open the doorway to your being so you can fly out into nothing. But what you're doing is you're saying, 'I'm experiencing. Ah, look what Rama is doing, showing us some scene or some other kind of thing.' That's not it—that's not my point. That's not why I'm doing it. What I'm doing is showing you where the sun sets so that you can become the sunset itself. That's what we're talking about."

Rama pointed out that he does the same thing in lecture halls as he does in the desert, but it's easier to see in the desert.

2

GROWIN' UP AMERICAN

Frederick Phillip Lenz III (Rama) took his first breath in an American body at 4:29 p.m., San Diego, California on February 9, 1950. He said that he selected his parents according to the classical Tibetan model: spiritual mother and successful father. Seeing the horrors that lay ahead for Buddhist monks in Tibet[1] and seeking a warmer climate than the Himalayas, he opted to incarnate in a culture that had no experience or knowledge of ancient lineage teachings but would at least be open to their practice.

His mother, Dorothy Gumaer, was a graduate of Sarah Lawrence University and a trained, practicing astrologist. His father, Frederick Phillip Lenz, Jr., had recently completed his line of duty with the U.S. Merchant Marines and was starting out in the field of advertising sales for magazines.

Dorothy and Fred had moved from Connecticut to San Diego, California, shortly before their son's birth. Although Dorothy was ahead of her time by about two decades with her deep interest in astrology, and Fred was perhaps behind the curve with his conservative, traditional Catholic beliefs, they were optimistic that the warm San Diego sunshine would melt their differences.

Baby Fred's ancestry ranged across Western lineages and cultures. His grandfather on his father's side, Frederick Lenz, was German; his grandmother was Irish (the McDonalds). On his mother's side, his grandfather, Albert Gumaer, was French-Danish; his grandmother was Irish (the O'Reillys)—making Rama half Irish, half French-Danish-German.

When Freddie turned three years old, his parents decided to return to Stamford, Connecticut, where they had met and where

---

1 Communist China invaded Tibet in 1950. There was a concerted effort to destroy Buddhism and the intelligentsia, with hundreds of monasteries destroyed, and thousands of nuns and monks murdered.

Dorothy's parents had a large home. The return was necessary—Fred Jr. had not found work in San Diego that could sustain his small family. For the next year, the young Lenz family lived in the Gumaer residence. Dorothy maintained and nurtured a vegetable and a flower garden. Freddie and his mother were very close, and she told him, based on her study of his astrological chart, that he was a rare soul destined to help many people.[2]

Rama recalled that his first experience of samadhi was at age three and a half. "My mother would play with me in her gardens. There were times when I would look at a rose or a marigold or daffodil, and suddenly time would stop. I would become clearly and cleanly aware of the presence of immortality. The rose garden became an endless eternity. I would wander alone in fields of light. I had no concept of time, but even as a child, I felt a surrender to divine ecstasy." It was only later, as experiences of samadhi returned in his late teens, that he understood what had taken place in the garden.

Freddie did not share his experience of merging with eternal light, even if he could, and instead assumed that all children and adults had the same experience, easily entering into states of awareness that were joyful, infinite and permeated with ecstatic luminosity.

When Freddie was four, the family moved to their own house in Stamford. Initially, he was enrolled in a Catholic school where he was an altar boy, which he loved. During the winters, the family went on skiing trips and Freddie quickly showed an aptitude for winter sports. During the summers, Freddie loved to go sailing on his grandparents' sailboat.

His parents' relationship, however, hit the rocks. The spiritual divide between Fred and Dorothy widened. It was the 1950s, very few people were practicing astrologers. The study earned zero to minus respect from most quarters and especially not from conservative Catholics. There were few to no outlets for intelligent, spiritual women to express themselves. The 1950s glamorized alcohol intake (and smoking). Increasingly frustrated by the marriage, she began to

---

2   Almost 40 years later, Gaye Nelson, a well-known Los Angeles astrologer, reviewed Rama's astrological chart at his request. She said that he had "the most gigantically overloaded stack of karmic contracts" she had ever seen. "Karmic contracts," meaning people he was supposed to help.

drink. After her third sojourn in an alcoholism treatment center, she announced that she wanted a divorce. In the Connecticut of 1957, divorce was unusual and handled with punitive measures. Dorothy won her divorce and soon remarried, but she lost custody of Freddie, who remained with his father. Freddie was now seven years old, his mother had moved far away to another town in Connecticut. He was rarely able to see her. She was lifted like a chess piece out of his life. For several years, while his father worked in New York City, Freddie was raised jointly by his maternal and paternal aunts and uncles.

Freddie's father relied on (or deferred to) the Catholic Church for advice and guidance. A member of the church to which he belonged was a recently widowed woman with two young sons. 1960—three years after the divorce—it was inconceivable that a woman could work and raise a family single-handedly, or that a single father could succeed. A friendly priest conceived the notion that Freddie's father and the recent widow, Joyce Slavin, should marry for the sake of the children. They did, in 1960, and the former Slavin family moved into the Lenz Stamford house. This was not a marriage of love and it was a challenging arrangement.

One problem was that young Freddie and his stepmother did not get along at all. She took an instant dislike to her new stepson. He was pulled from the stricter, more expensive Catholic schools and enrolled in public schools. By this time, his father was an account executive for the main publication of the advertising industry, *Advertising Age*. His commutes to work in New York City became longer each day and family time was sparse. Freddie's younger stepbrothers were in need of a father figure and often occupied the time and space that his dad had available to give for fathering duties.

Freddie often was left to spend time alone. One day, relegated to the house as it rained steadily for several days, he went into his father's library and found a set of eight unopened books on Buddhism. He avidly read them all. He found the teachings familiar and the explications of Buddhist canons and sutras easy to follow.

Freddie was brilliant and strong-willed. After altercations with his stepmother, or his father, he would leave his home and stay with his uncle and aunt for days at a time. His uncle, Edward Lenz, a former Marine who fought at Guadalcanal during World War II, was a patrolman on the Stamford police force. "Uncle Eddy" supported Freddie's strong will and provided wise counsel. He had faith in his nephew's abilities and gave him encouragement and perspective. Freddie respected his uncle for the hard work and service he put into his duties as a police officer and saw firsthand how service to a community is performed. Ed Lenz and his wife, Louise, were a stable, loving force in Freddie's youth. Nonetheless, from age 10 onwards, Freddie looked more to the support of friends than to his family for love, feedback and support. Fortunately, he made friends easily. If he felt despair, it was quickly countered by an innate brightness of spirit.

Rama referred to his adolescence as a "very confusing time." He started dating at age 14 and always had girlfriends from that time forward. In school, he did very well in subjects taught by teachers he liked, and poorly in subjects taught by teachers he did not like. He intuitively objected to being placed in a box of other people's ideas and expectations when he found them limiting. As a teenager, he mounted a sign on his bedroom wall, "To Thine Own Self Be True." Rather than limit his spirit, the indignities of his family life made him independent, self-reliant.

Rippowam High School in Stamford played host to a mixed demographic—poor mixed race to wealthy white professionals. Initially Freddie was a target for schoolyard muggings. He got tired of having his lunch money stolen and decided to enroll in a nearby Tae Kwon Do martial arts school.

"This was Korean Karate, and it was in the mid-sixties, before it was softened somewhat for Westerners," Rama later explained. "They made us do push-ups on our knuckles and thousands of kicks, and we'd run on the beach barefoot in the winter. It was torture but they taught us good martial arts. Before and after each martial arts session, our Korean masters made us meditate. We would sit on our knees and practice controlling our thoughts. Doing this, they claimed, would make us better martial artists. They didn't give us a choice, we just had to do it. That's how I became interested in meditation. I sat on my knees on the hardwood floors and stopped my thoughts completely." Freddie acquired the martial arts skills he needed to defend himself and the muggings stopped.

When he received his driver's license at 16, he was finally able to drive on his own to visit his mother. It was a milestone, something he had looked forward to for years. The regular visits began—to a nursing facility. His mother had become gravely ill. She gave him two pieces of advice before she died—to keep his sense of humor and to periodically see astrologers. Freddie was 16 years old when she passed away.

Rama recalled, "I remember that after my mother died, when I was quite young, I tried to find her. One day, perhaps just several months after she had left the body, I was driving in my car and suddenly I thought I'd go visit her. I lived in southern Connecticut and she lived in eastern Connecticut. I had forgotten for a moment that she was no longer alive, strange though it may seem. Suddenly I was about to turn my car—it was just an inspiration. I was driving along and thought, 'Gee it will be nice to go see Mom,' and suddenly I realized or recalled of course that she had died, just several months before.

"And I was surprised that it had slipped my mind. How could I not remember having gone to a funeral, all the things that occur when one we love dies, and it seemed strange to me. But yet she had always been there, and then she was gone. And I realized that she was no longer on earth.

"In other words, what I'm suggesting, and this is, I think, a common phenomenon for many of us, is that when a person first dies, someone we've been very, very close to, we intellectually accept that they have died, that they are no longer with us, but something inside of us doesn't necessarily accept that right away. It takes a while, and I think it's only until much later, when we're alone, that suddenly it dawns upon us what's really happened, that someone we've been very close to is gone. And I remember thinking, as I was driving on the Merritt Parkway in Connecticut, that my mother was no longer in this world, that I could search anyplace I wanted to and not find her, that that presence, whom I had called 'Dorothy,' was not to be found. It had returned to the source."[3]

In 1965, his father ran for mayor of Stamford, Connecticut and was elected. This was a source of pride and also pressure for Freddie—it was important that he toed the line—not easy for a free-spirited youth. In 1967, Freddie graduated from Rippowam High School with many close friends and a mixed transcript: A's in topics he liked, such as English and Music, and C's in the classes he was not interested in.

Rama described his childhood to his students.

"When I was very young," he said, "it was very clear. The way was apparent. Then they sent me to school, and things became very, very confusing. Fortunately, I had an interesting balance. I had two parents who were somewhat unusual. On the one hand, I had a father who was

---

3   Lenz, Frederick (Rama). "Death and Reincarnation." *The Lakshmi Series.* Los Angeles: Lakshmi Inc., 1982.

strong and kind and loving beyond, at least in my case, anything that I could understand, and at the same time, who was extremely puritanical, who had been raised in a religious tradition with extensive morality. I had a mother who was very developed psychically and spiritually, who was very remarkable in many, many ways. She was, in a way, an opposite [of my father], a complete liberal in every sense of the word, interested in women's liberation before it was the fashion, believed in reincarnation, psychic development, all kinds of things.

"It was interesting to have both a very conservative and very liberal parent, because we deal with both of these elements in the world, and we have both elements within ourselves. So at an early age, I found the world a very natural place to be. I was always in a meditative consciousness as a child, which all children are. Then they sent me to school. And school was a strange place, where they tried to make you into something. Not simply what they taught you, but they presented a description of the world to all of us which was very limited and narrow. While I don't doubt the intentions of the people who did it, what they passed along was incomplete. They only passed along, of course, what they had been taught.

"I found that the breakthroughs for me, as I went through school, junior high school and high school, came through sexuality, came through explorations of consciousness, in reading and in loving, through friends, through time alone in nature, and through psychedelic experiences. I had been pretty well made a prisoner by school, by society. I had been given this description that I couldn't accept, and it was projected from the televisions, the radios—the images of the world, the teachers.

"In reading, in literature and poetry, I found an artistic freedom that I didn't see at Woolworth's[4]. I was drawn to the arts because I sensed that I was by nature Bohemian, and yet, very conservative. How strange to have two natures. I would read a great deal, all kinds of things, everything from Shakespeare to science fiction. I read voraciously for years and years, sometimes a book a day. I learned a lot from my friends in school. I had lots of friends. Yet I was very indrawn.

"I didn't really want to be a part of the world because I found that the world was filled with unkindness. People didn't love each other.

---

4   Woolworth's was a five-and-dime variety store that was ubiquitous in American neighborhoods during the 1950s.

They didn't understand. In every home in America, in the world, there was cruelty and anger and hatred and things that I didn't feel. And so I found friends who were somewhat similar, a little bit, and didn't think about it too much—because life just takes us where it will.

"I found, growing up, that love and sexuality was a wonderful way to understand existence. When we love it takes us beyond our self, otherwise we're just absorbed with the preoccupations that we invent. But when we love someone, we can do something magnificent. We look beyond our own immediate needs and we become more concerned about the welfare of another.

"I was attracted to poetry, which is perhaps the purest of the art forms, where love is the medium of exchange, and the nobility of love is considered. It's a land of higher ideals. I was very drawn to music, all types of music from Beethoven to Jimi Hendrix—finding that a great deal of music offered nothing but the description of the world that I was given in school, but that there was creativity in music, there were musicians and composers who were expressing a vision that was beyond the mundane, beyond the ordinary.

"Then, of course, as was the fashion, I explored alternate states of consciousness at one period of my life through psychedelics, as was the fashion with all my friends—we all did. It was a time period, I suppose, in the 1960s, when a generation of souls, or part of a generation in a particular country, looked at the established society, looked at the pettiness, the greed, the hate, and rejected it and tried to create something new. Their creation neither succeeded nor failed. It was another experience. We sought a tribal society—to be close to each other, not to sit behind a television with our families and not see our families, not just to watch the evening news and the inane comedies designed to pacify the multitudes, but rather to explore ourselves, to come to some definition of what this world is, what life is, to at least live it while we are here. So we experimented and we experienced many altered states of awareness. We used the power plants, and I did that for a year or two."[5]

Freddie was a classic child of the Sixties, ready to throw off old conventions and not trust anyone over 30, but he had that strange secret. The moments of time out of time, the strange sense of past life

---

5   Lenz, Frederick (Rama). "Sophisticated Sexuality." *Insights: Talks on the Nature of Existence.* Los Angeles: Lakshmi Inc., 1983.

recollections, the samadhi in his mother's garden that made his blue eyes deeper.

In the U.S. in 1967, the hippie movement was in full swing on the West Coast. Right out of high school, Freddie decided to head west to experience it. He wanted to learn about life from the real world, not books in a college. He, a friend and a girlfriend drove across the country, found a small studio apartment in the Haight-Ashbury district of San Francisco and set out to live the free-wheeling culture of the time. His friends soon returned to the East Coast, but Freddie opted to stay. After several months, he decided to head south to San Diego to check out the surfing scene and pursue his fascination with board sports.

One of the first friends he made in San Diego was a neighbor, a pot-smoking, Grateful Dead-loving man in his 20s with long hair and an easy manner. He joined Freddie for social gatherings where marijuana was smoked, and Fred was glad to have a friend who knew the scene. He trusted his new friend completely. Several months later, Fred found out that his friend was a police informant who, as part of his parole, had been tasked to find "weed-smokers." In the fall of 1968, Freddie was arrested for possession of one ounce of marijuana (in California today, this is 100% legal), sent for trial and given a one year sentence—that was then reduced to nine months and later expunged from his record—at a fire fighters' work camp in the hills above San Diego.

The result of this betrayal was an intense and transformative education, and an awakening.

The Southern California mountains were known for exploding with fire in the hot summer months—one careless campfire spark could ignite a blaze that threatened homes and lives in a swath of small mountain towns. The minimum security work camp was nestled on a mountain top surrounded by miles of low shrubs that were capable of setting off a fiery blaze. The task given to Fred and his fellow inmates was simple—to clear and remove low lying brush and prevent fire from spreading, if it were to break out.

The work camp also offered education to its population of perpetrators of lesser crimes—many of them illegal immigrants who could neither read nor write English. Some were illiterate in their native language. In addition to his brush-clearing duties, the tall, poetry-loving East Coast teenager with the clear blue eyes was assigned to teach them English as a Second Language or simply to help them become literate for the first time.

It was at the work camp that Freddie discovered he had an aptitude for teaching. As a teacher, he could transform people's lives. He recalled the wondrous feeling he experienced when someone who had not even been able to write his own name could do that for the first time—the look of amazement and joy in their eyes. It was thrilling for him.

It was also there that Freddie began to seriously practice meditation. "The setting of the work camp was actually very beautiful, high in the mountains above San Diego," he later told a group of students. "We spent a large part of the day clearing brush. We were out under the open sky, the smell of rosemary and sage was wonderful. We were always seeing deer, coyotes and foxes. We were not busy all the time so I began meditating regularly, just to keep occupied.

"I would sit out there around twilight and focus on my third eye, and everything would become still. Rings of light would appear, and I'd go through them. Then suddenly I would be beyond time and space, beyond life and death. I would dissolve for what, an hour, a lifetime, eternity—there are no words. And I was changed by these experiences. I went into samadhi for the second time in my life there.

"I did not know what to think of it, but when I emerged from that timeless state, it was as if I knew something, an arm was pulling me—I had to visit the Himalayas. I still had about six weeks left at the work camp, but I knew that when I left the camp, I somehow would find a way to get to Nepal."

When Freddie was released from the work camp in August, 1969, he'd gathered new viewpoints and the love and respect of 55 Spanish-speaking work camp inmates and the work camp supervisor. As he said later, he made mistakes in his youth—who doesn't—and he learned from them. He now wanted to attend college and travel, and that meant earning money. He returned to Connecticut and landed a number of part-time jobs, including working for a nursery as a tree-topper. With the funds he collected, he was able to invest in a surfer's long board that he re-engineered for early snowboarding adventures with his friends in the local mountains of Connecticut.

In the late Sixties, small travel ads flourished on the back pages of most metro newspapers. In particular, the ads offered cheap flights to Kathmandu, a rite of passage for hippie youths. By December, 1969, Freddie had saved enough to book a multi-stop flight. He figured he could stay at youth hostels once he arrived. His luggage consisted of a backpack and his big, ungainly long board. He had no conscious desire to do anything other than snowboard in the Himalayas.

When he arrived in Kathmandu, the teeming town was packed with sadhus and Western hippies from many nations. Freddie checked into a youth hostel and found that the tallest mountains were several hours outside the city. The next day, the American youth with wild, long hair and classic hippy clothing set out early in the morning to hitch a ride to the mountains. The Nepalese were accustomed to such kids and he had no problem getting rides. He was dropped at the foot of what his Nepali driver designated the highest mountain in the region. Freddie was in excellent shape from the months of brush-clearing. He climbed many hours to get to the top.

Once at the peak, running out of daylight, he had two choices— to go back down the steep, unknown slopes on his rustic snowboard or to stay at the top and freeze to death. After double-checking his ropes and other gear from his backpack, including flares and a strong flashlight, he hopped onto the board and began his descent.

What happened next became the subject of Rama's 1995 book, *Surfing the Himalayas*, the chronicle of his teenage spiritual adventure and transformation in Nepal. Long before the book was written and published, however, he told his early students that his descent down the mountain had gone well, that he was nearing the bottom of the mountain and traversing a relatively mild slope when, to his astonishment, an old, short, orange-robed man seemed to materialize about ten yards in front of him. Astounded, Freddie did not even think of swerving until the very last minute. By then it was too late. The sound was somewhere between a smack and a thud. To his extreme embarrassment, he had snowboarded directly into a diminutive monk. They both toppled into the snow.

"I was too wild and full of teenage independence to ever have listened to him," Rama said. "But after I hit the monk with my snowboard, I felt guilty and indebted to him. I was shocked to the core of my being. That was the hook. It was only later that I connected him to the experience of samadhi I had at the work camp on the mountain top in San Diego. I realized that it was his call that led me to Nepal."

The monk he had slammed into was the head lama of an old monastery that was kept hidden, even from most of the Tibetans and Nepalese people. The lama said he had been waiting a very, very long time for Freddie, longer than this lifetime. He told Freddie that in the future he would be a great teacher in the West and that Freddie would carry on the teachings of a lineage that had almost disappeared. That he (Master Fwap) was passing along these teachings to Freddie. Master Fwap predicted that Freddie would become the new lineage-keeper who would revive the teachings and help millions of people. Naturally, Freddie was incredulous.

As he later wrote in his book, *Surfing the Himalayas*:

"Master Fwap," I began, "I don't understand any of this. I came to Nepal to snowboard the Himalayas, not to learn about enlightenment and the secret teachings of your Buddhist Order. I don't mean to complain, but are you sure you have the right guy here?"

Master Fwap smiled at me and didn't say a word. Then he closed his eyes. Several minutes passed and he still didn't respond to my question. As a matter of fact, the expression on his face was so peaceful, I was afraid that he might have drifted off to sleep.

As I sat on the yak-hair rug in Master Fwap's small, clean and comfortable room, a very strange thing began to occur. The air in the room began to thicken and turn a beautiful, bright, golden color—not all at once, but very gradually.

At first I thought it was "snowing" golden light around Master Fwap. I noticed the phenomenon first around his head; then the golden light seemed to spread all around his body, and finally it filled up the entire room.

Seeing the golden light surrounding Master Fwap's body, my first thought was that something must have happened to my vision. I rubbed my eyes with both of my hands in an attempt to clear my sight. But it didn't make the slightest bit of difference. The color of the air around Master Fwap and in the room remained a soft and beautiful gold.

As I watched in amazement, the golden light that was filling the room became even thicker. After a few more minutes, I could barely see Master Fwap at all, even though he was sitting directly across the table from me. Then I felt my entire body beginning to tingle with a prickly heat. It wasn't an entirely unpleasant sensation, just unusual.

I lost consciousness of the passage of time. Master Fwap and I could have been sitting in his room for five minutes or five hours; I couldn't tell the difference. I did notice, however, that my mind had become clear, composed and relaxed. In fact I felt very good, probably better than I had ever felt before in my life.

As timeless time passed, another awareness began to overtake me: without any apparent effort on my part, I suddenly understood everything. Not that there was anything in particular to understand; I suddenly just "knew" all about life. I realized that I was one with life, and at the same time a separate and unique part of it.

It was then that I first knew that Master Fwap was enlightened. Somehow I could feel inside of his mind—and I knew it was made up of the pure golden light. I also knew, without knowing how I knew, that the golden light in Master Fwap's mind, and the golden light that was currently filling up his room, was the light of enlightenment.[6]

Freddie spent several weeks in Master Fwap's humble monastery. Master Fwap embraced Freddie as an apprentice and brought him through a series of profound teaching experiences that would change his life forever.

At the end of their work together, Master Fwap counseled Freddie to go back to the USA, obtain an advanced degree in college, seek the best spiritual teacher he could find and learn as much as he could from that teacher. It would then be Freddie's role to teach on his own and carry on the knowledge and experience of enlightenment to others in the West, sharing the knowledge that he had learned from Master Fwap and reviving the ancient lineage of Master Fwap's Buddhist order, the Rae Chorze Fwaz.

Freddie left Nepal, intending to follow Master Fwap's advice. About the predictions, he was not so sure. Freddie could agree with

---

6   Lenz, Frederick. *Surfing the Himalayas*. New York: St. Martin's Press, 1995

Master Fwap that he return to college and do exceedingly well, and that he should seek a spiritual teacher in the U.S. But Master Fwap's prediction of his greatness as a teacher, as someone who would help millions of lives, was so far from his difficult upbringing, his life in America, his recent stint in a work camp and current circumstances, that he set aside the idea. Perhaps one day it would make sense.

3

ACADEMIA AND STUDYING
WITH THE GURU

As I am sure you are aware, sexuality is the primary focus of our culture, and almost no one has come to resolve it. Most people are terribly afraid of their own sexuality, and one has to respect another person's sadhana, another person's path. - Rama

Known for its liberal arts curriculum, the University of Connecticut at Storrs sprawls across a green, leafy campus in northeastern Connecticut. Freddie arrived there in the Fall of 1970 with strong motivation from Master Fwap to succeed. He received no financial support from his family so he had to balance work and study. He continued tree topping, something he could do on his own hours when not in class or studying. He also hand-crafted dulcimers and gave occasional performances in local coffee shops.

From his first semester at Storrs, he began a pattern that he employed throughout his academic years. Instead of waiting to interact with a professor after the class had started, he interviewed teachers in advance of enrolling in their classes, to ensure he was making the right choice. Freddie felt that the teacher was more important than the topic. Many professors were surprised to see a gangly youth show up during their office hours, during which, on a typical day, not a single student crossed their doorstep. Freddie sat on their worn office furniture and engaged them in discussions about their work and selected classes based on those discussions.

In this manner, he became close friends with many of his teachers at Storrs. In one of his recorded talks, Rama stated, "When you study at a university with a great professor, and I was fortunate enough to have many, if you observe them and not simply what they say, but what they are, you will learn a great deal. I was very fortunate. I had one professor, Dr. Charles Owen at the University of Connecticut, a Chaucerian. I spent a great deal of time with him, not only in class but I participated in a special group of honor students who would come over to his house because we all fell in love with him. He was this marvelous old man. He was an old scholar, but he had an animate spirit; he was alive.

"I would go to Dr. Owen's house, and we used to study certain archaic books, which I really didn't have much of an interest in, to be honest with you. But he was fascinated by them, and I was fascinated by him. So I was willing to put up with the books for him. I loved to be around him. There was something in this man, some deep truth that touched me. I would sit and listen to his lectures on these old texts and I would study them, just so we could be together because what interested me in him was what he was, his essence. That's what I fell in love with, and that's what I responded to, and I wanted to be like him. I felt a goodness that I responded to, and I fell in love with it."[7]

From his first semester, Freddie received straight A's in all his classes. It helped that he had a photographic memory, but he also became an enthusiastic learner, going beyond the assignments to read and question more.

During his undergraduate studies at Storrs, as he engaged in wide-ranging discussions with his professors, Freddie encountered professors who shared his interest in metaphysics. Two of his professors shared their past life experiences. These conversations spurred him to start keeping a journal that recorded such conversations, by whom and when.

There was no one to tell him of the concept of a *tulku*, a person recognized as the reincarnation of a self-realized lineage teacher. Instead, Rama said, "I meditated on my own for some time, read spiritual books, became a vegetarian and had incredible experiences every day, every meditation, where I was just thrown into the infinite—never realizing that other people didn't necessarily have those experiences in meditation that quickly. I never considered myself to be special. If anything, I considered myself to be awkward."

Soon after enrolling at Storrs, Freddie spotted a poster on a campus bulletin board. "Study with a Master," it proclaimed. The

---

7   Lenz, Frederick (Rama). "Love, the Fourth Level of Ecstasy." *Insights: Talks on the Nature of Existence*. Los Angeles: Lakshmi Inc., 1983

poster featured the photo of an Indian teacher named Sri Chinmoy. Sri Chinmoy was relatively new on the Eastern religion teaching circuit. He had obtained his Green Card in 1967 and embarked on teaching meditation classes at universities. Wherever he went, Chinmoy encountered students eager to learn and adopt classical ways of Indian philosophy. Chinmoy's mixture of meditation, devotion, extreme sports, music, poetry and art appealed to Freddie. He seemed to fulfill the assignment he had received from Master Fwap—to find the best spiritual teacher he could and to study with him.

According to Rama, "I entered a spiritual community when I was 20, which I was in for 11 years, with very strict meditative and eastern ritualistic practices. It was very much like a religious order. At the same time I went through college, graduate school, received a Ph.D. and started to teach. The training was rigorous, hundreds and thousands of hours of meditation and self-giving. But it was easy. I loved it. I would merge again and again with the superconscious in meditation.

"I liked my teacher very much and after some years of meditation, after mastering basic techniques and levels of attention, I began to teach meditation, teaching only that which I knew and referring all things that I didn't know to my own teacher. As the years progressed and I learned more, I tried to share that with my friends, because in meditation I found light. I found sincerity, purity, and a quality of experience which few people seem to have in this world. I became very convinced that by practicing meditation, one could have a life that was uncommon, remarkable, because I found that happening to myself."[8]

One of the first steps toward becoming a teacher on behalf of the guru's organization was to learn hatha yoga and teach it. After attending the yoga classes, promising students would be told about the Chinmoy seminars. Freddie loved hatha yoga. His stepsister, Lisa, recalls that when she was five years old, she and her brother Freddie would sit in the family's basement playroom as he enthusiastically and patiently taught her yoga postures, and from that she gained a lifelong love of hatha yoga.

At age 21, Freddie spotted a woman in one of his classes who captured his attention. Her name was Pamela Wardwell, age 20. "Marriage was his idea, not mine," she said. "He was the one who came

---

8   Lenz, Frederick (Rama). "Sophisticated Sexuality." *Insights: Talks on the Nature of Existence.* Los Angeles: Lakshmi Inc., 1983.

up to me and said I was the perfect woman for him." After a short courtship, they married on the Storrs campus. At that time, Storrs did not allow marriages on the campus, but several of Fred's professor/ friends took a stand—make an exception for this couple. The pair both wore white, and they were married under the trees in front of a small group of friends and family. Asked about his impression of the May 1971 wedding, one family member could remember only one detail— "It was outside!"

The honeymoon consisted of a camping trip in Iceland. Icelandic summers brought long daylight hours, wild flowers, abundant birdlife, travel through the uninhabited interior. Freddie loved doing a perfect job of setting up their tent, assembling the moving parts of the tent with care, creating a secure environment for the couple. After the honeymoon, Fred and his wife moved into a small apartment near the campus. Six months later, as Fred realized that he was not cut out for marriage, the couple separated and later divorced. Later, he often referred to his marriage as a painful but excellent learning experience:

"In my early life, in my adolescence, love, as I think for most of us, was a tremendous focus. I wanted to find the perfect partner—I did, I married her. Then I realized after being married for some time that, while I could go on being married and that was a wonderful way to be and I'd actually found the most remarkable woman or she had found me or whatever, it wasn't enough. It wasn't enough to lead an individual life where I loved one person and we created a world together. I couldn't be happy, I was too restless, too strange, too possessed by this love of light. I just had to be alone because I had to spend my time working for others; I just knew that I had to do that."[9]

After the marriage ended, he lived in a home that a friend described as a quaint, rural, one-story dwelling along a well-wooded country road in northeastern Connecticut. Fred assembled a photography darkroom in the basement. His house was done in the décor of the day—student Bohemian—with an unusual roommate perched on a pedestal in the middle of the living room, Ariel by name, a toucan by nature. Visitors to his house kept a respectful distance from Ariel, whose long beak was capable of maiming fingers and wrists. But

9   Lenz, Frederick (Rama). "Sophisticated Sexuality." *Insights: Talks on the Nature of Existence.* Los Angeles: Lakshmi Inc., 1983

she and Fred were gentle friends. Fred's admiration and kinship with birds was a constant throughout his life.

In the spring of 1973, Freddie graduated Phi Beta Kappa (A's in all classes) from Storrs. He was awarded a State of New York Graduate Council Fellowship and decided, based on the quality of the English Department, to attend the State University of New York (SUNY) at Stony Brook.

Compared to the Storrs campus, Stony Brook was a behemoth—1,039 acres of land, primarily forest, set a short distance from the Atlantic beaches of Long Island's North Shore and the vineyards at the East End. Fred achieved a Master's Degree in English Literature within one year.

According to a Stony Brook colleague and classmate, Christopher Chapple, now Professor of Indic and Comparative Theology at Loyola Marymount University, "Fred was respected by his peers for charting a smooth and efficient course towards his Ph.D. We worked on various cooperative projects together, including organizing a festival for yoga and meditation at the student union and a concert for a popular fusion band—John McLaughlin and the Mahavishnu Orchestra—at Stony Brook. Fred had a wide and eclectic music collection and an appreciation for all types of music.

"We shared stories about our gurus," said Chapple. "Fred was with Sri Chinmoy, and my wife Maureen Shannon and I studied with Gurani Anjali, founder and director of Yoga Anand Ashram in Amityville, New York. We met at Jones Beach on Long Island Sound and swapped different spiritual viewpoints."

In 1974, Fred was thrilled, said Chapple, to receive a spiritual name from his teacher.

In both Hinduism and Buddhism, receiving a spiritual name from a teacher is considered a major transition in a seeker's life. It means that at some point in their practice, the student achieved a high state of awareness that transcended their former, limited self. The spiritual name denotes a new self.

"Atmananda," a Sanskrit term for bliss of the soul, was the new name bestowed upon Fred. Going forward, many of his friends and all of his fellow guru students called him Atmananda. (This biography also will refer to him as Atmananda for the time period he used that name.)

In 1975, Atmananda applied for and was accepted into the Ph.D. program for English Literature. Stony Brook presented a gourmet menu of scholars and poets with whom he could study. Atmananda was most drawn to study with the Pulitzer Prize-winning poet, Louis Simpson. "I have this disease," Atmananda said. "I fall in love with people. In graduate school, it was the man who directed my dissertation, Louis Simpson, who's a poet and a marvelous scholar—I took as many courses with him as I could because I fell in love with him. I fell in love with that aspect of eternity that reflected in him—his strength, his beauty, his vision, his mental clarity—I fell in love with his consciousness."

Atmananda seized opportunities to interact with Dr. Simpson. He enrolled in all his classes, primarily to be around him. "It didn't really matter what the subject was. I learned what he said. I passed his examinations. I wrote the papers. By affixing my consciousness to him, I gained something. I didn't do it to gain something, to be honest with you, I just fell in love and found myself doing it. Love creates a bridge, a bridge between peoples, a bridge between nations. The absence of love is war, hate, enmity, fear."[10]

At the same time, he pursued his other study. Almost every Wednesday night, Atmananda, often sharing his old Saab with friends, embarked on the 50-mile journey to the chapel at Columbia University in Manhattan where Sri Chinmoy held meetings, and drove on weekends to Sri Chinmoy's converted warehouse in Queens, usually to meditate for hours with the guru.

The Queens facility featured high ceilings, a painted blue floor and white walls. The walls were decked with photos of the teacher and his artwork. The students practiced guru yoga—devotion to a teacher. Whenever the teacher entered or exited the main hall, the students stood and put their hands together. They sat down after he sat down. The male and female students sat separately, on opposite sides of the room, the women dressed in saris and the men in white pants and a plain shirt.

Atmananda always wore white pants to the gatherings, although he erred on the side of plaid shirts. He looked forward to the long meditation sessions. Once he took his place among his fellow meditators, he would close his eyes and merge with light. What puzzled him was the fidgeting, mental agitation and physical restlessness of his fellow meditators. Since meditation was natural for him, he couldn't

<hr>

10   Lenz, Frederick (Rama). "Love, the Fourth Level of Ecstasy." *Insights: Talks on the Nature of Existence.* Los Angeles: Lakshmi Inc., 1983.

understand why everyone else was having such a hard time. He also didn't "get" the emphasis on celibacy. In fact, after the long meditation sessions, he and a fellow Chinmoy student sometimes went to nearby bars to party (i.e., meet girls). According to the friend, all the women in the bar would soon flock to Atmananda's table while he (the friend) got dates because of his association with Atmananda.

As a chasm grew between his experience and the philosophy imparted by his spiritual teacher, Atmananda explored the theme of physical body versus spirituality in his Ph.D. thesis, *The Evolution of Matter and Spirit in the Poetry of Theodore Roethke.*

"It was interesting," Atmananda said, "because in Roethke's earlier poetry, he was very drawn back and forth. On the one hand, he wanted to have the spiritual quest; on the other hand, he was drawn towards love. And he found in the two this terrible dichotomy, that certain forms of spirituality seemed to set up, where the flesh is bad and the spirit is good, and he struggled terribly in that. I identified with that because I went back and forth. But then ultimately, in his later life, he came to see that body and soul are one, that everything is the same, that everything is spiritual.

"Roethke came to feel that both the impulses of his body and soul were holy. He no longer believed that his physical body was a stumbling block to higher spiritual realization and he acknowledged that simply suppressing his physical desires would not lead him to the enlightened states of consciousness that he sought. He had come to realize that instead of suppressing his physical desires, he had to transcend them. By doing this he believed that he would eventually attain a state of mystical illumination."

Atmananda struggled in real life with many of the same issues that Roethke's poetry explored. Love in all of its manifestations was a vivid daily realization, a core element of his growing ecstatic awareness.

"As my meditative experiences grew," Atmananda explained, "I had wonderful relationships. I met the most wonderful men and women who meditated and shared certain spiritual understandings that I had. And our time together was invaluable, as was my time alone. I was drawn to be very solitary as a scholar. I lived a very quiet life with my books, with my walks in nature, and meditating, of course, with my teacher, and living in the world of a spiritual community. At the same time, I was very drawn to people I loved, to my family, to my father, to my sister, to my brothers. So a large part of self-discovery was quite personal. It had to do with relationships, with people.

"Some of the most exalted states of consciousness I experienced were in bed with someone—or alone or with my spiritual teacher. There was never a difference for me. I became aware, as time went on, that this was not necessarily an ordinary experience, because I lived in a community where celibacy was the rule, with the word 'rule' underlined; where one, as a matter of fact, was expelled, from the community if you were not celibate.

"My own teacher knew that I always had a girlfriend. I never kept any secrets from my teacher. I saw many people asked to leave the ashram for so much as looking intensely at a member of the opposite sex. For some reason, my teacher never said anything to me about it, which I never understood. I wasn't going to argue! I loved my teacher and I wanted to be there. But I also knew that I loved other people too, and I just couldn't give up one for the other because it didn't make any sense.

"I seemed to be leading a very incongruous life from the point of view of the definition of the community I was in. Yet I noticed that my brothers and sisters in the community, my friends, were not too happy. They seemed to have a lot of trouble with sex. It was a very touchy subject for them. Some of them looked quite askance at me, as a matter of fact, because they knew that I had a girlfriend, which was, of course, against the rules. They didn't understand why my teacher tolerated it. But I had a respect for all the students of my teacher because I felt that if they were with my teacher, they were special.

"As time went on," he recalled, "I changed. The more I worked for others, the happier I was. The only incongruity in my life was that I had a girlfriend! Everything else seemed to be going well. I went through terrible times. I went through times of self-hate, thinking how undeveloped spiritually I was. [Out of] everyone else in the ashram, a thousand people, nobody had a girlfriend or boyfriend. I did. Honestly, I went through terrible, terrible times where I just took myself over the coals. I thought I must be the most impure person in the world, but because that is reverse egotism, I thought I must be the second most impure person in the world!

"Yet I found the experiences that I had with sexuality were wonderful, they were very uplifting—we had a good time—and they didn't seem to affect the level of my meditation. My meditation kept improving. I seemed to be able to help more and more people all of the time. So it was quite incongruous. But I perceived that other people couldn't necessarily do this. I realized that many of the brothers and sisters that I had, my friends in the ashram, needed to be celibate, because for them sexuality was a very tacky issue."

On the sexuality/celibacy issue, Atmananda later explained to his students, "Over the years of much self-doubt, I came to realize that whether sexuality was in my life or not, which at times it would be and at times it wouldn't be, it didn't seem to matter a heck of a lot, and I just surrendered the whole thing to God, and I said, 'God, if I'm supposed to be celibate I will be, and if I'm not I won't be. It's up to You, it's not up to me. Who am I to be so vain as to think that I know what's right? Only You know what's right.'

"As the years went on, I found that my relationships got better. They changed though, as I changed. In the process of the years of meditation and self-giving, self-analysis, I found that I no longer loved as I had formerly done. As I went on, the relationships got better and better. And they meant less. The relationships that I had became more and more impersonal, yet had more love in them. It's an odd incongruity. I loved more but I was less attached. In other words, my love was no longer bound by the body, it was a love of spirit."[11]

As he meditated more deeply, there were other spontaneous discoveries—the return of past life powers and realizations. He accepted his abilities matter-of-factly. When he met people or when interacting with friends, he often saw their past lives as visceral perceptions that momentarily overtook his present awareness. He could see their deepest tendencies and desires. His own past life recollections began.

"Psychic powers developed, my meditation increased and I found myself changing, over and over again, becoming someone new almost every day. The form that I had known, the person whom I had grown up with, went away. And someone else would come, another self that was a little more refined, that had a little more purity, a little more humility—not too much, a little more—because I was quite egotistical, I thought I was quite wonderful. I did very well in school, I had lots of honors, so I thought I was quite smart. I of course had to find out that that's quite ordinary, if you work hard."

11   Lenz, Frederick (Rama). "Love, the Fourth Level of Ecstasy." *Insights: Talks on the Nature of Existence*. Los Angeles: Lakshmi Inc., 1983.

Atmananda's intuition became perfectly sensitive. He loved long walks through the surrounding forest with its narrow, lightly maintained paths. Once, 20 minutes into a winding pathway through the Stony Brook forest, he realized he had lost one of his contact lens. He turned around and retraced his steps and at one point put his hand down. There was the tiny lens.

In 1977, he began teaching meditation for credit at the New School for Social Research in Greenwich Village. Every week for a year and a half, Atmananda and his Chinmoy student friends would poster the surrounding area to attract people to the talks he gave in a New School meeting room with pillars and a hardwood floor. New Yorkers of all types—students, Wall Street bankers, lawyers, yoga teachers—sat on pillows in an open space. Atmananda spoke and meditated and then, if people came back, he invited them to see his guru.

Atmananda also offered weekly meditation classes at the Stony Brook student union, a 4 p.m. and a 7:30 p.m. class. After the classes, the group would be invited to a house on Dale Road that several of the Chinmoy students shared. Chief party chef Atmananda would cook and serve vast amounts of student fare such as Mexican food and huge omelets.

"12 Dale Road was like Camelot," said a fellow Chinmoy student. "In the guru's world you never had men and women together. In Stony Brook, we were always together. When Atmananda came to the house and did meditations with us, it was way off the charts compared to the guru. Atmananda's energy was a celebration of life in myriad forms. That's what came out in Dale Road. He was going into samadhi. I saw someone in a professorial, collegial structure. He was love, celebration and creativity. He started blossoming spontaneously, he was teaching everywhere in New York. He would fill the East West center with 300 people, but it was not the guru's energy, it was him. He was pulling far away from the guru but still kept within the formal group.

"When Atmananda cooked, I had never seen so much food in my life. He would invite people from the student union meditation classes to Dale Road and stuff them with food and light. He invented a board game called the reincarnation game. One night, I had a vision. I told him about the vision, that he was going to become enlightened. After that, he humorously called me 'The All-Seeing Duck.' We were all close friends who loved each other like family."

As he worked diligently towards his Ph.D., Atmananda built up his physical strength. He took up sailing, taking the college's small sailboats into the bay. He ran long distances and was a powerful swimmer. One friend recalled that in the summer of 1978, he and Atmananda were chatting as they hung out on one of the beaches off Long Island Sound. They often swam together in an inlet and looked across the water towards a small peninsula, about one quarter mile from the beach. They knew that to swim to the peninsula, they would have to go into the water at peak tide, otherwise the currents in the Sound would sweep them out to sea. That afternoon, at peak tide, the pair set out to try it.

"We swam from the shore at a brisk pace, and I soon became aware that the current was much greater than I'd anticipated," the friend recalled. "Nevertheless, we continued swimming. About two-thirds of the way across, I was tiring rapidly and falling behind Atmananda. I mounted a desperate effort to catch him, as he looked like he would make it. I failed. I looked up, utterly exhausted, only to see myself drifting past the peninsula. I noticed Atmananda had just made it to the tip. I had absolutely no strength left, and I was being dragged well beyond land. I was surprisingly calm and resolved to my fate, although it did seem sad to be dying so young. I looked over at Atmananda and saw him jump back in the water. It really didn't register that he was coming to save me. I was about seventy-five feet past him but he reached me in seconds.

"Atmananda held me up as the two of us floated in the current, waiting for my strength to return. Atmananda had brought hope with him. I felt we would make it, though the odds were against us. We were well away from land, and there were no boats in sight. Our best chance appeared to be a swim of about three-quarters of a mile in to shore. Atmananda assured me my strength would return, and that we'd make it.

"At that moment we saw a boat, and miraculously it was heading in our direction. The boat came right up to us, and the people on board lifted me to safety. Our friends back at the beach had flagged down this boat to help us. To my total amazement, Atmananda stayed in the water and decided to swim for shore. I urged him against this, but he insisted and said he'd see me at the beach.

"The boat took me back to our friends. Our concern immediately shifted to Atmananda because he had a long swim still ahead of him.

We spent some anxious moments, but Atmananda soon came walking towards us along the sand."[12]

One hour later, Atmananda was home again, reading homework and writing papers.

Films such as *The Last Wave, The Deer Hunter* and *Star Wars* became part of the Stony Brook group's seeker vocabulary, even though the Chinmoy set thought movies were generally low-vibe and unspiritual. References to current films became part of how Atmananda taught. In the classes, he also started playing music he liked—electronic music by Walter Carlos and Tomita, and classical music such as Bach. This was frowned on by the Chinmoy crowd. Atmananda developed his own teaching format, where people would describe their meditation experiences. Even then, said a friend, people had powerful experiences that were still, transcendent and different enough to come back and participate regularly.

Atmananda also traveled extensively at his teacher's request. In addition to the New York teaching, he taught meditation classes in Germany, France and London. Often, his talks would cover the topic of reincarnation.

Local radio shows in the U.S. began to contact him to speak on reincarnation, and Atmananda often spent hours on the phone, talking to skeptical radio hosts and the public. He often shared the true stories he had gathered since his early days at the University of Connecticut— stories of ordinary, non-mystical people suddenly plunging into vivid experiences of a past life. Whenever he spoke of his story collection on radio shows, either during or after the show, more people would contact him to share their own past life experiences.

By the middle of 1978, Atmananda had amassed 127 past life stories, and he shopped the idea of a book to East Coast literary agents. James Seligmann liked the book proposal and the funny, articulate, 28-year old author. On Atmananda's behalf, Seligmann landed a book deal with Fawcett Crest. Atmananda was to deliver a completed manuscript by the end of 1978 in order to meet Fawcett Crest's 1979 publishing schedule.

Atmananda presented his Ph.D. thesis in August of 1978, and it was accepted. He was now Frederick P. Lenz III, *Ph.D.*, and his next task was to deliver a completed book in a four-month time frame. In the

---

12 John. "Journeys." *The Last Incarnation*. Los Angeles: Lakshmi Publications, 1983. PDF p. 187.

meantime, the guru asked him to go to Switzerland and give talks on meditation, which he happily did.

Atmananda's approach to *Lifetimes, True Accounts of Reincarnation* was formal and disciplined. He analyzed the 127 stories from the point of view of place, age of the experiencer and other statistical data points. He mapped the stories to *The Tibetan Book of the Dead*, the ancient Tibetan treatise on death and dying, and demonstrated the similarities. He used the book to introduce readers to the main concepts of reincarnation, describing the different viewpoints of Buddhist and Hindu philosophy.

As he worked on the book, Seligmann used the first few completed chapters to pitch another book by his budding author. The new book would be called *Total Relaxation, The Complete Program to Overcome Stress, Tension, Worry and Fatigue*. Bobbs-Merrill Company liked what they saw and commissioned Atmananda to write it.

In mid-1979, having delivered the *Lifetimes* manuscript to Fawcett Crest and started work on *Total Relaxation*, Atmananda met privately with his guru who suggested to Atmananda that it was time that he open up a laundromat in Queens and spend the rest of his life running it. For Sri Chinmoy, this was not an unusual idea. Professions such as running laundromats and selling food from street carts were standard fare for Chinmoy's students. Atmananda, however, was disappointed. He had hoped that because he had earned a Ph.D., had authored two books and taught all over the world on his teacher's behalf, his teacher would divine a better recommendation. Atmananda pondered a way to end the dilemma.

Several days later, Atmananda returned to his teacher and suggested that, rather than open a laundromat, he instead try to make a living by opening a Chinmoy center in San Diego. To Atmananda's delight, Chinmoy agreed, and on July 31, 1979, Atmananda and five of his close friends and fellow Chinmoy students boarded an airplane and flew to San Diego. Several other students who had been attending Atmananda's lectures in New York came separately.

They had no idea of where to live or how the center might come to be, but they trusted in their friend Atmananda's increasing hours immersed in samadhi, vision and competency. That, plus their friendship, their white pants and saris, comprised the assets they carried with them to the golden state.

4

SHIFTING WEST

July in San Diego—the sun shone brightly with a clear, dry heat. The sky vibrated like an iridescent blue bell. The flight had been smooth and the luggage collected safely. Two rental cars, with Atmananda at the wheel of one of them, wound their way north on the eight-lane Interstate 5 freeway. Inside the vehicles sat a unit of friends in awe of their good fortune. The road ahead looked spectacularly clean, wide and beckoning.

They drove to the home of a fellow West Coast guru student. Soon, with his help, a small La Jolla house on Cliff Ridge Road was rented. To keep costs down, Atmananda shared the new house with two of his old friends from the Dale Road house in Stony Brook. The friends enrolled in computer science classes at the nearby University of California San Diego (UCSD) campus, and Atmananda formed the San Diego Meditation Center.

The center began modestly. Atmananda taught public meditation classes in several locations—Balboa Park in San Diego, UCSD and San Diego State. The New York friends, accustomed to wrangling posters onto the crowded windows of jaded New York deli owners, found it much easier to place their intriguing signage, with quotes from Carlos Castaneda or a range of Eastern spiritual books, on the windows of San Diego's shopkeepers. The posters included Atmananda's picture—a clear-eyed young man with short hair and a tailored, preppy shirt—inviting all to learn to meditate.

The La Jolla home's small backyard was private, covered with grass and filled with flowers. There, Atmananda sat on a meditation cushion, not willing his meditation to start but simply absorbed in light. As he sat, eyes closed, for hours at a time, a smile played on his face. People noticed a radiance around him. When his roommates returned from school, they would enter the house quietly so as not to disturb him.

At age twenty-nine, Atmananda was going through his astrological Saturn Return, a time when people who have been enlightened in past lives are likely to regain their enlightenment. The San Diego setting served as a nurturing and powerful place to ignite transformation. To augment that transformation, Atmananda increased his teaching schedule.

Initially, attendance at his talks was small, perhaps ten or twelve people, typically young college students. After the talks, Atmananda invited those who wanted to learn more to come up to the front of the room to meet him. He then assessed the person's readiness to join the smaller group of students whom he worked with at the house. Atmananda stated that he taught on behalf of his teacher, and that if they wanted to attend his smaller classes, they would have to sign up to be accepted by Chinmoy.

One of the first new students to join this matrixed organization was Helen Frith, a freckle-faced 16-year-old high school student whose stepfather taught at UCSD. Her stepfather had picked up one of Atmananda's posters and taped it to the family's refrigerator door. While searching for the pepper jack cheese, Helen would study Atmananda's photo and read, "Let Me Share with You the Coolest Thing I've Ever Found—Meditation—and Experience It for Yourself."

Helen tagged along with her parents to a UCSD classroom in the Fall of 1979. The family found Atmananda's presentation to be clear and the meditation experiences to be light and high. They found him impeccable in his motivation, which he stated repeatedly—to help people, to be of service.

When Helen showed up at the smaller classes at Atmananda's house, he acknowledged her ability to see into the psychic realms, telling her she had "20/20 vision in the inner worlds." She spent most of her free time at his house, helping and observing her new teacher.

In late February, 1980, a student who was an avid hiker told Atmananda about a little-known spot in the Anza Borrego desert that seemed to have a special resonance. The next day, with his housemates and Frith packed into the front and back seats of a small car, Atmananda drove east to the desert. The group left La Jolla at 9 a.m.

Two hours and countless mountain switchbacks later, they parked alongside a deserted two-lane highway that snaked across the desert floor. The air temperature had risen 25 degrees from their La Jolla starting point. Shouldering their daypacks, they walked together along a dirt road that led into a small, canyon-like area. It initially seemed unremarkable. Four-wheeler tire tracks marked the surface of the brown and ivory sand. Because of recent rains, the ground was relatively firm. Tall, spiny ocotillos bloomed with brilliant red flowers. A soft wind blew. The group walked down the road for about half a mile.

"I observed Atmananda walk, stop and still his mind," said Frith. "Earlier, at one of our meetings, he had spoken about the guardians, an ancient race of enlightened beings that guard access to inter-dimensional planes that exist in specific places on the Earth. When I was a kid, we used to go camping in the desert. But I'd never felt guardian beings before. I never felt ancient, native warriors around. This time, I could see and feel the guardians in this small canyon, and I knew that Atmananda saw and felt them as well.

"I observed that he simply created a polite greeting. It was utterly respectful, a touching lightly. Atmananda did not have a relationship with them yet. This desert visit seemed to be about getting acquainted—a hello, how are you. I suddenly experienced a familial feeling with all the beings there that I had never felt before. I felt we were in a sacred place. Atmananda spent less than an hour with us in that spot.

"On the drive back, Atmananda was very quiet. I think he had already been recognized by those beings. The same energy band that was in the desert was going right through his house in La Jolla. There wasn't that much between the desert and him, just a few mountains."

The group returned home before sunset, hiked down to the beach and meditated. A week later, Atmananda returned to the same spot with 18 of the San Diego students. This time, they walked further into the gorge and meditated together. They stayed until almost midnight, and Atmananda experimented with showing them some of his returning siddha powers—exploding vast auras of light across the desert sky. He told the group that ancient guardians were watching his antics with delight.

"He led us on incredible adventures, yet he was older-brotherly, making sure that everyone had eaten and no one was dropping out of school or work at whatever level," said Frith. "He was like a black belt teaching on behalf of the master. His whole motivation was for people to be happy. He would ask his friends, 'What can we do to help people? What do you think they need?' It was all he focused on.

"He always kept a yellow legal pad on his table. I once looked at his TO DO list, and everything on the list was a specific, actionable idea to advance the cause of meditation to help the students. He sat down every morning to see ways to make the students happy and then he would write up his list. When I saw the list, I felt the level of sacrifice he made. But in his mind, it was just a good use of his time."

In this small, microcosm La Jolla teaching environment, Atmananda "the student," "the writer," "the best friend," "the athlete" fell away. He was those things, but he became something more. He began to meditate throughout the night. Experiences of ecstasy, pure stillness, dissolution in light were not intended, they simply happened. At times, the limbs of his legs locked into place as he meditated. He told his friends that his mind was merging with planes of light. When he emerged from his experiences of samadhi and made lists of ways to make his students happy, he wrote based on deep inner seeing. He was learning and becoming selfless.

By early October, a consistent group of 20 people, almost all college students, regularly showed up at Atmananda's house. Atmananda's powerful energy, the freedom and joy in thought-free meditation, was infectious. And he loved sharing. Every week, the group would go to movies together. Atmananda usually selected the film to see, finding just as much truth in over-the top-silliness as intense drama. 1979's iconic films included *The Muppet Movie*—Atmananda lip-synching Kermit the Frog—"I want to go to Hollywood and make millions of people happy;" *The Jerk*—Steve Martin one-liners; and at the end of 1979—*All That Jazz*—with the one-liner, "It's showtime!"

The 20 became a small group of friends with Atmananda, sharing what he was feeling and learning why he was doing what he did. The Chinmoy link was peripheral. "Some people were into it but I just ignored all the Chinmoy stuff—like big photos of the guru and people wearing saris—because we had so much fun together," a student noted. "Going to the movies was like a high meditation. We'd watch the screen and suddenly, we were in this different level of knowing. It was remarkable."

1980 began with increasing signs of success for the San Diego Meditation Center. Atmananda drew larger audiences at his public talks. University students spread the word about this new meditation teacher—young looking and funny, college professorial, yet so clear in his presentation and practice that a palpable transformation was available for everyone who sat and meditated with him.

It was noted repeatedly by newcomers to his lectures that when he first came into the hall or classroom, his demeanor and dress were so modest that they had no idea he was the instructor they'd come to hear. But as soon as he began to speak, and once the meditation had started, there was no doubt who was the teacher in the room.

At the house, he interacted with each person individually, checking people out to see if he wanted them in that room. To a young woman clad in barely-there dancewear, he said, 'You have to be really committed to be here. You have to work hard at it. It is not casual, you have to give it your all. It may seem casual on the surface but there's a lot going on beneath the surface."

Atmananda spoke of a truth and a conundrum. On the surface, he purposefully presented a laid-back, informal demeanor. He rejected the pageantry—such as bowing when the teacher entered and left the room—of the Chinmoy group. The surface—the casual dress, electronic music for meditation, fun interactions at dinners, movies, outings—comprised Atmananda's sensibility about a different way to teach. But beneath the surface, as the year went on—with a busy teaching schedule, numerous teaching/learning excursions to the desert, a commitment to the transformation of students and ever deeper and more luminous immersions in samadhi—a formal change took place within Atmananda that required recognition.

5

THE TEACHER EMERGES

In early September, 1980, the Chinmoy student who had helped Atmananda move into the Cliff Road house purchased a home on La Jolla Farms Road in La Jolla and rented it to Atmananda for a nominal price. A California ranch-style house, it featured a spacious living room with high plate-glass windows, a pool and a grassy back yard. Perched on the bluffs near UCSD with a spectacular view of the ocean, it was a pristine setting—a place of power—a place conducive to higher seeing and meditation. The new dwelling charged, changed and accelerated everything.

Before the move-in, the house was in poor condition. All the friends got together, repainting everything from sash to ceiling, putting up dry wall, creating a Zen garden. Atmananda chose a sky blue color for the carpet in the large living room because the color would make it easier to meditate. The house was polished to immaculate cleanliness.

When the house was ready, Atmananda and his roommates from the previous home moved in, sharing the rent. Immediately upon move-in, Atmananda was drawn to a sunlit spot on the cliffs, a small, triangular point jutting out into the sea. The first time he meditated there, sitting in a full lotus position, he entered into samadhi, later explaining to his students that the term was "salvikalpa samadhi."

> Salvikalpa samadhi doesn't just mean having a really high meditation where the room fills with light and everything is bright and shiny and you feel one with the dharma and the flow. That's not salvikalpa samadhi, that's a high meditation.
>
> Salvikalpa samadhi means that you lose your individual awareness as a person. You no longer have a name, an address; you're no longer in this world at all. There's

no sense of the earth, time, space, past history, future possibilities. All of that goes away. All of that is completely erased. You dissolve, but in your dissolution you become something. You become God. You become eternity.

There is a sense—not in the human sense, not in the way of thinking, 'I'm God' or 'I'm eternity'—if you're thinking these thoughts you're not in salvikalpa samadhi—that you are the all-pervasive existence, that existence has an awareness which cannot be described in words. That is salvikalpa samadhi.

As Atmananda spoke these words, it was noted, he manifested them. If he spoke of salvikalpa, the students felt he became salvikalpa. Atmananda—Frederick Phillip Lenz, III, Ph.D.—surrendered himself to the process taking place inside him, the immersions in salvikalpa that would culminate in a new state of awareness, termed nirvikalpa samadhi. He told his friends he was not in the state of nirvikalpa yet.

For the rest of the year, he meditated for hours at a time starting at noon, seated on the bluff overlooking the sea. He meditated in a full lotus position, the soles of his feet facing the azure blue sky, his back erect, his chest erect. From a particular vantage point on the UCSD campus, people could see him—motionless, his hands folded in his lap, his eyes closed, a half smile on his face. Hours passing with no visible movement.

Many students came by after school to see him and found him physically present, often clad in running shorts and a golf shirt, but gone in terms of awareness of their presence. Often, at the end of each afternoon, several students would be seated around him, meditating. The students said they could feel the increased light and energy permeating and emanating from him.

Atmananda explained that every time he entered samadhi, he came out a different person—less self, more light. "You can observe a person going into the superconscious states," he said, "you can watch them dissolve. They can't explain to you what it's really like, but if you sit and meditate with someone who's in samadhi, who goes into the superconscious states, a field of energy is generated around their being that is so strong that you will experience to some extent what it's like. You'll get a feeling for it."

The small, supportive, light-buzzed group around Atmananda got the feeling.

Once, when Atmananda slowly ended a long meditation and stood up from the grass, several students seated nearby jumped up to their feet and folded their hands. Atmananda walked by them as if he did not see them, then turned suddenly. "We don't do that here," he said sternly, emphasizing each word. No one ever went the guru salutation route again.

Perfect for inviting students into Atmananda's increasingly broadband field of light, the new home also served as an ideal venue for meditating. Outside the windows, the sky and ocean merged into an endless vista of golden sun pouring through the glass. People entered the front door and found a spot on the cerulean blue carpet. They faced an empty bamboo dining chair with a little table that had a candle and yantra (a visual meditation symbol) on it. Up to 60 visitors could sit cross-legged on the living room floor while Atmananda sat on the chair and spoke.

The house's layout also worked to feed large groups of people, and as he had done in his New York grad student days, Atmananda often hosted dinners for visitors and students with several large table cloths set down on the living room floor. The students sat around the edge of the table cloths as he playfully served the food onto plastic dishes and plied second portions. Among the memorable entrees—the hottest chili some people had ever tasted and, on other occasions, chocolate chip pancakes that oozed melted chocolate. Laughter was a constant on the menu.

At La Jolla Farms Road, Atmananda again had one room to himself—a bedroom that also served as his office. The room featured a walk-in closet with three or four pieces of clothing and a small record collection. His desk was made of a file cabinet and several pieces of wood. It had a tray for whatever book he was working on.

The months passed, Atmananda seated on the grassy backyard cliff overlooking the Pacific, without visible movement or breath, meditating for hours. After meditating, he performed yoga and strength work. He would run, sometimes twice a day. He swam in the ocean. People saw that his hair got large and curly when it dried and suggested to him that he let it go curly, so he let it go natural.

The small group of meditators enjoyed hiking along the flat rocks and red cliffs of Torrey Pines Beach, where Atmananda showed his friends his new found powers. "He wasn't showing off," said Debby Saracin, a U.S. International University dance major. "He would just humbly do something miraculous, like disappear and reappear in front of us. We'd follow his gaze up a cliff and the whole side of the mountain would start to wave and turn gold. And he would say, 'Isn't that cool? I'm starting to cycle my past lives.'

"You'd look at him and he would be wearing shorts and sneakers and a sweatshirt, and his hair was big and curly, his arms were folded across his chest. He still behaved like one of us, but he was doing uncharted things, effortlessly. The only reason he wanted us to see his shifts in consciousness was to inspire us. It was always, 'If I can do this, you can too.' As a group, we shared a sense of awe about what was happening to Atmananda, and, simply by being there, a sense of awe of what was happening to us."

How to generate more income to teach? Atmananda and a fellow student decided that, based on Atmananda's love for birds, raising and selling macaws might be a profitable venture to help support the San Diego center. They purchased nine brightly colored macaws and one toucanet. The birds were placed on perches throughout the house and in the garage. Within weeks, the birds chewed all the walls in the garage and ate a hole in the roof. The only person who could enter the garage was Atmananda; all others were overwhelmed by the screeching and biting. Atmananda tended the birds with love and care. "Beak" was an affectionate word for him. "Hi, Beak!" was a favorite salutation he often called out to friends.

Frith, now 17, and Atmananda bonded over the birds. "He taught me how to talk to the birds," Frith said. "Atmananda could put his hand in their cage and draw them out to pet them, and they'd nestle against his cheek. When any other student tried to do that, they'd get their fingers bitten. I loved birds and was the only other person that could touch them."

The toucanet named Flash was extremely hyperactive. After Atmananda started going into samadhi on a regular basis, Frith reported, he would come out of samadhi, tap the bird's beak with two fingers and talk to it. All of a sudden, the bird would lie on his back and Atmananda would sit and rub its belly while the bird slipped into samadhi. Then, to bring him back, he would feed the bird a grape.

"You have to give up yourself when you're with them," he explained. But after several months and no bird sales, he ended up donating most of them to the San Diego Zoo, except for Flash and one macaw named Samadhi.

The San Diego students arranged for Atmananda's first lectures in Los Angeles. To navigate the two hour-plus drive, the group of friends chipped in to buy him one of the least expensive cars on the market in 1980, a small, round French coupe called LeCar. He loved the gift, but when he went to sit in it, his 6'3" frame hit the car's ceiling. He drove it long distances anyway, hunched over, pushing it to its slow max speed.

One day, Frith had a vision of Sri Chinmoy and shared it with Atmananda. When she told him of her seeing, he said it was exactly what he had perceived as well—a transit was taking place within himself, while his teacher was going in another direction. He felt it was time to end the association, and he wanted to do it cleanly, if possible without drama or fanfare.

As anyone who has studied in a close-knit spiritual community knows, the departure of a highly visible student is often dramatic for the student, the teacher and the community.

On October 16, 1980, Atmananda journeyed to Eugene, Oregon to meet with Sri Chinmoy at a running marathon. Several of Atmananda's student friends accompanied him to Oregon to attend and help set up for the events. Nancy Winkler, who had met Atmananda one year earlier in a UCSD classroom, joined him in his rental car at the Eugene airport. She recalled that he seemed inwardly conflicted and uneasy, as if rehearsing what he wanted to say to his teacher of 10 years. "I think it was a conflict between head and heart. He was aware that it was time to leave Sri Chinmoy but he had spent years loving him."

The next morning, they awoke at 5 a.m. to help prepare for the day's events and stayed up very late participating in meditations, songs and other activities with other Chinmoy students from all over the West Coast. In a large public gathering, the guru praised Atmananda for his success in establishing the San Diego center and held him up as an example for his other students. Atmananda was silent.

"Atmananda had the briefest of meetings with Sri Chinmoy," Winkler said. "The gathering further confirmed for Atmananda that he needed to break away. His relationship with the teacher had followed the path of love, devotion and surrender; Atmananda had embraced that fully. But because he had started to go into samadhi on a regular basis, had been to the desert and had attracted several of his past life students, he was in a new place in his consciousness. He was gaining back his past life enlightenment. He was seeing things in an entirely new way. His love was growing too strong to be constrained in any way.

"Sri Chinmoy told Atmananda not to show the new powers that were naturally and easily bursting through him. But he could not and would not do that. He was not focusing on or boastfully showing off powers. They were an integrated part of his enlightenment."

Prior to leaving Eugene, the group drove to Spencer's Butte, a mountain in Eugene's backyard with sweeping views of the surrounding valley. They hiked to the top of the treeless butte, enjoyed the beauty and meditated. Driving back to the airport Atmananda was much more at peace, Winkler said. He knew what he had to do.

After Oregon, the intensity of Atmananda's samadhi experiences increased. He balanced the intensity with humor, laughter and hopping. "You'd come into the house and he'd hide in the bathroom and then he'd leap out, tickle you and yell some funny words from a movie," said Saracin, "'I want to make millions of people happy' in a Kermit voice became our group chant.

"There was so much sparkling, bubbling energy running through him. He would emerge from samadhi and hop around the kitchen on one foot because the energy was so intense. He and his housemates would laugh for hours, it was joyous and infectious. Sometimes Atmananda just jumped up and down like he was on a pogo stick to distribute the intense kundalini energy that passed through him. Sometimes he'd hop and sing out 'beaks!' while the birds around the house squawked merrily in support."

"He would talk to us very cheerfully about where he was in meditation," said Frith. "'Oh, did you see that towards the end? I was in salvikalpa samadhi.' A week later, he'd say, 'OK now I've done this meditation and I was able to go into nirvikalpa samadhi.' Then he would explain to us what it was. He'd say, 'You dive into it fully and don't expect to come out, and you have to be fully OK with that. That process of diving in and being in that state sands you. It sands all of you from the inside, so light comes through you. You have to feel you may not come out, there's hardly anything left. You become like a lens.' Everyone laughed when he said that, because it was a play on his name. 'You know what I mean—so you can focus on the light.'

"He gave darshan, although he never called it that and probably never thought of it that way, blessings of light and presence. After a little while, he said, 'OK, I'm now in my saint phase. The saint phase is when you've given up yourself to give light to others.' He used the word 'saint' but he was sitting on his dining room chair in his jeans and sneakers, and the word had no sense of elevation, it was just a description."

As he told his roommates—his student friends from New York—of his total and blissful immersion in light, they listened respectfully and with wonder, but could provide no feedback. There was no one for Atmananda to talk to about the transitions he was experiencing—no teacher, structure or guides.

As Atmananda's body burned with intense kundalini energy flowing through him, humor became the salve. Drinking intense hot salsa helped move the energy through his body; another salve—putting his feet into gallon tubs of ice cream. He and his housemates kidded around. "They were like little goofy kids, playing pranks," said a frequent visitor to the house. "They were so high. It was sweet. The more he went into samadhi, the more playful Atmananda became. We'd hang out and have more fun."

To further lighten the intensity of Atmananda's high-rev transformations, he and one of his housemates masterminded a call to the eternal lightness of the seeker's soul—*WOOF!*

A 20-plus-page, hand-typed, legal paper-sized handout, *WOOF! The Voice of Southern California* was ostensibly a means to draw new students to meditation. In fact, it was an outlet for multi-hour, gut-busting laughter sessions.

Atmananda and his housemates lay on the welcoming blue carpet of the La Jolla home and dissolved in pools of giggling bliss at the foolishness they created for *WOOF!* They wrote advertisements for "Guacamole Hot Tubs" and news stories such as "Dead Sea Scrolls found at Fed-Mart." Pages of wacky articles sent up new age teachers and told zany yarns.

WOOF! was printed and distributed to various stores, new age restaurants and college campuses throughout the San Diego/La Jolla area. Somehow, *WOOF!* brought people to Atmananda's talks. As one of his later students said, "When I saw a copy of *WOOF!* in the grocery store, I went to the lecture. I had to find out who would write such a crazy little newspaper."

In spite of the powers, the meditations, the light and the humor, Atmananda was careful to tell the small band of students that he was not fully enlightened. He said he was being thrown into samadhi for five to six hours a night. Atmananda was in a state of euphoria, losing his body consciousness for longer and longer periods.

As winter approached, Atmananda realized that he could no longer accept any inner connection with the guru. He felt the guru was trying to inwardly impede the new San Diego students, and he could no longer teach on his behalf.

Atmananda flew back to New York in mid-December, 1980, to attend one last gathering at the Chinmoy ashram. On December 17, at the Columbia University chapel, Atmananda approached Sri Chinmoy on the stage, planning to ask for his blessing to leave and start teaching on his own. Instead, the guru pulled a switch. As Atmananda sat on his knees before him, waiting for his chance for a polite farewell, the older man placed his hands on Atmananda's head and said to the assembled group that Atmananda was his best disciple, and he again thanked him for bringing so many students over the years. With that public call out, Atmananda did not feel it was the appropriate moment to tell Sri Chinmoy goodbye. His goal was a clean but quiet departure, not a public diss.

When Atmananda returned from New York, he worked carefully on a formal departure letter that a number of the original students signed. He rewrote it many times and asked several of his friends to edit and comment before he put it in the mail. The group that had been Chinmoy students gathered some money to include in the letter as a formal gesture of thanks. Atmananda conveyed his gratitude in the letter and asked for his guru's blessing.

A few days after sending the letter, Atmananda re-assembled his closest student friends, about ten people. At all meditation sessions at Atmananda's house before this time, a picture of the guru was displayed prominently. This was now removed. He told the Chinmoy student/friends of his decision to teach on his own. He said, "I think we should go and do our own thing, and if you want to come along—there's nothing wrong if you don't—but if you want to become my student, just sign this yellow legal pad." Frith signed up as student number five.

"I loved becoming Atmananda's student via yellow legal pad," said Frith. "It was perfect. Atmananda was all lists. He even made a joke one time that he had lists of his lists. For someone who was so driven to help beings, the amount of distraction and obstacles that come up—you have to be so driven, so completely focused, and Atmananda's focus was impeccable. He used his will and the sharpness of his mind to focus on the goal of teaching, and therefore extraordinary results occurred."

Once the yellow pad list was in place, Atmananda was now free to tell this first group of New York/San Diego students to make a change in their practice. Until then, they had followed the traditional Hindu mantra chants and meditations. Now, Atmananda could say, "Hey, I can show you how I meditate so look at me while I meditate."

"He wanted to show us because he was excited and wanted to share the changes in his awareness with us," Saracin recalled. "He meditated and opened his eyes and all this love would come through. All this light. It was very childlike and innocent. All of us were in a huge period of discovery."

On December 31, 1980, he assembled the entire group of 40 people who then constituted the San Diego Sri Chinmoy center. He explained what was happening. He was respectful to the guru. He told the people in the room that they could decide if they wanted their own San Diego guru center, and he would be happy to help them start that, but that he had been going into samadhi every day and it was time for him to do his own teaching. He explained that every molecule in his body was changing. He said he had to hop up and down because the energy he felt surged so intensely that it was physically painful. He would run on the beach and jump into the ocean to integrate the energy. He said that even his skin texture was changing.

He told the group they had a choice—to study with him or go with the guru. He said they should decide from their heart, that it was a matter of personal feeling, and that he was neutral regarding their decision. Any choice would be just right.

Approximately half of the people in the room chose to stay on as Atmananda's students and the others in the room chose to leave. Of those who left, a number opted to start a different Chinmoy center in San Diego, and still others dropped out altogether.

Atmananda/Rama later described the decision to leave his teacher:

"As the years progressed, my spiritual evolution seemed to increase in speed. I stepped outside of this world, the selves reordered. The combination, the aggregate of beings that I was, dissolved in the white light of eternity. The realization of existence returned, or we could say, it became manifest. At a certain point I left my spiritual teacher because I began to see the limitations of my teacher. While I loved my teacher, my love was a bit blind. I didn't really so much love my teacher as what my teacher represented, although my teacher had many wonderful sides. But it's like with our parents. When we're young, we look at our parents and we think that they're gods, and we grow up and we see that they are. But gods have limitations sometimes, and goddesses, and we see them.

"As I grew up spiritually, as I entered into enlightenment, I saw the limitations of my own teacher who was a very powerful occultist, but who I thought was, to some extent, limiting others in their spiritual growth. So I went off on my own and started the process of spiritual teaching.

"And I found myself in the world, outside of that community. I started to teach, without any effort. It all came back. I remembered my past lives as a Zen monk, as a Tibetan master, many, many things— jnana yoga teacher, mystic. I've had hundreds of lifetimes as a spiritual teacher."[13]

---

13 Lenz, Frederick (Rama). "Sophisticated Sexuality." *Insights: Talks on the Nature of Existence.* Los Angeles: Lakshmi Inc., 1983.

6

1981 - ESTABLISHMENT OF THE ECSTATIC CULTURE

When I give of myself, I expand my consciousness infinitely. When I share my inspiration with others, I live love. When I choose to share my life with God, I become a flame of perfect perfection. - Rama

Thirty-One Days and Nights

Ecstatic love. This is the path of bhakti yoga, the love of light, of God, a love so intoxicating that it burns up the shards of self. The human self drops away, burned away in waves of love—the snapshot of Atmananda in January 1981.

Atmananda's life as a spiritual teacher was about to begin. Atmananda knew about the importance of beginnings. He was about to *perhaps* take on the role that had been predicted for him when he was a teenager, that of a great teacher for the West who would help many people. To create the foundation for such an undertaking would require a magnificent gesture and great strength. Many obstacles lay ahead, including moving past the old teacher. Atmananda had no set plan, rather he had a deeply felt knowing of what to do.

He had to reach new levels in meditation to help all the new people he felt would come. The current students had to become stronger in their practice in order to support each other and the mission. To do this, he would merge with and transmit divine love. Love would transmute the awareness of all of his current and future students, and they would learn the path by observing and interacting with him. The fullness of his heart would protect them, hold them high and dissolve them in the light of eternity.

To launch the public start of his life as a teacher, Atmananda announced that every weeknight during the month of January, commencing January 1, 1981, his 25 enrolled students were invited to attend a meditation at his house at 11 p.m. as well as a Saturday midnight meditation. During the day, Atmananda said, he would meditate and fast.

The month of nightly meditations would be a ceremony, a rite that aligned the teacher with the dharma and the sangha. Together, he and the students would form a circle of power to support the work ahead.

Every evening during the month of January 1981, as the waning and waxing moon danced on the waves outside the large living room windows, the students meditated with their teacher. Atmananda often asked the students to meditate with eyes slightly open and to verify with their own "seeing" what was taking place.

Did they see anything? They did. They saw golden light consuming Atmananda and radiating out in waves towards them. They sat with him for long hours that seemed to last for minutes and meditated to music from the "Star Wars" theme, to Berlioz Requiem, Mozart, the Pachelbel Canon, Debussy, Ravel, Walter/Wendy Carlos, Tomita and Jarre.

"After one midnight meditation," said Steve Diehl, a UCSD computer science major who had joined Atmananda's meditation classes during the Chinmoy days, "he explained that he was going through a transit—being pulled into samadhi sometimes all night— like the blazing light of one thousand suns. It was taking him over. He was remembering teachers he had in past lives. He said he had been enlightened in past lives and the enlightenment was returning. He couldn't stop it if he tried. He was being pulled into a vortex of rapid transformation. His friends who lived in the house with him told us that they often sat up with him all night. They felt they were being lifted by the energy from him and saw gold light radiating from him."

"It was the first time we practiced gazing meditation by looking at Atmananda," a student recalled. "I had incredibly strong experiences. His face became the tiniest little spot in a sea of molten gold. At times I could see just two little pin eyes in this sea of gold. My shirt was soaked because my eyes poured tears, I was moved to the depths of my soul. It went on for hours, the same every night. He was being consumed by light before my very eyes."

The students had a sense of the miraculous. Their friend was becoming, what? A saint, a teacher, a walking miracle? The students and Atmananda sat together in meditation, often until dawn, when the sky outside the house grew lighter and a pinkish-rose light covered the horizon.

"Atmananda would talk for a while, then his voice would start to sound distant and he would stop talking completely and just sit on the couch with his legs crossed, eyes closed, and remain still and silent for a long time," said Francis Wang, then a sophomore at UCSD. "Soon, the room began to fuse with bright golden light. At times the golden light would grow so intense that I lost all sense of time and felt an immense sense of inner stillness, subtle joy and clarity. Invariably, around four or five o'clock in the morning, Atmananda would start opening his eyes and, seeing us still there, tell us it was time to go home."

Some students felt skittish about Atmananda's transformation. "We had been very good friends in the guru days," said one student. "We were studying with this older, East Coast teacher. I told him I was getting nervous, and Atmananda would say, 'You know, there is no difference between us.' But a lot of us were having moments of feeling unsure of how to proceed—Atmananda was changing before our eyes, dissolving in light. It was like being washed in this very strong and fluid and gentle, loving light, like being dipped in light every night. All the consciousness expansion we experienced with him was extremely light-permeated. There was no playbook. We felt like pioneers and renegades in illumined states of consciousness."

"As the month of meditation went by," said Lila Jenner, a tall, blue-eyed UCSD student, "I remember Atmananda telling us that no matter how advanced a soul you are, when you go through the enlightenment cycle in any given lifetime, it's like a quick recapitulation, like packing in all the essential blocks of consciousness that you had in all your lifetimes. You have to go back and absorb all the knowings you had at some point during your chain of lifetimes. In Atmananda's case, it was pretty quick. He loved the light so much that he just dove in and cycled through realizations and understandings from many lifetimes. The light loved him back and he was absorbed, giving himself over to the ravishing of the brilliance, as it soared through his soul."

"Our midnight meditations were wonderful," said Winkler. "We all saw the shimmering gold light that emanated from him. I experienced the most incredibly pure and beautiful states of mind. It became so easy to silence my thoughts and enter into realms of indescribable beauty and love. On the seventh night, I was meditating when quite suddenly my awareness lifted completely out of my body. I felt blissful and totally free. It was exquisite. Atmananda looked at me and smiled. Our eyes met in this beautiful cloud of ecstasy.

"He had a telepathic ability to know exactly what we were experiencing. Atmananda smiled with delight whenever one of us had a high experience. He shared in our experiences with love and oneness. Atmananda was exploring his ability to lift and transform us using his teaching siddhas. Love, of course, was rampant among us. Love makes the connection. And love is the network, the ring of power."

"We came as often as we could," said Saracin, "because it was so amazing to be in the room—going into samadhi higher and higher. It was the first time he meditated on us with his eyes open. He would go around the room and make eye contact with each person. To each person, he transmitted waves of light and energy with his gaze. When he opened his eyes, the wave of energy was pure love. It was all about the heart chakra. It created lovely bonds among all of us because we all felt so lucky to be experiencing this."

According to Frith, "Atmananda wanted to purify himself and clear his aura of past associations. He wanted to accelerate the profound transformation that was already taking place. When he was going through the samadhis, it changed his physical body. He would go through physical ecstasies that were so intense they were actually painful. For a short period of time, he was drinking nothing but juice and cocoa and not eating anything. He couldn't walk anywhere—that's why he started hopping. The hopping happened because his body was on overdrive with light."

"I am who you will be," Atmananda said to the students. The transitions they witnessed in him were their future. "One day you will be like I am. You can't tell yourself from God. There is no difference anymore. You become existence. You have merged back with the source. Yet you will still be a person with eternity expressing itself through you as a person."

The house was kept impeccably clean. After every evening's meditation, students would stay to vacuum the beautiful blue rug. Spotless—Atmananda's own room and meditation table, with a picture on his meditation table of Sri Ramakrishna, standing in samadhi, being supported by his students. During the days, Atmananda often rearranged the house to create greater order, a tighter "tonal" in Castaneda terms.

He cleaned the pantries and the fridge every week. As he cycled through awareness, he used physical surroundings to reflect that.

A human self in the final stages—from finite to infinite. Atmananda wanted the students to witness his transformation. It would seal the energy inside them for their own process of enlightenment. They were there to verify—this was not an imagining or a stunt. It was real.

Nor were students the only witnesses. "When we sat in the room with Atmananda," Diehl noted, "there was a sense of many presences. I saw luminous shapes around him, like rainbow-colored butterflies that hovered in his aura. As the days progressed, it became like a hidden party in Atmananda's living room."

Atmananda would emerge from the meditations radiant, barely aware of his body. His transition period consisted of heading towards the kitchen for juice.

Small details had to be handled. To create a new teaching center, he and the students explored a number of suggested new names. They selected "Anahata," the Sanskrit term for the heart chakra. Prior to leaving the guru, the students had ordered yellow windbreakers with "San Diego Sri Chinmoy Center" emblazoned on the back. When Atmananda announced his teaching plans, they immediately phoned the printer to flip the order to "Anahata Center of Light." The new Anahata students proudly wore their bumblebee-colored jackets to the late night gatherings.

Atmananda's enlightenment process was the most powerful transformational gift he could give a student. "It's going to be so easy for you," he told the group, "because now I have regained enlightenment. You are my students and you are here at the beginning and I love you all so much. All you have to do is listen and receive and I'll take care of everything."

"His purity and the light and ease of his enlightenment—there was this innocence," Saracin stated. "He was a conduit for giving and love. He thought it was going to be a sure thing for the students, and he was so excited for us. Initially he thought he could take the students where they would all become enlightened, every single one. He wasn't aware yet of all the students' samskaras—past life tendencies—that were going to come up."

"The gold light when Atmananda meditated during January 1981 was extremely intense," said Diehl. "While clearly Atmananda's ability to bring the highest light through him improved throughout his life, nevertheless, I felt it was easiest to see the gold light in his living room in January 1981, sitting on the floor a few feet in front of him as he meditated in his chair—while he started to integrate the experience of nirvikalpa samadhi into his being. The gold light was so intense that many times nothing could be seen in the room at all, except gold light.

"The January 1981 meditations provided us the opportunity to see enlightenment take place within a being. This is as close as I can come to a 'purpose' for the January 1981 month of meditations with Atmananda. He wanted as many people as possible to benefit from witnessing the loss of the personal self as it becomes absorbed into nirvana. This witnessing, by our causal bodies, would remain with us forever."

As the month drew to a close, Atmananda's students had received bountiful infusions of light and energy. They had bonded in trust, friendship and support. Atmananda had empowered and refined his own meditation practice and reached nirvikalpa. With this new beginning, a ground state of ecstatic love from which all subsequent teaching would emanate, anything was possible.

> *I have seen the silver fountains of eternity. At the eternal springs of timelessness I have renewed myself. Now— drenched with the immortal nectar of happiness and bliss—I roam alone in a world of changeless change. I am alone with my own pure delight. I am existence itself.*
>
> - Rama

WOOF!

How many students does it take to support a teaching center? Atmananda set a goal of finding 250 students by the end of 1981. The students would either have past life connections with him or past life experience in meditation. If he met the goal, it would be an omen—were the predictions of the monk who materialized in front of his snowboard when he was 19 actually correct?

At the beginning of February, working with two of his women students, Atmananda planned an ambitious lecture schedule, expanding the number of talks he would give in the San Diego area and scheduling a series of talks in Los Angeles, starting in mid-March. Atmananda personally checked each location to feel if it was conducive to conducting light. At each venue—UCSD, San Diego State, The

Humanitarian College in La Jolla, the Los Angeles Convention Center and UCLA—he stood on the stage where he would speak and felt the psychic resonance of each room. If it could hold strong waves of light emanating from his being, it was booked.

The core group of San Diego students took on postering duties, interspersed with spontaneous celebrations—flower parties, bird parties, cheer up parties, graduation parties—hosted by Atmananda. "We would get drunk on hot chocolate," said Frith. "We ate delicious food. We were all so blissed out no alcohol was necessary."

WOOF!, the publication that had started during the Chinmoy days, continued to bark the spirit of Anahata, with new style and wilder humor. Not only was it a way to create hilarity among the core students involved, it had earned its stripes as a way of advertising, a way to find students who would "get it."

WOOF!, during its brief publication span, wore many colorful hats. Breaking away from Chinmoy had given Atmananda and his New York students a sense of freedom they had not known before. They sought to redefine spirituality, announcing that being a 'spiritual' person doesn't mean acting serious and heavy, like a know-it-all. The path should be fun. The fun balances out the discipline of meditation and the powerful inner transformations.

According to Winkler, "*WOOF!* was about dissolving the ego, being yourself, no pretensions, a continuation of the love and innocence we felt in the month of meditation. It was a parody of the New Age scene which Atmananda thought was pretty 'off'—a lot of pretentious people and silly ideas but not much real enlightenment. Atmananda wanted to reach out to people who would sense something genuine. He wanted the handout to be funny because that reflected who he was."

Casting the San Diego net for past life students, the February 3, Issue Four edition of *WOOF!* upped the ante from earlier publications. Headline stories included "Employment Service for Jobless Atlanteans," "Unicorn Weds Housewife (ceremony performed in the little church of Our Lady of the Artichoke)," "Not Feeling Mellow? Would You Like To? Fer Sure?"

It also contained, if you searched for it, a small column titled "Anahata Calendar" that listed Atmananda's public talks on Tuesdays, Wednesdays and Thursdays at UCSD, sometimes two talks per day at different locations. What topics would bring the past life students? Topics that resonated with certain seekers: The Way of Zen, Kundalini

Yoga & Tibetan Secret Doctrine, Samadhi & Cosmic Consciousness, Carlos Castaneda's World of Power.

Who came in the door? In San Diego, old souls in unlikely packages. Waitresses, surfers, rock band members, holistic health practitioners, massage therapists, plant waterers, more college students. "Atlantis" and "Carlos Castaneda" were particularly appealing subjects for young people.

At the beginning of March, the next issue of *WOOF!* hit the sidewalk real estate occupied by free publications. Headlined on the front page: "GOD RESIGNS - Replacement Sought," "PROOF that Ancient Civilizations Exist within Your Nose," "Ancient FEDMART discovered beneath Great Pyramid."

An ad for a 2 a.m. talk by Swami Ugula Ugle noted that the Swami had "personally assisted in the baking of several LARGE rye breads at the Sri Aurobindo Ashram." The ad for the fictional event promised "LOTS OF POMP AND CEREMONY FOR YOU WESTERN TYPES WHO CAN'T ACCEPT THAT ENLIGHTENED SOULS CAN LOOK AND ACT LIKE NORMAL HUMAN BEINGS."

For the first time, teaching articles were written by Atmananda on the foundational topic of meditation: "Meditation, Yantras & Meditation Techniques" and "Meditation Primer."

From the primer:

Focus your attention upon the center of your stomach, in the area of your navel. Feel that this is an area of tremendous strength. Visualize a clear sphere, a dome of energy surrounding your entire body, which is supported by your own willpower. Positive thoughts, feelings, ideas and vibrations can pass through this sphere and reach you. As long as you visualize a sphere of clear energy surrounding you, negative thoughts, hostilities, anger, and aggressive feelings of other persons and situations cannot enter you.

While you imagine this sphere of clear energy surrounding you, feel that you are consciously directing energy from the center of your body, in the area of your navel, throughout the sphere. Feel that the energy of your willpower can easily deflect tension-causing feelings and frustrations that are directed inside you from the outside world. You will find that with repeated practice it becomes easier and easier to visualize this sphere of energy, and that you will be able to stop the negative energy of others from entering you.

The back page was also handled differently, standing apart by a small sidebar titled "Paid Advertising":

Dr. Lenz is a spiritual benefactor. ... Dr. Lenz believes that in addition to having a good conceptual understanding of the workings and laws of the inner worlds, it is equally important to have direct spiritual and psychic experiences in higher consciousness. In order to help you enter into higher states of awareness, Dr. Lenz meditates with you during the meditation section of each of his workshops.

During meditation, Dr. Lenz enters into Samadhi and directly channels Peace, Light, Power and Ecstasy to you. Having this direct experience in Cosmic Consciousness will give you a psychic "boost" that will add to your own feeling of well-being and will increase your spiritual awareness. No words or techniques can equal this experience in Self Discovery.

With Issue #7 in early April, 1981, Atmananda and his small student staff went out of print grinning. The final *WOOF!* rocked the world of self-published handouts. "Rye Bread Captures Poland;" "The Tequila and Peanut Butter Diet;" "Horrorscopes" such as, "Aries Man—Rich, happy, strong, powerful, none of these attributes apply to you, in one of your past lives you were an alcoholic squid;" "The Revenge of the Beast of Norf, A Delightfully Absurd New Musical." Photos pictured students in ridiculous garb. Celebs included Pope Evilnose the 23rd. Ads included "Asbestos Carrot and their Hot New Album, *Court Appointed Attorney*—featuring their smash hit: 'The Void Stops Here.'"

Writing about the restaurant where Atmananda often went with his small band of students for salsa-drinking contests:

Here at WOOF!, scarcely a day passes without our thinking of eating at our favorite Mexican restaurant, El Ranchero. We are hardcore consumers of south of the border specialties, and our weekly visits to El Ranchero have become a semi-sacred ritual.

From the wide variety of native Mexican dishes, we recommend Chile Rellenos, Quesadillas, Guacamole Tacos and our favorite, Special Cheese Crisps. Their Margaritas are the best in San Diego. ...

The atmosphere is Mexican, nouveau snit: piñatas hang from the ceiling, artificial flowers adorn the tables, and Mexican blankets and colorful paint brighten the stucco walls. However fabulous the food and charming the atmosphere, Tony, our favorite waiter, makes a trip to El Ranchero complete. Tony embodies south of the border charm; he always smiles, works hard, and makes everyone feel welcome. Tony also has a wonderful sense of humor.

We've tried several of the Mexican restaurants that San Diego offers, and we haven't found one comparable to El Ranchero. On a scale of four tacos, El Ranchero deserves all four.

Also in Issue #7, a surprise guest graced the front cover, a puppet with a large nose and a fuzzy white mane of hair. Atmananda called the puppet a "bliss." He said that the silly, happy innocence of a bliss puppet was the state of mind that offsets the flatness that often creeps into spiritual practice. He loved that blissful state of mind and said he expressed it often.

¡ WOOF ! Issue No. 7

The wave of new students from the winter of 1981 entered the study on the path of innocence and humor. "Sometimes we laughed for hours on end, and when I would leave Atmananda's house, my mind was completely still," Saracin said. "We made fun of ourselves too. I felt light in every part of my being. The group of us working on the *WOOF!* publications experienced pure happiness."

> *Enlightenment means having no human mind, no limitations. Your awareness is eternity, timeless, infinite, beyond boundaries, and yet it exists within all things.*

WOOF! spoke the language of no limitations.

Finding Students/Teaching Students

> *My happiness comes from doing all I can for my students. To help them, what else could there be? To see them succeed, to see them improve, that is what matters.* - Rama

As he reached out to the public with the indomitable *WOOF!*, Atmananda's calls for students from past lives continued on the inner planes.

On a day early in February, 1981, as he sat meditating in the house, he heard a knock on his front door. When he went to the door, a college student stood at his doorstep. The student had once attended a talk by Atmananda. But on this day, he didn't know why he was knocking on Atmananda's front door. He just found himself doing it. Atmananda invited the student into the house and spoke with him.

"He proceeded to tell me a little about his organization and as he talked I felt a weight being lifted off of me," Ken, age 19, said. "After a while Atmananda asked me what it was that I wanted. I didn't know what to say. I didn't want anything as far as I knew.

"Come on Ken, what do you really want?" he asked.

"I don't know. I don't even have any idea why I came here," Ken replied.

"Ah, that was wisdom, my friend."

As Ken and Atmananda sat in the living room, Ken felt that everything was energized. Finally Atmananda just looked at Ken and said, "Come on, fess up. What is it that you really desire? Fess up with yourself and say it out loud."

"I don't know," Ken said, struggling for words. "'Enlightenment' is a pretty scary concept."

At that, Atmananda started looking around the living room with an exaggerated, puzzled, frightened look on his face. He looked under the rug they were sitting on and Ken started laughing. "What do you mean, scary?" he said. "You want to learn how to love, and be happy and all good things, right?" Then he told Ken that he would shortly be having a series of public meditations and that Ken should come. He did and enrolled as a student.

By the middle of March, approximately 55 students had enrolled to study with Atmananda in San Diego. The group fit nicely into the La Jolla Farms living room. Beginning meditation was the first key teaching. Perhaps the souls coming to the lectures had meditated in the past, but now, back to basics.

Atmananda recommended starting meditation by chanting AUM aloud seven times, gazing at a yantra with eyes slightly closed for about five minutes in order to build focus, and then closing the eyes and focusing on the heart chakra in the center of the chest. After thirty minutes, end the meditation by offering it to eternity. Sit quietly for several minutes. Don't judge your meditation.

In early March, Atmananda released his entire spiritual book collection to his students in the form of a library in the kitchen. He encouraged the students to read the books while they were there. In particular, he said that 12 of these books, from a variety of traditions, had the highest vibration of the many thousands of books he had studied. He taught and spoke about the books; he had internalized them. The book titles (he recommended specific translations) were:

- *The Bhagavad Gita*; Swami Prabhavananda and Christopher Isherwood, translators
- *Shankara's Crest Jewel of Discrimination*; Swami Prabhavananda and Christopher Isherwood, translators
- *Patanjali's Yoga Sutras*; Swami Prabhavananda, translator
- *The Supreme Yoga / "Yoga Vasistha"*; Swami Venkatesananda, translator
- *The Way of Life* by Lao Tzu; Witter Bynner, translator
- *The Tibetan Book of the Dead*; W.Y. Evans-Wentz, translator

- *The Upanishads*; Swami Prabhavananda and Frederick Manchester, translators
- *The I Ching*; Cary F. Baynes, translator; Richard Wilhelm, editor
- *The Gospel of Sri Ramakrishna* by Mahendranath Gupta (M.)
- *Journey to Ixtlan* by Carlos Castaneda
- *Tales of Power* by Carlos Castaneda
- *Walden* by Henry David Thoreau

He spoke of a book that was central to his teaching and his life: *The Little Prince* by Antoine de Saint-Exupéry, "It is only with the heart that one sees rightly. What is essential is invisible to the eye."

In one of the living room talks in La Jolla, someone asked, "We're studying all these traditions. What do we take as truth?" Atmananda replied it was important to follow the path with the greatest heart. He said that each student should use the tools he was presenting that worked best for them.

Early in March, Atmananda began prepping the San Diego students for imminent change. "He began talking about Los Angeles and referred to it as a whole different world," said Saracin. "He said the people there were more sophisticated and professional. He knew that a lot of his potential (and past life) students resided in Los Angeles, many of them working in the entertainment/music industry. He was going to try to figure out the best way to reach them."

On March 14, the day before his meditation classes were set to start at UCLA, Atmananda walked outside of his house, emerging suddenly from the thick tall hedges that surrounded the home. He encountered his student, Lila Jenner, who had been bicycling past the house on her way back to the university campus.

"I stopped the bike dead in its tracks," she said. "He stood about five feet away from me, smiling, casually drinking a Tab. I was speechless. His eyes sparkled, knowing I was stunned. Finally he said, "Well, don't just stand there—why don't you come in and have something to drink?

Inside the house, over diet soft drinks, Atmananda predicted that there would soon be an L.A. meditation center with hundreds of people. "It's the beginning of a new cycle," he explained. "It's time for Los Angeles. It's time to explore the dimensions that the L.A. area has to offer. L.A. is very powerful, very complex, and also very sophisticated and tricky."

As a San Diegan, Jenner abhorred L.A. but was open to learning. "Beginnings are always interesting," Atmananda said. "You have to pay particular attention to omens, indicators, signs. When I begin teaching in a new city, I extend a broad-band psychic message that is picked up on some level by people who are in some way right or appropriate structurally for the study of tantric mysticism. Maybe some of these people have past life ties with me, maybe not. It's a real free-for-all in the beginning; you never know who's going to show up. Later, the ones who stick it out, who show interest, aptitude and affinity will stay."

They arranged to meet the next day to drive together to the UCLA college town of Westwood. During the drive north, Jenner played navigator as they weaved in and out of dense freeway traffic. At the UCLA campus, Atmananda parked at the top of a four-story parking structure and they walked across broad lawns and open spaces to the lecture hall. Jenner took a seat at the back of the hall, near the top of the sloping structure. Atmananda went to meditate in a separate, dedicated guest room. At the appointed time, the hall filled quickly. Jenner had no idea so many people were interested in meditation! There were at least ninety people quietly taking seats and staring at the empty stage.

"Atmananda came out and delivered an incredibly funny and moving lecture," Jenner recalled. "I suddenly realized that he was changing, becoming more—what was it? More powerful, more formless, more forceful? I felt him rising to meet the L.A. challenge. I began to feel my own life changing in response this new L.A. module."

During the drive home, they shared their perceptions. "The people you are going to meet in Los Angeles will need me to do different things," he told her. "I have known some of these people for many lives and some of them are adept and skilled. Some of them are older and have studied with other teachers. You're going to have to try to keep up. Be prepared, it's going to speed up."

And it did. Quickly.

The first set of UCLA talks was presented as a ten-week series, at the end of which Atmananda would accept student applications. The topics included Kundalini Yoga and Tantric Mysticism. But it was not the subject matter or Atmananda's easy and eloquent speaking style that walloped the urban sprawl mind.

Seeing emanations of golden light, stopping thought completely in meditation, perceiving colored lights around Atmananda's hands, witnessing effortless miracles—this is what intrigued would-be students.

In Los Angeles in 1981, experiences of light and siddhas did not go unnoticed. Soon, several hundred people filled the sloping lecture hall at the UCLA chemistry building, primarily working adults, coming to assess Atmananda's teaching chops with a considerably longer judgment checklist than the San Diego crowd. During and after every class, Atmananda patiently answered questions and spoke with potential students.

From mid-March forward, packed teaching days and nights became the rule—Atmananda logging two nights per week in L.A., five classes a week in the San Diego area, Sunday afternoon meetings with the full group of students, Saturday afternoon meetings with smaller groups of students. There were teaching handouts to be prepared, applications to be reviewed and replied to. Postering teams met and carefully prepared their routes. Atmananda continued meditating throughout the night— the more he taught, the more intense his samadhi experiences became.

During his talks, at some point in every lecture, usually towards the end of a meditation session, he asked people to open their eyes as he would slowly make eye contact with every person in the room. When that happened, something visceral happened. Atmananda absorbed that person's pain and suffering. The gaze he returned was pure light, free of pain and suffering.

In Buddhism, this practice is called *tonglen*. With inhalation, all the suffering, the causes of suffering and the bad karma that beings have amassed are drawn into oneself. With exhalation, the suffering and bad karmas are transmuted into happiness and all the causes of happiness, in the form of gold and white light rays. These light rays go out to all beings to touch and renew them, so that they obtain present temporary happiness and the cause for the ultimate happiness of Buddhahood.

Atmananda performed *tonglen* in every interaction, public and student gathering he engaged in. It occurred naturally because real *tonglen* is not a theory, it happens in perfect stillness, at the cusp of being and non-being, where Atmananda's mind was poised. He breathed in suffering, and exhaled renewal. Not metaphorically, literally.

"Many nights, when he returned from teaching in Los Angeles, he shook with pain because he had absorbed so much negativity," Winkler recalled. "He had to take muscle relaxants because of the cramping." And he said, that was his choice. As a teacher, that was what he did. How else could the people who came to see him truly change and transform?

In late April, Atmananda and his small staff of friends/students embarked on a new newspaper designed to jog and awaken his future, geographically dispersed, would-be, past life students.

Geared towards the Los Angelena, the May 1981 edition of *Self Discovery* featured a front page drawing of a woman seated in meditation posture with the English and Sanskrit names of the seven chakras (energy centers along the spine that move life force up through the subtle physical body).

In the *Self Discovery's* editorial, "The Unity of Spiritual Pathways," he stated themes that were repeated throughout his teaching years.

> *The pathways that lead to the Infinite are many. Whether you call yourself Christian, Vedantist, Jew, Hindu, Taoist, or simply a follower of the way, you are a seeker. All true seekers of the Infinite Light are united in their quests. The names that apply to their quests may vary but their goals are the same.*
>
> *No matter what you call it, your goal is union with your own highest Self. There is no greater challenge in all of life. One might say that the very raison d'etre of existence is to return to the Source of all Existence.*
>
> *When human beings are able to see and accept the unity of all spiritual pathways, then and only then will they be worthy of that which they seek.*
>
> *To my way of thinking there is only one real measure of a person's spiritual development. It is the way one treats those around them. You may have had thousands of religious or mystical insights, you may even have hundreds of followers who admire your spirituality, you may feel that this is your last incarnation, but unless your spirituality expresses itself through kindness to those around you, then it may be time for you to realize that your 'enlightenment' is incomplete.*

In the world of Atmananda, there were no dry and boring tasks. Every interaction performed well, in a happy state of consciousness, included an empowerment. "One evening," said Leah Morrell, then a college student and singer in a local rock band, "after working at the house to help put together the first *Self Discovery* paper, Atmananda announced a late night meditation at Torrey Pines State Beach. About 30 of us piled into 10 cars and drove a few miles down the road from the house.

"We parked our cars on a narrow strip of gravel off the Pacific Coast Highway and scrambled down the sand bank to the shore. We walked south in between the craggy orange cliffs and the roaring ocean. When the tide was high, it could hit against the cliffs making it impossible to walk, but the tide was low and the sand was wide and smooth. We walked about a half mile down the beach and stopped at a rocky cliff projection, a natural jetty. We stood along the base of the cliffs and watched Atmananda stroll toward the water. The waves lapped gently up onto the beach and around the rocks at the tip of the jetty.

"Standing at the water's edge, Atmananda threw his hands up in the air. As he did this, the water became alive and luminous, like a sea of mercury, moving in slow motion, in circular patterns, dancing. And he began to dance with it. His body became liquid light, moving with the water. His body disappeared altogether as the light that had originally been part of his body began to slowly spin upward, hovering above the water. Then he moved slowly up onto the flat rock of the jetty, and he appeared to be an extension of the ocean itself, moving in a brilliant rhythm of tide, sea and cosmos. Standing there, my heart beat with the waves. It felt like I was a part of the fluid movement, dancing through air and water with Atmananda. He danced and the ecstasy of being sparked off of him like fireworks, into the air and into our bodies and minds.

"Everything dissolved into liquid light until we were transported through formless realms of brilliant silence. We glided back to our cars, still liquefied, and stopped for a moment of gratitude at the bottom of the sandy bank. We stood motionless, looking out into the black void of the ocean and sky."

To produce 200,000 eighteen-page newspapers, in order to find past life students, required funding. Atmananda did not seek wealthy students, he sought enthusiastic and inspired students. In an April 9 letter, Atmananda reached out to his enrolled students for more help with advertising.

> *The key to self-realization is selfless giving. No one has ever achieved enlightenment without selfless giving. Enlightenment and all spiritual realization has come through studying with an enlightened teacher, associating with highly evolved persons, meditating and selfless giving. … Our organization operates through selfless giving. We feel that everyone who is a member cares for the welfare of other human beings. It has always been our policy to give all that we can for others. At the same time we never ask anyone to give more than they are either capable of giving or are inspired to give.*

The students got it and supported the newsprint handouts and big print ads that would serve as a beacon for other students to join.

In June, 1981, Atmananda presented another foundational teaching in a new *Self Discovery* magazine. The article centered on a fictional character named Suzie.

> *Suzie surprised herself by directly asking the teacher why she felt drained from her relationships with men. The teacher paused for a moment, and after looking deeply into her eyes, he told her the following:*

> *From the psychic and spiritual point of view, men are the downfall of women. As you may be aware, very few women have ever attained total enlightenment, while many men have.*

> *The reasons for this are many; you yourself are an illustration of this phenomenon. There are three primary factors involved: your self-image, the amount of lower energy that enters your consciousness, and the amount of personal power you lose in your relationships with men.*

> *Now let us look at these things one at a time. First of all, let us consider your self-image and the image of women in general. Most women are conditioned from the time of infancy to think of themselves as being less powerful than*

men. Actually, quite the opposite is true. Women have much more personal power than men do and theoretically it should be easier for them to attain enlightenment than it is for men. ...

Women are constant victims of the negative energy of men. Men may not consciously wish to hold women back in their spiritual development, but they do. Their attitudes are repressive in the outer world, and in the inner world they often unknowingly hurl negative sexual forces into women's consciousness and also drain them of their power.

Women have been taught from their earliest childhood to make themselves attractive to men. This teaching weakens women. Instead of simply being themselves, they try to become something that will attract or please others. After doing this for a number of years, women lose their identity and self-awareness. ...

My advice is to be aware. ... Be conscious of your relationships with men. When you are with a man you are close to, try to feel what is taking place on a deeper level. Don't take my word for it, experiment yourself and see. Pay particular attention to the way you felt before you were with a man, and then notice how you feel after he has gone. If you feel less energetic and happy than before it is because he has drained some of your power.

Try to associate only with those persons who help you and not with those who use you to their advantage. There are nice people in the world although you have to look a little harder to find them.

Atmananda's first feminist bell ringer, this issue of *Self Discovery* was directed not only at the public but at his current population of female students. The result—more women and men of all ages began to attend his public talks.

In early June, as the ten-week UCLA series drew to a close, of the 1,000 people who attended the talks, over 100 people applied to become his student, and he accepted 60. The new L.A. enrolled students drove south to La Jolla on weekends for classes at Atmananda's house, while Atmananda drove north on weeknights for public lectures.

The mellow San Diego seekers and the intense Los Angeles seekers created a strange confluence of energies. "The L.A. group was very confusing to me," said Jenner. "They knocked me for a loop. We had lived in a rarefied environment. The San Diego students were mostly the same age, going to college, very young and inspired. There's not much action in La Jolla. The L.A. students were older and played a different game. I was getting knocked on my ass, the vibes were so rough. I did not understand the L.A. students at all. They were a different breed of cat—dressed up women, coming on to Atmananda like a rock star, some of them quite sure of what they were doing. It was a whole new level of worldliness."

Once the L.A. students joined the San Diego students in the La Jolla Farms living room, they filled every corner. To the old San Diego students, he became something new every day.

"We all watched him transform before our eyes, on the stage. We saw him turn into a 'teacher,'" Frith said. "And he called us on that one. He said, 'You guys put me into a role. People have the habit of having 'a teacher'—a dodge so you don't have to do it yourself. It creates a distance so you don't have to feel the reality.'

"I saw that his transformation was caused by the current and future students. When the students required him to dress differently, he did; to live in a different location, he did; to play a particular music selection, he did. At a certain point, the transformation into a 24/7 teacher became an organic part of his being."

Just weeks after their enrollment, Atmananda invited new students to his spiritual sanctuary, the Anza Borrego desert, for a nighttime hike, meditation and empowerment.

One new student recalled, "Because of the moonlight, I saw everyone in the group quite clearly but once we had assembled on the sand, Atmananda blinked in and out of physical sight like a lantern on a buoy. At times I could hear his deep voice with no physical presence. He asked us to lie back and look up at the stars. I unfurled a jacket from my pack and placed it under my head and lay back on the sand. I felt my heart swell just looking at the panoply of desert stars—millions of stars, the Milky Way a swath of white. And the moon—what was the moon doing? It had split into two moons and was dancing around in a wild, erratic manner. Atmananda asked us to sit up and tell him what we saw. He said that speaking our experiences in the desert would help us to retain them, and also help ground our awareness amidst the diffuse power of the surroundings. Someone said they saw the moon split in two and dance like drunken orbs. Others saw lines of white light in a grid pattern across the sky. One student said she saw bursts of brilliant colors in the sky.

"Atmananda then asked us to focus on the ridges of the mountains. I saw a bright band of light along the ridge and figures that resembled huge American Indians on top of the ridge. Atmananda asked us what we saw. Several people reported seeing large Indian-like figures at the top of the mountain, which they called guardians. Atmananda said that the seeing was correct."

"On this trip," said another student, a veteran of previous desert journeys with Atmananda, "I had to arrive late and walk in by myself. It was dark with little moonlight but I easily found where the group had assembled, at the base of a mountain around a mile and a half into the gorge. There was a golden dome of protective light around everyone there, and I just walked towards the dome of light."

Throughout the summer of 1981, Atmananda invited all his students to join him for the Shakespeare plays performed at the Old Globe Theater in San Diego. "He meditated during the play as we watched the players on the stage," said David Silver, a blonde-haired, 22 year-old computer geek. "It was extraordinary—he lit the whole place up. In another way, it was something we came to expect. If we were going to spend time with Atmananda, it was going to be truly magical."

"He would take students to the movies and it was another type of meditation," said Morrell. "We went to the beach and played in the water and ran on the shore and it was another kind of meditation. It was not just about sitting in meditation but also expressing light in your own life and decisions. That's what he was doing. There wasn't a party line. Not with him. There was tremendous effervescence bubbling through, even going to a restaurant, he was silent in a way but not. The light didn't stop flowing because we were out of the meditation hall. It was fizzling and emanating from Atmananda to his students in all venues, at all moments.

"When we were at a Denny's restaurant, on the surface we were ordering fries and Diet Coke; the waiters had no idea. But light was literally bubbling through; the walls would sparkle. It was an unspoken, very humorous experience. It was the cosmic joke that was always riding through everything we did in the world."

The Denny's restaurant chain, with its 24-hour diner ambiance and locations on the major Southern California freeways, became the eatery of choice for Atmananda's students. "We would meet up with Atmananda on drives back and forth to L.A. or the desert," said Diehl. "There were usually a lot of other people in the restaurant, but he would go around our tables and make everyone laugh. We called it dharma at Denny's."

Atmananda was becoming enlightened and was having a ton of fun with it. He was showing the students it couldn't be what they thought. "It was all an experiment and it was happening anew each moment" said Morrell. "We were just inside of the experiment. I often had the sense that I had come upon the greatest treasure that has ever been, and we were sharing that treasure with the world."

But by the fall, Atmananda had quickly journeyed beyond the role of innocent new teacher on the block. He had received threatening phone calls. Christian fundamentalists had taken umbrage at ads and stories in WOOF! "Christ Materializes in Fed-Mart" had raised some hackles. Another set of calls with actual death threats, possibly from a former boyfriend of a female student, were left on his answering machine. Atmananda took the death threats seriously. He asked a small group of his male students to accompany him when entering and exiting public lectures. He announced that he had purchased a handgun and would keep it on the nightstand in his bedroom.

Threats did not, however, deter Atmananda from his use of advertising as a modern lure for past life students. For Atmananda, the chance to meet a past life student, "to intrigue people with the possibilities of their own immortality," trumped fear of personal harm every time.

In November, 1981, full page ads in the San Diego and Los Angeles Reader (free urban newspapers) threw down the gauntlet. The ads featured a photograph of Atmananda, freshly emerged from samadhi. Beneath the photo was a lecture schedule and his past life resume.

Occupation: Spiritual Teacher

Objectives:

1. To find my students from past lives and finish their liberation;

2. To meet new persons who are interested in studying the meditative arts that lead to illumination and self-realization.

Experience:

1531 - 1575 Zen Master, Kyoto

1602 - 1671 Head of Zen Order, Kyoto, Japan

1725 - 1804 Master of Monastery, Tibet

1834 - 1905 Jnana Yoga Master, Madras, India

1912 - 1945 Tibetan Lama, head of Monastic Order, Tibet

1950 - Self-realized spiritual teacher. Director of spiritual communities in San Diego and Los Angeles.

Interests:

Running, swimming, film, yoga, perfection

The resume listed current life publications, teaching positions, lectures, media appearances. The headline: "This man can turn a room GOLD in 60 seconds. Imagine what he can do to you."

Atmananda held a different view of advertising than the average Madison Avenue executive.

"Many people say that the type of advertising I do is controversial," he explained. "I am not sure what that means. I feel that advertising is a creative medium and I enjoy it. I try to make each advertising campaign a little bit different; I write all of the copy myself. I try to catch the interest of people who might be looking for truth. ...

"My ads list my past lives as a teacher. How do I know I've been a teacher in other lives? I remember. When you merge your consciousness with the superconscious, when you practice psychic development, it's not very difficult to remember. Past lives are not ultimately important. They are when you're in them, but I think what matters is now.

"I like advertising. I think advertising is a very creative medium and I try to use the medium as effectively as I can to entertain and enlighten.

"One day I was running on the beach with a friend and we were talking about what would make an interesting advertising campaign. We wanted to break through the stereotypes that meditation and spiritual groups have created.

"A great many gurus came to the West in the 1960s and created a certain image of what meditation is, what teachers are like and how it all works. But what they taught as meditation is not what I experience as meditation. Their methods of teaching are not mine. They became involved with changing people's lifestyles and teaching them Sanskrit and making them bow down to the guru as an authority figure. Most of their followers seemed to suffer spiritual burnout—they didn't become enlightened and often appeared worse for the study. ...

"Real self-discovery has nothing to do with any of that. It's exciting and it creates quantum leaps in your awareness. Eventually it leads, through much silliness and seriousness and beauty and hard work, to enlightenment. The whole journey is a circle. You end up back where you started, except that when you get back there, you're different. I seek ways to bring about or transmit the essence of this experience, and I use radio and newspaper ads and posters in order to intrigue people with the possibilities of their own immortality.

"So we were jogging on the beach and I said to my friend, 'Suppose I use a resume, as if I were looking for a job, as an ad. I could list some of the things I've done in this lifetime—where I went to school, where I got my Ph.D., books I've written, things like that. But suppose I list my other lives too. Suppose I list when I was the head of a monastery in Tibet, when I was a jnana yoga master in India or when I was a Zen teacher in Japan? Wouldn't that be fun?' The resume is the theme. It says, 'Purpose: looking for students from my past lives or individuals

I've not encountered so far who are interested in learning the art of meditation and psychic development.'

"I like advertising. I know it rocks the boat, but what is there to rock? Life is a strange thing some days. The so-called spiritual groups that object to the type of creative advertising I do have only been in existence for a few years.

"Before Alan Watts and a few pioneers like him began the counterculture spiritual movement in the late 50s and early 60s, only a few individuals had heard of meditation. Now all kinds of small and large groups have sprung up, and they've created a kind of spiritual establishment. Even though they've only been around for ten or fifteen years, it seems that they've constructed some kind of oral code of do's and don'ts. I find it rather ironic that there's supposed to be an established way to advertise or not advertise if you're trying to bring people closer to an awareness of God and immortality. It's funny that these individuals are setting themselves up as paragons and judges.

"I think if I'm irritating people a little by the methods or style of my advertising, I must be doing something right. Self-discovery is a creative process, and I try to bring that creativity into everything I do, all hopefully with a touch of humor, much of it directed towards myself."[14]

From November 1981 forward, Atmananda's past life resume became the print ad of choice, bringing thousands of people to his talks. The ad sometimes sparked intriguing experiences.

"The Yellow Submarine Subway Sandwich shop on North Judah Street in San Francisco was the site of my first encounter with Atmananda," said Paula Steep, then a science major at San Francisco State University. "I was laughing aloud at what seemed an absurd poster, until suddenly, the first line in the resume, 16th century Zen Master in Kyoto, became vividly real. Suddenly I was standing along the roadside of a Japanese village and I could smell and taste the dust after horses rode past. I never had an experience like that before." Paula attended the lecture and enrolled as a student.

How did the advertising really work? Atmananda spoke about old cycle souls, about Atlantis and ancient Egypt and times before this one when things were less solid and everything had more light in it. The light of the superconscious was more accessible then, and people

---

14 *Interview with Rama*. Los Angeles: Lakshmi Corp., 1985.

navigated their incarnation with more light. The knowledge of how to do that had carried into the folks who would come to find him, even if they were not aware of it yet.

"Even with *WOOF!*," Frith said, "only somebody with a crazy, multi-life sensibility could get that. The person who responds to the ad has to be kind of out there and complex. Atmananda had to do those crazy things. It had to stand out. He was willing to go to all lengths, multi-city tours. He'd send out a group with ads and posters, he'd travel with a group of people whom he was also teaching. He would do his thing. It was grueling and beautiful. It was all about being of service. He was fearless, looking for people who knew what enlightenment was, in their soul."

November brought a sense that bringing Western students to enlightenment was going to be more difficult than it had seemed at the start of the year. Some people who he had been close to were using the energy they received from him to strengthen the unrefined, adolescent side of their being—forming cliques, feeling superior, keeping others away. Atmananda stayed in his room and meditated, rather than playfully hanging out with the students. He frequently became sick with debilitating colds and nausea. He told the core group that his illness was due to processing his students' karmas, which he had the power to do, and therefore did.

"In mid-November," Saracin said, "I arrived at the house and I could feel that Atmananda was not happy. I felt something had changed. I did not know exactly what caused it but we were a small group of core students. I knew that some of the students had become jealous of one another if Atmananda was paying more attention to one person than another. I knew that a few students were not even trying to meditate. There was a different feeling in the La Jolla Farms house."

Twenty minutes later, Atmananda entered the living room without saying a word. He sat down, crossed his legs, then lifted up his coffee cup and took a sip. On the front of the cup, it said "No More Mister Nice Guy." He made sure all the students present—the group that he worked with most closely—saw the message.

"He basically told us off on many levels," Saracin said. "He said he was not attached to us. He said we could not control him. 'We're not the same. I take care of you, but we're not equal.' He sounded hurt. He looked so tired, with dark circles under his eyes. He said, 'I don't look like this. This is not my level of awareness. I'm eating more to cut through all this energy and karma I'm processing for all of you, and I don't think you're getting it.'"

Forgiveness was swift and total, but Atmananda had changed. In order for his physical body to survive past a few more years, the teaching process had to shift. "Things can change in a second," he said. He was no longer a wide open sieve—he began to seek and require more private time to give him the strength and stillness he needed to find past life students, unravel the public's and the students' samskaras, to dissolve tough egos and transmit light. His love grew, so did his detachment.

The Castle

The Chinmoy student who had leased the La Jolla Farms Road house to Atmananda was not pleased about housing an infidel, particularly one who drew easily twenty times more students than the local Chinmoy center. And Atmananda was no longer at ease in a full-time student drop-in spot.

Atmananda began to look for another place to live. In late November 1981, while shopping for groceries in Del Mar's small supermarket, he ran into a couple who owned a local landmark called the Del Mar Castle. They struck up a conversation. The couple offered to lease it to him at a reduced price.

Close to 200 students were now paying modest monthly tuition fees, and public lectures were pulling in big audiences. The rent was covered. A deal was struck, with December 1 set as the move-in date.

Moving was also a teaching. "Atmananda told us that whenever we leave a place, even if we have just been there overnight, we should seal off the energy lines between ourselves and that place," said Frith.

"He said to feel we are pulling in lines of energy from the room or house into our solar plexus, and then cut the lines. I helped Atmananda do the final walkthrough of La Jolla Farms Road. He did the absolutely impeccable final check of the house to make sure that nothing had been broken. Someone had pulled down a curtain, so we added that to a yellow pad list of fixes. A water cooler had to be moved. He was sweating the details, as he always did.

"As he walked into each room, I felt him drawing into his solar plexus lines of energy from the areas where we had meditated, talked, laughed and eaten sumptuous food. I witnessed him cutting those lines.

As Atmananda stepped through every room of the house, he sealed or closed every square inch of the past history.

"I was the last person out and walked to the car with him. Perched on my arm was Samadhi, a scarlet macaw of vivid red, blue and yellow, a very sweet tempered, loving and gentle bird whose red tail alone was about a foot long. Atmananda helped me and the beautiful bird-ness get settled into the car, where we filled up the whole passenger seat. Then he went back inside and did two more minutes of 'final' check/close. When he re-entered the garage and got into the car, he was already moving into the transition.

"He did not say anything the whole way to the castle. You know when you see in the movies where things go to light speed? What happened on the drive from the old house to the new house was like that. We drove past Torrey Pines State Park, which is a power spot. What I saw Atmananda do next was absolutely real. I saw him move all the way through time so he did not leave a single thing behind.

"He folded space and time so that by the time he arrived in the new place, he was 100% in the new place and it was as if the old place had never happened. All the offerings, samadhis, transits, realizations, talks—everything that had happened, good bad or indifferent—was gone from that location.

"When I was in the car with him, it was scary because I also felt myself being divested of the past that did not need to be brought forward and I felt a new self being integrated with what needed to be brought forward.

"Atmananda was in meditation the whole time he drove. He was a very good driver. Some extra-logical piece of him—his second attention—was like the sub-layer of whatever he did. By the time we got to the circular driveway of the new house, he had completed folding time in the former house. He turned off the car and was completely in the present moment.

"He walked around the car to the passenger side. He took Samadhi and gently placed her on his shoulder, her long tail streaming brightly down his back."

Atmananda's explanation on moving to a new house: "One of the things I like to do when I move—after all the furniture is gone, we clean the place up that we're leaving, everything's done, everyone's packed and gone away—then I come back for a few minutes and I walk through the house and I look at the empty rooms. Because I'm fascinated by absence. Because I see as much reality in absence as I do in presence. Because as you walk through the rooms that are empty, you're not only dealing with that which was, which you can still feel traces of—it's like when a meteor falls and you can still see traces, which is what our lives are really like—but also that absence is nothingness. And nothingness is perfect existence."

"When he opened the castle's front door," said Frith, "it was mayhem. There were more than 20 people unpacking, setting up the office. There were boxes, plants and furnishings all over the place. The plants in the entryway had been left by the previous occupants and drooped forlornly. First thing he did was look at me and say in a soft voice, 'Hel, these plants need attention.' I felt grateful to have a task that I could focus on."

With Samadhi ensconced on her tall human perch and nibbling occasionally on Atmananda's earlobe, he then went to speak with students who hauled a large, heavy, boxy personal computer up to his new office—the first ever edition of the IBM PC.

Installing the bulky PC in the new office was an important task, more art than science circa 1981. The castle would be the first setting where a number of students installed applications and tested them, pushing the new IBM PC to its considerable limits.

Atmananda's fine-tuned vision into computer science had started in 1980. He noticed how well some of his students functioned when they engaged in computer science in school or at work. He observed their focus as they reached a new level of concentration that was very good for meditation. He saw that they were excited about their work and did not come home drained by the world. He saw that his students needed to be on a money track to survive as meditators and to tighten up their minds. He told several of his disbelieving students that computers and software were going to be huge. He got involved and saw how it worked.

The first IBM personal computers hit the market in August 1981. One month later, Atmananda phoned Winkler and asked if she wanted to go to the IBM store to check out the new PCs. Few people then owned or were interested in them; the clunky, heavy boxes had little memory; the graphical interface was non-existent. In fact, the first IBM PC came equipped with 16 kilobytes of memory, expandable to 256k (today one photo can take up more disk space than that.) The PC came with one or two 160k floppy disk drives and an optional color monitor.

Atmananda and Winkler clambered into his LeCar and drove down to La Jolla Village. The salesman showed Atmananda the computers and let him try them out. Atmananda typed in various spiritual aphorisms.

Atmananda told Winkler that computers were going to become very popular in the next few years. He said it would be a very smart idea to learn to program them, because then you'd always have a job and you wouldn't have to interface with people all day. He said Mary, his friend from New York, was giving up nursing and going to computer school because it was very hard on her to be around sick people all day.

Late on the night of the move-in, after the 20-plus people had left, Atmananda padded around the castle alone, with one roommate on a separate floor. No longer was his office just a table in his bedroom. His bedroom did not open onto a central hallway. The gated property provided security. The castle's thick rock walls were cave-like. He continued his intense meditation practice at the top of a turret, rather than a bluff.

Other differences emerged. While the La Jolla Farms Road was an open, sea-facing, classic California ranch-style home, the Del Mar castle was formal and cool. The interior rooms were large, and the home retained a slightly chilled temperature (given that the outside air averaged 80 degrees). There were three levels—the vast living room, dining room and kitchen on the first floor; the second level that included bedrooms and a loft that overlooked the first floor; and a turret. The turret became Atmananda's meditation room, reached by a circular staircase, where you could gaze across the city of Del Mar out to the sea.

The dining room, with its long, dark oak antique table that came as part of the rental, easily sat twenty for dinner. The kitchen, a favorite room, had two stone fireplaces, a huge stove, two sofas around one of the fireplaces and a kitchen table. It was usually the room where Atmananda and some of the students gathered after returning from his meditation lectures in various cities.

"We overhauled that castle," said Maryann Vibraye, a rosy-cheeked, dark-haired UCSD student from France. "We almost lived there while we worked on it. It was full of wood—everything had to be oiled, the windows were layered in dirt. It was dusty and grungy and we cleaned it until it shone." Steve Diehl recalled washing a window, looking up and suddenly seeing Atmananda, making eye contact, and "the glass, the window frame and the wall dissolved into light."

At the La Jolla Farms Road house, the San Diego students could visit as often as they wanted, typically several times per week. At the castle, the students had to be invited. There were many invitations for large and small groups; the planned and impromptu trips to the desert continued. But now there was more space for Atmananda, literally and psychically. Just as he advised his students to spend time by themselves, he too acquired the right setting for renewal.

The castle served as a teaching gesture—to enter the castle, if you are interested in becoming enlightened, show me. Show me with your meditation practice, your personal transformation, your increasing happiness. Don't pull from my energy without making changes in your own being. I will help you, I want to help you, but you have to do the work, too.

Atmananda purchased an electronic synthesizer with a piano-style keyboard and installed it in the loft overlooking the main floor. Saracin recalled sitting on the couch in the living room and listening to him playing music on the synthesizer. "The music was melodic, from very gentle to strong and blasting. Atmananda pushed eternal awareness through the notes. Everything stopped," said Saracin. "When I heard it, I felt out of time and exactly where I wanted to be."

"The castle in Del Mar was a Tibetan move—the stone, the big chimneys and the tall ceilings," said Vibraye. "Atmananda lit roaring fires. One night I had dinner in the castle with Atmananda and one other student. We spoke of Tibet the whole evening. Atmananda would generate an image of what we spoke about, and I could see it. That night, he reminded me of being in Tibet with him. We walked in huge, barren plains with horses and yaks, travelling from one monastery to another. Atmananda reminded us of the gorgeous sunsets and sunrises and I could see them."

To his student friends from San Diego, he said that he was changing so fast that different people would be attracted to different levels of energy. New people would come and others would fall away. Because he was hitting higher levels of samadhi he would find different friends from different lives.

Among the San Diego enrolled students was a group of people who all worked at the same health clinic. The clinic's office manager, Kathleen Forge, had attended one of Atmananda's talks in a large meeting room at The Lodge at Torrey Pines but had not enrolled. She thought he seemed too intellectual and yuppy.

Soon after taking up residence in the castle, Atmananda invited all the clinic employees to dinner, including Forge. "When I arrived, Atmananda greeted me at the door," she said. "He was about to go upstairs, so he suggested that I venture into the kitchen to see if the gals needed any help. I entered the kitchen and saw three women baking up a storm. I had never met them in this life but I recognized them as soon as I saw them. I suddenly had a past life remembrance. We had been nuns in a French convent!

"When I returned to the living room, I joined my colleagues and sat down on a beautiful lama hair rug. Several students joined us. We were all very quiet. Soon Atmananda came down the stairs and took a seat on his living room couch. He wrapped his legs in a full lotus position. He said hello and welcomed us. We chatted a bit and then he suggested we meditate. I closed my eyes and stilled my thoughts. Time and thoughts slipped away, replaced by waves of ecstasy. Waves of energy shot up my spine and emanated out of my heart, it was overwhelming and tears began to fall from my eyes, while a mile-wide grin formed on my face. When the meditation ended, I sat absorbed in pure happiness. I walked up to Atmananda and told him he literally won my heart. He replied, 'It's about time!'

"Over the years of my study, he and I often laughed about the French convent lifetime. He said that several of his women students had been there and that we all drank a lot of wine and partied heavily!"

Morrell visited the castle in December 1981. Atmananda had been experiencing profound changes in his meditation practice. He became more and more dissolved in light. "It was a birthday party for someone," she recalled. "Everything was still and radiant. We had dinner and meditated. As he sat and talked to us, he was in samadhi the whole time. There came a moment—it was very simple on the surface. Someone brought out the cake and served it. They brought a piece of cake to Atmananda as he sat there, totally gone. He took the plate in his hand, and it slipped right out of his hand as if he had never made contact with it. He went to pick up the plate as if it hadn't happened.

"I watched something click inside of him. The disconnect between him and physical objects had been happening more and more. He was so in the superconscious that the physical was becoming less and less. People had to do more for him in the physical. When he picked up the plate, I watched him come to a powerful insight in his own being, that he was going to shift tracks on that count. It was so simple— dropping a piece of cake. I sensed him willfully bringing himself into the physical while remaining in the superconscious. I saw it happening in Atmananda, starting in that moment.

"There was a new sensibility that it was not just about being in the superconscious. It was about everything coming into play. He was feeling he could do more for people if he could be more present in the world. The saying is, 'Samsara is nirvana,' and he would manifest that in his life."

During the still-sunny month of December, seated in his castle office, Atmananda wrote and published a small book, a poetic paean to the core practice of Buddhism, *Meditation: The Bridge Is Flowing But The River Is Not.*

The only thing that stands between you
And the infinite ecstasy of existence are thoughts.
When you stop your thoughts,
You stop the world.
When the world stops, time stops.
When time stops, matter stops.
When matter stops, self-consciousness stops.
When self-consciousness stops, there is nothing.
Nothing left to stop, start, begin or end.
The person who did all of these things
Has gone away,
Vanished without a trace in the
Ecstasy of existence. ...

I have longed to be with you. I felt you in meditation so
long ago. I waited as long as I could
and then, when you didn't come, I had to write these
words.
So they could be with you when I could not be.

On New Year's Eve, 1981, Atmananda's multi-dimensional job—finding the students, sanding down student egos—took a new form. He invited his growing number of Los Angeles and San Diego students to a UCSD lecture hall to perform a Gong Show, a takeoff on a popular TV program where absurd acts went on stage and kept going until they heard a loud gong. Atmananda wielded the long padded stick that struck the gong, swinging it around his head and comically exaggerating the long arc of movement before the stick hits brass. In between the gongs and the acts, Atmananda's comments kept the students laughing long after the gag was over.

That evening, I drove to La Jolla with a friend, Renee Locke, and brought with me a style relic, a floor-length red velvet peasant dress. As we drove south, we devised an act, an imitation fashion runway show. Renee would read an elaborate fashion commentary on the red dress and I would send-up modeling it. For the next fashion design, Renee would read a different commentary and I would come out wearing the same funky dress. We created a commentary for about four iterations of that red velvet number—day wear, evening wear, lounge wear and swim wear.

Two hours later, we sat nervously in the audience as, with suitable tongue in cheek fanfare, Atmananda announced the Gong Show. Some of the acts that preceded us were "Stop in the Name of Love" by three guys in drag, several women dressed as dancing cans of household cleaners, and a juggler. I felt shaky as I slipped on the red dress in the nearby restroom. We walked out on the platform that constituted a stage. Renee read our notes and I performed awkward model moves.

We made it through the first reading and I walked off the stage. Renee began reading the second description. As soon as I came back with the exact same dress, Atmananda's face reflected mock dismay. He gleefully imitated my model send-up moves. The audience rocked with laughter and we got gonged. As I walked back to my seat, I looked back at Atmananda.

He met my gaze with a strong, grateful look. Yes, it took a bit of work to put together the skit. I had taken a chance and dropped my guard. Renee and I had created an opening for him to work with the other students as they laughed. To me, he transmitted a blast of powerful, clear energy that lifted my mind like an updraft from a tornado to a clear, thought-free plane of intensely powerful awareness, filled with expanding love. It was a powerful physical sensation, as if

I were standing next to and drawing from an energy generator of indescribable force. I learned later that Atmananda's students called this 'getting blasted.'

When Renee and I drove back to L.A. that night, I felt pulsating ecstasy throbbing through my being. This was not just Happy New Year, 1982; this was Happy Infinite Possibilities, 1982.

Two hundred fifty enrolled students—the result of Atmananda's vision, meditation, *tonglen*, advertising, travel, lectures, his inner calls to past life students, student postering, handouts and brochures—laughed together at the Gong Show that night.

7

1982 - WHAT'S IN A NAME?

If you have an abundance of happiness, then life is bright. We see it more correctly. - Rama

Lakshmi

To launch the New Year, Atmananda chose "Lakshmi" as the name of his teaching organization. In Hinduism, the goddess Lakshmi represents beauty, harmony, abundance. As a mantra, "sring," Lakshmi represents access to planes of delightful bounty. Students used the Lakshmi Sri Yantra[15] as a way to develop concentration and mental focus.

The Neptunian Women's Club in Manhattan Beach, an ocean-facing suburb southwest of Los Angeles, became the new Los Angeles meeting place. A small, white, bungalow-like structure set amidst side streets and cottages several hundred yards from the sea, the Neptunian Club offered an intimate and protected setting and an almost unobstructed view of Atmananda as he sat on a narrow couch on a raised stage at the front of the hall. A linoleum-tiled entry, a vintage 1950s kitchen, thin white poles holding up the ceiling and up to 120 people seated on folding chairs added to the sense of a small town theater.

As one L.A. student said, "The Neptunian Club was the first place where I really noticed what Atmananda did to a room. Well before he arrived, the space filled with waves of stillness, intense and vibrant, enveloping the brain and being. All I did was drive from Santa Monica to Manhattan Beach, park my VW bug, and suddenly I'd enter a magic kingdom. I didn't question it. I loved it."

The early Los Angelinos were characters. Esmond, the British playwright who liked to ask about the meaning of life;

---

15 A yantra is a visual meditation tool, usually consisting of a symmetrical concentric pattern with a dot in the center.

Vanessa the young teenager who simply grinned all the time, glad to be there; musicians, dancers and actors, some of whom had not become successful in their chosen careers so were attending computer school just in case; UCLA students who found Manhattan Beach low key and quaint. Atmananda held them all in a protective aura—a pulsating, palpable, still energy that permeated the room.

The first meeting at the Neptunian Club was celebrated with a pot luck dinner. Students were asked to bring enough to feed the entire group. Long tables set end to end in the Neptunian Club kitchen overflowed with intriguing offerings, from vegetarian chopped liver to lasagna for 120. Beauty and abundance reigned as an expression of higher awareness.

In reference to a desert trip that had taken place several days earlier, Atmananda again explained his stance on the siddhas or mystical powers. In some Hindu and Buddhist traditions, it is considered somewhat gauche to display the siddhas. Omitting the possibility that a teacher does not have sufficient kundalini (because they are not going into samadhi regularly or at all) to display a siddha power, the classical concern is that the student will mistake powers for substance. Or that the teacher will make a similar mistake. Atmananda pointed out that he displayed the siddhas for only one reason—to help students become enlightened. And of course, since he manifested a wide range of siddha powers, he did it for sheer, silly fun.

Building on this theme, several days later he retired to the Del Mar castle turret and wrote on his yellow legal pad some thoughts to be shared with the students.

> "At the age of thirty-one, my self-realization returned. I am happy that I am self-realized because it gives me the ability to do more for the world. ...

> "Sometimes I wonder if you know the resource that you have. If you did, you would use it wisely. In the 'I Ching' there is a hexagram for the 'Ching.' It is symbolized by a well. I and all self-realized spiritual teachers are like wells. People come to us and they take as much as they need. If their need is great, they bring a large vessel to fill. If their need is mild then they bring a smaller vessel.

"Don't be fooled though. If you feel that you have gauged the depth of the well by the amount you have taken from it so far, then you have not understood the nature of the well. The well is Eternity. A self-realized person has melded their conscious awareness with eternity. When you reach into their awareness, you touch the wellspring of the void. It is endless. When you meditate on or with a person who is self-realized, you draw from the well of eternity. The more that you take from the well the more there is to take."[16]

Atmananda set a new goal for the year—to quadruple the size of the student body from 250 to 1,000. He said he had run monasteries of that size in past lives, and it was a reasonable number of students for him to work with. He also added San Francisco to the teaching quest. He said that opening a center there would be a lot of work, but it was the right thing to do and he hoped the current students would support him.

Atmananda restated his mission: "This year, in 1982, what we're doing together, besides just having a generally good time, is trying to get you to walk through the doorways to eternity. Because each time you walk through those doorways your perfection will manifest in a new and exacting way. ... What I'm trying to do is to have you not be pedestrian or plebeian with this study. That is to say, we're not simply studying how to get high in a new way. You're studying existence itself, to become it."[17]

Atmananda booked the 770-seat ballroom at the Miramar Sheraton Hotel in Santa Monica for weekly public lectures.

Before each talk, students came in and helped to prepare. The teaching space was spotlessly cleaned, far beyond what the facility's own cleaners accomplished. Flowers covered the stage. This was Lakshmi. The physical beauty and cleanliness would help raise the consciousness of the attendees even before Atmananda arrived. Then, when everyone in the audience sat with Atmananda, they were physically aligned to perceive and meditate well.

A lore of first time impressions developed:

16 Lenz, Frederick (Rama). *Lakshmi: Notes from Atmananda*, Issue No. 1, Del Mar, CA, Jan. 12, 1982.
17 Lenz, Frederick (Rama). Student meeting. Los Angeles, CA, Jan. 9, 1982.

"Atmananda went into the lotus position and began meditating, after telling us to meditate with eyes open a few moments into the meditation. Almost immediately after I opened my eyes, I saw rings of gold and pure red light around him. I was no stranger to auras and other paranormal phenomena. I had seen other teachers and a number of natural psychics manifest various phenomena. However, I had never experienced anything as intense or vivid as this before, and particularly had never experienced anyone who could emanate energies at all resembling what I saw here, who was so unselfconsciously humble about it."

"I was so moved during the public workshops in February 1982. During a question-answer-comment session, Atmananda was sitting and responding to the audience, but the light kept on emanating from him as if he were still in deep meditation. The light behind him flickered in gold and pure crimson, and suddenly I saw the serenity that I had sensed and experienced in Tibetan Buddhist figures I was surrounded by as a child. All at once I knew in an inexplicable way what it was that the Tibetan craftsmen had captured—only instead of being in the presence of a statue, I was in the same room with it manifesting as a living being."[18]

"Atmananda suddenly stopped talking about the unspeakableness of 'Nirvana.' He said it was time to experience meditation ourselves. With our eyes open, Atmananda began formal meditation by turning up some cool electronic music including sections from Tangerine Dream's *Exit* and *White Eagle* as well as other electronic music groups on his cassette player. As we all stared at his form, per his request, the light surrounding him turned gloriously golden and spread evenly throughout the room. The back of the heads of the audience sloping down in front of me changed colors and polarized like a huge negative print, and Atmananda himself appeared and disappeared within his own blinding light. Atmananda was for real."

On February 9, 1982, for Atmananda's 32nd birthday celebrated at the Neptunian Club, the students chipped in to buy him a vehicle in which he could sit up straight—a BMW.

On this birthday evening, I sat a few rows back from the stage at the Neptunian Club. I still couldn't believe I'd found this teacher—

---

18 Brian. "First Meetings." *The Last Incarnation*. Los Angeles: Lakshmi Publications, 1983. PDF pp. 21-24.

American, funny, iconoclastic. It struck me every time I saw him. That night, he wore a simple white sweater and tan pants. He announced some future events. Then he said that we would meditate. He settled into his bench-like seat and closed his eyes. I also closed my eyes.

Suddenly I found myself in a tunnel, swept along with no ability to move or change course. I was moving very fast, conscious but firmly held in the grip of the journey. In this tunnel, I realized that everything that weighed on my mind—concerns, fears, angers, desires, doubts, grudges—did not exist. They were phantoms that dissolved in the tunnel. I next had the realization that everything in my life that was "real" was not real at all. Everything I knew as solid and real was an illusion. NOT REAL. My individual existence dissolved in the tunnel.

And yet, there was something, an essence of "me" that was dragging along. It was making my journey more weighty than I wanted. The weight was my life of judgments, not laughing enough, not being happy enough or giving enough. The sensation was like sludge on the bottom of a race boat. And then I realized that the sensations and realizations I was having were *very* familiar, as familiar and as frequently repeated as an automatic physical mechanism, like batting an eyelid.

Eyelids open—*life in a body*. Eyelids closed—*life out of a body*. Over and over again. I calmly realized this tunnel was the experience of dying. At that moment, someone in the hall coughed and I came back into the present moment with a *thunk*. No tunnel. I opened my eyes and looked at Atmananda. He sat in front of me, eyes closed, a light smile on his face.

Twenty minutes later, during the break, I approached him and tremulously said I had experienced what death was like. I felt shaken but I said I would no longer be afraid of dying. He looked at me sweetly and said, "Death is nothing to fear." Then he went over to blow out the candles on his cake.

Atmananda and his five-tier 32nd birthday cake

Overcoming the fear of death was Atmananda's 32nd birthday gift to me. Our student gift to Atmananda, a BMW, had a more transient effect. Although very grateful for the new car, it was not his vehicle of choice. Not a match. Two weeks later, he drove the Beamer to a car dealer and traded it for another type of chariot, one that could outrace the fundamentalists still furious with him over *WOOF!*, and one that conveyed the message he expressed—NOT plebeian, NOT pedestrian. Self-discovery is fun, contemporary and exciting, and an enlightened teacher's ride should reflect that!

In choosing his new car, in the same spirit as taking out the large ads, Atmananda combined practicality, teaching and leaping beyond boundaries.

What vehicle could provide much-needed horsepower and convey the message of enlightenment for the West? No-brainer! A maroon Porsche 911 Carrera, naturally. Fast, sporty, the un-Buick. THAT was a match.

"He loved the car," a student said. "It was his toy. He bought a small frog for the dashboard and joked that it was a traffic cop detector. He kept the car spotlessly clean. The long drives to L.A. suddenly became fun because he could maneuver the car in and out of traffic with ease. Even the fact it had only two seats became helpful. Instead of groups of people mashed into his back seat, he could drive with more privacy. Enlightened teacher in a Porsche, deal with it! It was another koan."

In the second half of February, Atmananda spent late nights in the castle working with his students on the Spring 1982 issue of *Self Discovery*. The publication had become more sophisticated, reflecting its target audience. A large illustration of a clear-eyed Western woman seated in a full lotus position comprised the cover. Inside the paper, the lead article—"Why Don't More Women Attain Enlightenment, Part II"—contained another layer of integral feminist knowledge on the energy and inner workings of women and men.

> *Women are far more powerful than men. The kundalini energy is usually much more active in a woman than in a man. It is the essential life force that moves within all beings. The kundalini power is necessary for any type of worldly or spiritual success. The more a person has, the more successful they will be in their chosen field of endeavor. ...*
>
> *In most relationships between men and women, men use women as a power base. This concept is quite simple to understand. When a person opens their heart to someone, they place themselves in a place of total receptivity to that person. ...*

If you open your heart to a person who is filled with problems and anger, then those qualities will enter your awareness field. ... Love creates a two-way circuit between people. Unfortunately, most men take power from the women they are close to. This usually happens when they are making love. ...

In order to attain Enlightenment, it is necessary to have all of your power. It is necessary for women to begin to reclaim their power from men. This does not necessitate a complete breakdown between men and women. It does mean that women must become more conscious of the energy transpositions between themselves and the men in their lives. ...

The public lecture series commenced in the San Diego area, bringing seekers old and new, including several who had known Atmananda in his earlier graduate school/Chinmoy years.

"There, in a Del Mar supermarket on a laterally sliding glass door, I saw my old friend from the Chinmoy days, Atmananda," said a former Stony Brook student. "Placed on a poster, his visage bounced back and forth in front of the housewives, the construction workers, and the kids trying to get change for Pac-Man. Its proclamation offered a 'Journey through The Void' and it struck me like something out of Jules Verne, but *then* there was the most outlandish resume I had ever read. It spanned 450 years! Hey, Atmananda, I'm a sucker for spiritual hoopla, but this is really going out into the ozone.

"However, his photograph revealed someone's face that, while it had a resemblance to my old sidekick, was somebody somewhere else. It glowed, it shined, the eyes, something about the eyes. And there was another zinger, a little passage concerning his desire to help his students from previous incarnations. From deep within the vault of my own hidden self the faint click of a tumbler falling into place was heard. I again read the double live garbanzo resume. Images of life in the zendo, mother India, and the vast, eternal snow-clad ranges of Tibet raced through my mind. Were these the shadows of forgotten lives, or was my own desperate need for truth manipulating my imagination? 'Why ask dumb questions at a time like this?' I thought. I attended the talks and became a student."

The lectures series migrated north to 1982's new city, San Francisco. At the 500-seat Unitarian Center, lines stretched out the street. Not everyone who stood in line was able to get in; the hall filled and people were turned away.

"I saw Atmananda at his first talk in San Francisco," Sanford Knaff, a Russian mathematics student, said. "When we meditated, there was a mega-ton of energy. It was like one of those things they describe in science fiction, like a stunning radar type machine that hits you and does something to your brain, mind and body. Your body starts vibrating. I had been to other teachers but had never experienced anything like this.

"When I talk to people, I say that in one of the first meetings I attended, one of the big things I remember is that I always considered spirituality to be adding things to what you are. Atmananda said that YOU have to radically change. He also spoke of computer science, which was interesting to me since I had a strong engineering background—I was intrigued by the idea that an engineering computer mind-set would promote spirituality."

While Atmananda looked baby-faced, he did what he advertised. Using the power of his awareness, he took the public on journeys through the void. There was a distinct tech to doing that, which he related to Tibetan teachings.

> *Tibetan yoga is founded on several principle ideas. The first idea is that all human beings are part and parcel of consciousness, that consciousness is existence itself, and that consciousness has a field of attention through which it becomes aware of different particles of reality—or eventually it becomes fully conscious of all of existence, which is, as you know, what we call enlightenment; that there are specific ways that this enlightenment takes place.*
>
> *In other words, enlightenment isn't an accident, it's rather a science with specific principles: that there are universes other than our universe, universes not so much in the physical world as universes of mind, of spirit. That all of the*

universes operate through specific types of laws and once you've learned and mastered these laws you can operate in and through these different universes; and that you are capable of uniting yourself with the void, with eternity.

For many who attended Atmananda's talks, the journey through the void started prior to the lecture, continued during the talks, the Q & A's and meditation sessions, and usually continued on the way home. Then it was up to the participant to change in ways that would allow light and power to remain and grow in their being.

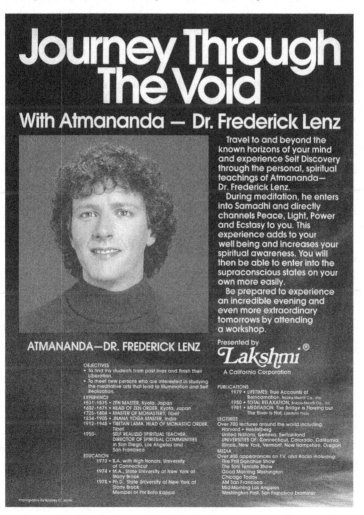

As the weeks and months passed, Atmananda became increasingly airplane- and car-bound. He drove from Del Mar three times a week to Los Angeles, gave classes for San Diego students twice a week, flew to San Francisco weekly, and hosted smaller groups at the castle on weekends. The weekend castle perk: students helping with small chores at the castle often were invited to journey with him to the desert.

I drove to Atmananda's castle on a Sunday afternoon, where I pecked at cleaning an already spotlessly clean white flokati rug. The exercise seemed pointless, but I was glad to be out of L.A. and spending time in the spacious grounds of the castle. The smell of jasmine floated into the living room from the open windows. At least ten of us were there, doing similar non-taxing tasks. Less than 45 minutes after I arrived, Atmananda—wearing T-shirt, jeans, casual demeanor—came downstairs and announced that everyone there was invited on a desert trip, and we should all share several cars and meet in front of the house in about 20 minutes. I vacuumed a few more square feet of white shaggy wool and headed for my car. Two other students joined me for the ride.

Instead of the Anza Borrego, we drove to Joshua Tree National Park, arriving at 8 p.m. Joshua Tree, with its remarkable, dramatic rock formations and exotic collection of *Yucca brevifolia* (Joshua trees), some of which live to 1,000 years old, is the Anza Borrego's cosmic cousin. Tall, with thick trunks and branches flung at every angle, the trees look like unique characters in a Dr. Seuss book.

That night, the moon was half full. With our caravan of six cars, we were able to park in a small turn-off area surrounded by mid-size boulders. We walked for less than ten minutes, following Atmananda into a clearing surrounded by what felt like a family of Joshua trees, and sat around him. We meditated for a long time. I opened my eyes occasionally. I saw that the light surrounding our group kept getting brighter until, at one point, the circumference of our circle was filled with clear white light. Streaming down from the sky towards Atmananda was a ray of soft white light that stopped just above the top of Atmananda's head—his crown chakra. I felt I was viewing grace.

The stillness and clarity of the meditation deepened. We meditated for almost two hours, but it felt like minutes, or like no familiar time at all. Then Atmananda stood up to leave and started speaking. We stood up around him, and I was a bit towards the edge of the circle. He made a humorous remark about frogs.

This is true.

Suddenly, I found myself the size of a speck of dust. I was looking at a grayish-brown frog, sitting on a rock at the edge of a moonlit pond. As my being had become the size of a dust particle, the frog seemed *huge*. He was croaking, his giant craw bulging in and out rhythmically. His all-seeing eyes surveyed the pond with intense, crystalline vision and complete dispassion. In my tiny speck-like state, unnoticed by the frog, I observed the frog's strongest qualities—perfect powers of observation and total dispassion. Then my awareness flipped back into my body and I stood, full-sized, on the edge of the circle around Atmananda, listening to him speak.

Less than a minute passed. Atmananda said the word "bee" in the context of speaking. My awareness suddenly flipped into the speck-size state and I found myself staring at what, given my perspective, was a *huge* yellow and black, spiky bee. The bee was poised on a textured, shiny surface such as the inside of a hive, and every bristling fiber of its being pulsated with energy. It was like an airplane poised for takeoff. It was still, but ready to explode into action at any time. It was a worker bee, and I sensed its intense dedication and loyalty to the Queen bee. The power and intensity of the bee were there to serve the Queen (whom I did not see). I perceived the bee's strongest qualities—focused, intense power and loyalty. Then my awareness snapped back into my body, like a sharp flick of a rubber band, and the group around Atmananda started to walk out of the desert, back towards our cars; I walked with the group.

I knew from past studies that in Sanskrit, words *are* the thing spoken of in vibratory form. The words of a fully enlightened teacher ARE the thing they speak of, and Atmananda just demonstrated this to me.

"When I take you to the desert or when I present subtle physical light shows for you at our meditation meetings," he said, "I am demonstrating the fluid nature of existence. The reason I do these sorts of things is to help you understand that the world around you is not really physical, but subtle. It is a web of light. ... Together we are trying to establish an awareness of light in the physical world. This is our play."[19]

---

19   Lenz, Frederick (Rama). *Lakshmi: Notes from Atmananda*,
     Issue No. 2, Del Mar, CA, Jan. 26, 1982.

On Sunday afternoon, the Spring Equinox, March 21, he met with the 80+ students remaining in the San Diego Center. He talked about the importance of a strong, mentally challenging career to support powerful meditations. He encouraged everyone to look into computer science. He said he was thinking of opening a computer company where Lakshmi students could work. He said there was a strong possibility he would move to Malibu.

The San Diego student resistance factor shot up—computer science, no way! Moving to Los Angeles? Ugh!

But Atmananda had already selected Malibu as the next physical nexus of teaching. A few days later he tapped his student and fellow adventurer, Lila Jenner, to explore the new terrain.

They met in the morning for coffee at his house, Jenner said. Atmananda laid out the day's plans. "I've seen that Malibu has a particularly interesting dimensional substructure which I'm interested in tapping," he told her. He also said they would be looking at several rental properties in Malibu, and the goal was to "see" the proper home.

He explained that the place where you live and base your energy greatly affects your state of awareness and the experiences you will have. Your overall state of mind is on some level determined by the place you live. Consequently, selecting a new home required being in a sharp, clear state of attention, with very few surface thoughts, in order to maximize your seeing abilities.

The pair arrived in Malibu in time for their first appointment with a realtor.

Said Jenner, "The first house was a very clean and ultra-modern beach house with strange sculpted and molded furnishings. Neighboring houses were ten feet away on either side. There was no breathing room, it felt too cramped. The second house was at the bottom of a canyon. The house itself was impeccably clean, with Japanese trimmings. It didn't feel right either. We walked through both houses very quickly and were glad to get back in the car. Atmananda told me that he had intuited that the third and final house we were about to see would be the right one, but he had to see the other two just to make sure.

"At the tip of Point Dume, we drove up to a tall wooden gate and stopped. The realtor opened the gate with an automatic door opener and it smoothly and quietly retracted to the side, revealing a long down-sloping hill. We drove through the gate and down the grade. The house at the bottom of the hill was a large, two story, light yellow and white Victorian doll house. The owner of the home was the actress Goldie Hawn. As soon as I saw the house, a strong vibration circuited through my being. It was on the edge of the high cliffs, overlooking the ocean. I didn't need to see any more to know that this was the right house. I walked out into the backyard to the edge of the cliffs. It was late afternoon and the sun was just beginning to get low in the horizon. It was incredibly beautiful, incredibly powerful yet peaceful, and it was easy to feel the timeless dimensions from the edge of these cliffs. Atmananda had found the place."

The move-in date was set for May 1 and packing at the Castle began.

Before the move, however, student house-cleaning was in order. At the end of March, Atmananda sat with yellow pad and pen in the castle's turret and composed his third and final "Notes from Atmananda." The topic was sexuality and the Lakshmi student. His notes were typed, printed and handed out to every enrolled student.

In the year-plus he had been teaching on his own, hundreds of young, mostly single people had signed up to enroll in Atmananda's classes. As they met their follow students, they discovered other bright, spiritual, people with whom they shared similar interests. To this mix, add habits and hormones, and you get—the dating game! In addition, as the teacher, the students focused on Atmananda's relationship status. Did he or didn't he? The time had come for an announcement regarding policy. It was important; people needed to know. He wanted to set things straight before he moved to Malibu.

> Perhaps the most difficult task facing anyone on the path to Truth is dealing with sexual relationships. In the following few paragraphs I would like to offer a few insights into this mysterious subject.
>
> Sexual relationships, like all things, are neither good nor bad. They do, however, have a volatile effect on your awareness. Traditionally most spiritual teachers have advised their students to avoid having sexual relationships. They feel that the emotional complexes that occur within these relationships reinforce the ego and limit and bind a person to the physical consciousness.

I do not feel that this is necessarily the case. As you know I have an extremely liberal policy regarding relationships for students at Lakshmi.

My policy is that you must run your own life and relationships. If you wish to avoid having sexual relationships, that is up to you. If you feel that you cannot handle them and that they do you more harm than good, then naturally I feel you should avoid them. If, on the other hand, you feel at your current stage of development that relationships are necessary and actually aid your spiritual evolution, then you should have them.

There is, of course, one catch. The single rule that I have for my students is that no student shall in any way interfere with the spiritual growth of any other student or of the student body as a whole. In my opinion, if a person who is a member of Lakshmi engages in a sexual relationship with another student, they are violating this basic rule.

Atmananda went on to describe exceptions—people already in a relationship before joining Lakshmi. Someone dating a non-student who then becomes a student.

The reason for this rule is simple. In a spiritual community everyone is trying to evolve their conscious awareness. In order to do this it is necessary to come together with your teacher and with other students in an atmosphere of trust. When you come to a spiritual center you should be able to relax in an atmosphere of purity and meditative awareness. You should leave your sexual preferences and energies outside the meditation hall.

If this is not the case then it is virtually impossible to bring people into the superconscious. It means that every time a woman or man enters the meditation hall, they are examined by the other members of the spiritual center as a possible partner. The sexual energies that flow back and forth pollute the consciousness of everyone present in the meditation hall.

Atmananda then described a soap opera of endless reformations of gay and straight meetups, breakups and flirtations.

My solution means that you can view everyone on the planet Earth as a possible partner—if you want to—with the exception of the few hundred persons who are my students.

Atmananda explained that some self-realized teachers are celibate and others are not. He was not.

A number of famous self-realized Zen and Tibetan masters have had sexual encounters after attaining realization. From their point of view, making love is an experience, like any other experience. They attach no more significance to it than anything else. They feel that to either be attracted or repulsed by sexuality is an attachment. It should be noted, however, that they are in a state of completion and when they engage in sexuality they are like small children who see perfection in everything. They no longer have attachments or an ego that can get caught. ...

I am not celibate. Like the Zen and Tibetan masters, I do not feel that sexuality matters any more or any less than anything else. I feel that to be either attracted or repulsed by sexuality is an attachment. I have gone through entire lifetimes, however in which I practiced celibacy. This was necessary at a certain stage of my development and now is no longer necessary.

Atmananda also spoke of tantric sex. True tantric sex is practiced in or near a state of samadhi, when the act of lovemaking is not physical but energetic and spiritual. It can be a form of teaching. Some Tibetan, Bhutanese and Zen teachers have taught in this manner.

Some self-realized persons occasionally use sexuality as a way of transferring kundalini. During the act of lovemaking, a person lowers their defenses to someone else more than they usually do. This is particularly true of women. If the person whom the self-realized person is having sex with is in a very high state of consciousness, it is possible to accelerate their growth with a very powerful transfer of the kundalini, for at that moment they may have opened themselves up completely. This is sometimes done on the path of mysticism.

Naturally the kundalini can be transferred in many other ways. Normally the kundalini is transferred in meditation with your teacher, the way I transfer it to all of you. But occasionally a teacher will use the mystical method if they feel it will help someone who was spiritually advanced enough to participate in sexual intercourse without getting caught up in their bodies.

Message: Date whomever you want, but not fellow students. Atmananda was not celibate, and he might use sexuality as a mystical method of transferring kundalini to a student. Read my lips. There was nothing to hide.

One other element of student house-cleaning—at the end of April, Atmananda met again with his dear friends, the San Diego students, the people with whom he shared the longest history. He spoke about the wild beauty of Malibu, and the refined beauty in the Neptunian Club. He asked them to sense the abundant job opportunities in Los Angeles. He saw that they would learn something and change in new ways if they made the move. He asked them—HINT HINT—to raise their hand if they thought they would move to Malibu with him. About one third of the group raised their hands. He did not push them further.

Malibu

"Malibu is a dream vortex," Atmananda said. "There are places where, particularly along the ocean or up in the mountains above it, it's very, very easy to change dreams. La Jolla, most all of San Diego, certainly, but La Jolla is a dream vortex. You'll just find you'll go through changes faster living in a place like this. The energies cycle and recycle constantly. It's very disconcerting sometimes. It's as if you're in a place where the weather changes constantly. It's raining, it's sunny, it's raining, it's sunny. So in Malibu, La Jolla, places like that along the coast of

California, you'll find that the dreams can change constantly. It's easier for you to view the different cassettes of existence in these places.[20]

According to geological surveys, the Malibu area is a rare coastal Mediterranean ecosystem, found in few parts of the world. The beaches occupy the Western portion of the Santa Monica Mountain Range. The geologic structure of the Santa Monica Mountains is exceedingly complex after tens of millions of years of geologic activity, evidenced by many ancient volcanoes and a long history of earthquakes. The main mass of the Santa Monica Mountains dates back approximately 100 million years.

In Atmananda's terms, he did not see Malibu as a contemporary playground for rich and famous people. He saw it as an ancient place of power that attracted seekers of power, including rich and famous people. When he flew over Los Angeles, he spoke of the sprawling city as the former location of a highly advanced and powerful nation. Malibu, as an advanced dreaming vortex, would be supportive of reaching his goal—1,000 appropriate enrolled students by the end of the year.

On Sunday, May 2, he moved out of the Del Mar castle and into the Hawn house in Point Dume, Malibu. The students helped to pack and load up several trucks. Three hours later, when the caravan of U-Hauls arrived at the bright yellow Cape Cod-style house, Atmananda was there to help oversee the unloading of furniture and boxes. The previous renters had left the house in shabby condition, so boxes were piled in the center of rooms while the students undertook the re-painting and cleaning. During the next several days the house was detailed into impeccability.

In addition to a spacious living room, dining area and kitchen, the Goldie house downstairs contained two family rooms. The students painted one room blue and called it the "Lakshmi room," the other was painted deep red and called the "Kali room," evoking the red colors of the Indian goddess, Kali. The upstairs was home to Atmananda's bedroom, his office, a library, the "art room" where all the brochures, ads and other media were created, and the "computer room" where the newest PC resided and all the administration work of the Center was handled. All the west-facing rooms had spectacular views of the ocean.

---

20 Lenz, Frederick (Rama). "Dreaming." *The Lakshmi Series.*
Los Angeles: Lakshmi Inc., 1982.

Atmananda enjoyed finding furniture for the house. He planted flowers all over the garden. Tibetan thangkas and Japanese scroll paintings were hung on the walls.

In Atmananda's room, large windows opened to the sea. His bed was covered with a colorful knitted afghan. To hear music ranging from classical to heavy metal to the latest Top Ten, he set up a Bang & Olufsen stereo system.

On the mantle of the bedroom fireplace rested copies of the twelve books he recommended for his students. A highly polished and lacquered oriental trunk, adorned with a fresh flower arrangement, served as his meditation table. Flowers lasted a long time in his house, especially in his room.

To meditate, he sat on a blue oriental rug which lay on top of a flokati carpet. His meditation table faced the windows that opened to the ocean. Two big pothos ivy plants hung symmetrically on either side of the table. His bedroom was his only private spot, yet even it was open. The only lock was a decorative door chain consisting of an eight-inch braid of wicker.

The library shone with dark wood, with shelves that went up to the ceiling. Every shelf was filled with an extensive selection of spiritual books from East and West. He collected many of the works of Vivekananda, teachings and stories of past Tibetan Dalai Lamas, teachings and stories of Tibetan teachers such as Tilopa, Naropa, Padmasambhava. The library contained a range of Buddhist texts from all traditions—Zen, Hinayana, Mahayana, Vajrayana. Numerous books represented Hindu teachings and teachers. Atmananda had read them all. Nestled in between the books were spiritual artifacts and relics.

"I used to work in the Malibu office," said Forge. "Shoes were not worn in the house and a clean consciousness was expected when you came in. It was assumed that when you walked in the door, you were to leave your ego behind with your shoes.

"If you worked at his house, you had to have mindfulness down or else you were Swiss cheese. I worked in the office on evenings and weekends. You had to be conscious of what was in your mind and have no thought at all, if possible. I always had to do that, and he used to comment on it when I was successfully practicing mindfulness and when I was not.

"He would emerge from his daily meditation practice in the late afternoon and be in very sensitive, dissolved samadhi mind-states. He was very sensitive to the states of mind of those around him."

With the Malibu house, a new etiquette evolved. Atmananda's awareness was becoming more and more merged with light and less able to relate on a familiar basis with students. There were still no overt signs of deference, no bowing or standing when he entered a room. He still strongly shunned such trappings (and always would). But there was a growing sense on the part of the students of the process their teacher was going through and the effect it was having on them. And that was naturally awe-inspiring.

"We would work at our own jobs during the day, go over to Atmananda's house in the evening and on weekends and help in the office or with other tasks," a student said. "Then he'd sit with us in the living room and we'd talk. He would tell us of the nature of existence. One of the talks was about women and kundalini. He told us what happens during menstruation, why some women have cramps and some don't, how it works with the energy body. He correlated the energy body with the physical body.

"While he spoke, it was as if a woman was talking to us. He explained that women are capable of conducting fantastic amounts of energy and kundalini power, much more than most women are now aware of. During menstruation, the kundalini gets unleashed from the base-of-the-spine chakra and comes up through the higher chakras located along the area of the spine. When energy is contracted or blocked in the lower chakras, particularly the second or third chakras, it causes cramping. It's a contraction of the energy body in that area. Kundalini yoga done properly will release the energy. As a woman, when you have your period, your power is up because the kundalini is flowing so freely."

Atmananda humorously pantomimed the kundalini energy blockage that would cause cramping, and the relief when it was released. "It was so right on. We all laughed so hard. So much of his humor was based on telepathic perception. We had many talks on the nature of existence. The topic was whatever was going on with the group working at the house. He always addressed who was in front of him."

The people working in the house learned selfless giving by watching Atmananda. Although the Malibu house was like a fortress of beauty, as he took on more students and engaged with their psyches, he had a rougher time dealing with their energy arrays. Also, as the older, original students began to go through intense changes, his openness and love for them affected him strongly. During the first year in Malibu, he gained about 75 or 80 pounds. "There was a sense that he was in a lot of pain," one of his old student friends said, "but he wasn't focusing on it. It would surface casually in a conversation."

To help clear out the energies he picked up from his seven-nights-a-week meetings with students and the public, he established new, vigorous workout routines. A steep staircase dropped precipitously down the cliff from the back yard of the Hawn house to Windward Beach, a wide, often-deserted stretch of white sand and pounding surf. Atmananda took the stairs to the beach and ran about one mile south on the shoreline, then jogged to the right, up the narrow, steep road that wound uphill to Point Dume. From there he ran up the hill to the end of the Point and often jogged up the circular path that led to the tip of a promontory overlooking the Pacific Ocean.

There, in an open, windy space, far enough from the street to be protected from the eyes of drivers, Atmananda often stopped to meditate. The occasional hiker might see him—a curly-haired man in a jogging suit sitting perfectly straight in a full lotus position, the soles of his feet skyward, eyes closed, a soft smile on his face. He was immobile, barely breathing, but not to worry. This was Malibu. Normal.

"The ultimate spiritual balancing act is to have one foot in eternity and one foot in time," Atmananda said, "and to not know which foot is which."

"One day I went running on the road in Malibu," a student recalled. "A shiny maroon convertible Porsche whizzed by, and I realized it was Atmananda. I waved and kept running. A few minutes later, I was still running, and up a hill. And what came flying over the hill—fast—but another shiny, maroon convertible Porsche heading right towards me—as if to mow me down. I must have had the most surprised look on my face as I jumped into the air to get out of the way. The car came to a screeching halt a few feet away from me, with Atmananda inside laughing happily. He said, "Hey—we're having Chinese food. Why don't you go home and change and come on over for dinner?" The crazy look of fear on my face must have instantly changed to pure ecstasy as Atmananda mirrored me and we both laughed as he drove off and I ran off."

The Malibu outings mirrored the madcap variety of L.A. A new, Friday night movie game was dubbed, "Where's Atmananda?" Students' intuitions were tested. The challenge—to find which movie Atmananda would go to that Friday and to be standing in the line as he showed up. Usually, at least 50 students figured it out. Most often the movie (no matter the genre or the reviews) was a new release opening in Westwood or a screening a week later over the hill in Calabasas. The reward for getting it right: an inner high five and a film screen transparent with light streaming through the images.

Even if a student didn't find Atmananda, the movie's name was circulated and—if the film contained a teaching point—added to the student movie list. "I learned to look at film in a new way," said Leah Antigne, a petite, bubbly UCLA student. "Atmananda used movies as a modern day teaching model. His point of view was different. The film plots represented what was in people's conscious minds. It was his way of studying what was out there in peoples' attention fields.

"He was fearless in his viewing of film. If you went to a scary film, it was to learn not to identify with the dark side, but to be detached and observe the hero. He was teaching us not to operate from a fear-based perspective but to move beyond your fear—or neuroses or stuck patterns. Most of us were very timid. He taught us—don't be a wuss."

"The film is to this century what the novel was to the 19th century," Atmananda said. "The only difference is that we experience it in another way. I don't think that film will ever displace the novel, I think it's added a new dimension to it. Films are a wonderful place to learn. Drama is probably the oldest of the communicative arts. Now instead of actors having to travel all over the country and do thousands of performances, they can do it well once on celluloid and many people can enjoy it.

"I think film is far better than television in the sense that commercials create unnecessary syntactical breaks in the drama. There's a lot to be learned from film, from cinematography, from camera angles, from the situations that are presented. You go through an emotional catharsis when you see a film. You see yourself on that screen. It is a cleansing process."[21]

At the movies, Atmananda often bounded up to people in the movie line and exchanged one-liners. Even an "I like your red jacket"

---

21 *Interview with Rama.* Los Angeles: Lakshmi Corp., 1985.

had meaning, a transmission of a packet of knowledge. Atmananda complimented people on their state of awareness, not just their clothes.

"Around July of 1982, I was sitting next to Atmananda at the movies when a preview came on for the movie, *Pink Floyd The Wall*," a student recalled. "I became very excited because I thought Pink Floyd was 'so cool' and assumed that since Atmananda was 'so cool', he would love them too. I turned to Atmananda excitedly and said 'Don't you just love Pink Floyd?' Atmananda looked at me and answered with a deadpan 'no' that left me hanging and floored—with my mouth gaping open, which caused him great laughter. Then I had to laugh at my obsession with Pink Floyd. I got, just from that one moment, a packet of information. That they were sort of obsessed with being dark and brooding, and that wasn't interesting to Atmananda."

Many films inspired Atmananda. He loved the film, *Conan the Barbarian* and recommended that the students watch it. The film represented tenacity, courage, not caving to sophistry; the destiny of an unloved, unrecognized youth to overcome opposition and grow to become a great leader.

Atmananda accompanied many of the students to see *E.T.* at the Pantages Theater in Hollywood. He loved the movie—the innocence, the courage, the yearning for our real home, the magical imagery of the kid's bicycle rocketing into the sky silhouetted against the full moon. When he left the film, tears filled his eyes.

Later he said that yearning for home is a yearning for higher awareness that is our birthright—a yearning for yoga, for union with eternity, with God. Atmananda added *E.T.* to the recommended student film list.

Soon after moving to Malibu, Atmananda sat on the flowered couch in the Lakshmi room and spoke of hard work to the small group of students who sat before him on the white flokati rug. Occasional pops and crackles from logs burning in the fireplace punctuated his speech. The words served as an antidote to the dreamy, movie star Malibu environment.

> *When you work, you should do a superlative job. When you work, you should do it with excellence because whenever you work with excellence, that adds to your consciousness. Whenever you don't, that detracts from it. Even if it's a simple filing job, typing, computer programming, being a*

doctor, lawyer, student, whatever it may be, you should succeed. Success is a sign of a good spiritual consciousness. You don't have to be success oriented, you should just do it. You should do everything perfectly and keep working at it. Because if you feel that your work is part of your yoga and you do that eight hours a day, all the energy you put into it will advance your consciousness, your meditation and everything else. ... I work from the moment I wake up until I go to sleep. I wouldn't know what else to do.

"One night I was giving Atmananda a shoulder rub," said a registered nurse who had known Atmananda since the New York days. "We sat in his living room in Malibu following one of the weekly Lakshmi meetings. I noticed my forearms were cramping. I thought it just meant my muscles were out of shape. Gradually the pain kept worsening. I reached the point where I wanted to run out of the room screaming. I knew that I was picking up on, but to a much smaller degree, the pain that Atmananda experienced. We began to talk and I told Atmananda what I felt. I asked him if it was a particularly difficult night or if for some reason I was just feeling more. He told me that he frequently was in that much pain, but that I usually was not sensitive enough to feel it.

"I kept trying to minimize the huge hard knots in his shoulders. As I rubbed I could feel or, I should say, sense, a kind of black sticky substance. It spread across the muscles of his lower neck and shoulders as if it had been laid there. It had a truly awful feeling to it. The densest areas of this substance corresponded to where in his shoulders these knots were located. As I rubbed these areas, I began to see mental images of different students of Atmananda's. Some were students that had been with him for a long time. Some were newer students at Lakshmi. I could somehow sense that each knot I was rubbing actually related to the person I was seeing. I also sensed that for one reason or another, these people were angry at Atmananda. I told Atmananda about this but I didn't mention who I actually saw. I asked him who he thought could be angry at him and sending him negative energy. He named five people straight off that I had been perceiving.

"I asked Atmananda why it was that he experienced so much pain. Did all realized beings have to go through this? He told me that it was because he had made the decision to work with people. It didn't have to be this way. He could just go away and live in the forest if he wanted it to stop. He told me he was feeling a little better and that I should be heading home. It was late and I left."

Early June in the Neptunian Club—several students brought tall, angular potted pine trees that framed his small on-stage couch in a comical way. Surrounded by the trees, Atmananda spoke of his teaching experience: "You see, spiritual teachers just sit at home at night waiting for someone to ask them out. And if no one asks them out, they stay at home. They try and look their best, you know. [Student laughter] No, really, I mean, you try and look attractive, put out a nice *force*, you know, stuff like that. But you just wait by the phone. [Laughter]

"It's true! You're waiting for somebody who's happening, who's glowing, who's ready to really go along. On a certain level. I mean you're out there doing the best you can for humanity, but another part of you that could be doing things just has to wait by the phone. And you'll know if somebody calls, immediately. (Atmananda snapped his fingers.) The student pops into your consciousness. Pow! They're there. Even if it's for an hour. What the heck."

On his reading of his students' progress: "You're doing fine, but I'd like to see you reach more into eternity itself, in this lifetime while we have—who knows how much time we have together? I don't know. I bet the birds do, but they would never say. But if you reach a little bit more, it's endless. I'm trying to tell you that life is so much better than you can imagine. That eternity is so complete, nirvana is so perfect and shining, but you're just skimming it. You're missing it. And that's a part in the process. But if you just reach a little more, if you just extend your self-giving, your love, a little deeper, if you just try a little harder in your meditations, it's endless, it's perfect, it's beyond anything that you can imagine. And I would like that for you. It would be quite wonderful. But you'll never know. You might even think that you know. But you'll never know. Unless of course—just some thoughts on a Wednesday night for you. For your scrap book. Should we meditate?"

Across the small hall, chairs rumbled and squeaked along the hardwood floor's surface as the students straightened their spines and either replanted their feet on the floor or folded their legs into a cross-legged position. Atmananda waited patiently for the scraping, like the tuning of an orchestra, to settle.

On a whim, I raised my hand to ask Atmananda a question about meditation. For many years, I had studied with another teacher. Because of that, I felt I had earned my stripes in spiritual practice, and I considered myself more advanced in meditation than many of Atmananda's students. Because of my self-appointed status, I usually pushed my way to the first three rows of seating in the Neptunian Club. I felt I had earned that placement and on this night I was in the front row, about five feet away.

He looked at me, acknowledging my raised hand. His eyes became two piercing lasers fixing me to my seat. Before I could even process a mental 'UH OH,' I heard him say, "You think you know SO much. You think you're SO important. You think you're more important than anyone in this room." The energy behind the words was so intense that it caused me to feel flipped out of my body, wishing I were anywhere but in my folding chair. He did not let up. "You think that you know everything, you have an answer for everything. You are so smart, you have nothing else to learn."

No, I wanted to yell back, I'm insecure and I put this on to compensate. But this was not a dialogue. It was a sandblasting. As he spoke, and he continued—"*You* can't learn anything because *you* already know it all"—he sent force fields of energy against my shoulders, my neck, my head, my arms. He seemed to be criticizing me for hours, although it was probably one minute. Then it ended. My awareness was in confetti strips and smithereens. That this takedown had happened in front of my fellow students made it all the more painful and embarrassing.

He closed his eyes and clicked the start button on his cassette player. The "No Exit" track from Tangerine Dream wafted into the room and he began to meditate. The students closed their eyes and followed suit and I was left to squirm.

At the break, no one spoke to me. It was as if I had acquired some illness they didn't want to catch. I felt like a leper. I drove home that night in disgrace. When I got home, my awareness, dislodged and flopping like a load of silver fish freshly dumped onto a fishing boat's deck, pushed out of my body, not wanting to inhabit such a know-it-all, insecure body.

My chopped-up self managed to go to sleep. When I woke up the next morning, I felt the strangest sensation. I was enveloped in what felt like a warm bath of soft, bright awareness. It was like a soft cloud around me. Wherever I went, it went. This gentle happy envelope of awareness sweetly put the pieces of my being back together. It lasted the whole week, until I drove to the next Lakshmi center meeting. I never would have quit Lakshmi because Atmananda yelled at me. He was right. I had become his student thinking I already knew it all. Over the week, I looked at that. As painful as it was to be publicly critiqued, I felt Atmananda had shifted my being in a powerful way.

At the next center meeting, I sat about ten rows back. At one point during his talk, he spoke of the need to sometimes speak harshly to people, then he stopped and looked at me. He said, "I only do that to people when I trust the quality of their love."

That moment endures.

With divergent student groups requiring different levels of teaching, Atmananda for the first time recorded an audio tape to be handed out to new students, and he also asked all his current students to listen to it. Titled "Welcome to Lakshmi," Atmananda communicated facts and feelings that remained true for the rest of his teaching life.

> The reason I've accepted you as a student is because I recognize your spiritual potential and your sincerity. Certainly I'm aware of your liabilities, problems, difficulties, karmas and so on. But at the same time I see something in you that suggests to me that you have the possibility of reaching a very high state of spiritual evolution in this lifetime. This doesn't mean you will, that's really up to you. But you have that potential. I won't accept a person as a student if I don't see that potential.
>
> I'm really not a personal advisor. You have to make your own decisions in life to become strong. What I do is teach you how to integrate your awareness with light and learn the sophisticated processes. And with that knowledge you can then make all of your own decisions. If I decide things for you you'll become dependent, and I'm into your independence, not your dependence.

I don't want you to over-focus on me. I want you to focus on realization and perfection. Not on a personality. I do have a personality, or a number of them actually, they come and go. When you attain realization you'll still have some personality but it'll be very thin, it's like a thin crescent of the moon. It's just enough to function in the world. And when it's not necessary it's not there at all, then you're just absorbed.

But there's a feeling of heart that we have in the Center. I mean, that's why we're here, and I don't know if you'll understand that yet. We do this out of pure love. We don't have to do this. I can just sit at home and write books, that's enough these days. But I come in every day to the Center meetings and open my being up to you and take in all your energy, good and bad, and go home later and sit around in pain as I watch my muscles contract from the bad energy I pick up, I mean that's not a whole lot of fun, but it's done out of love.

You have to understand that this whole thing takes place out of love, and if it's going to work for you, then you have to love. And I don't expect you to do that right away, it grows in time.

I worked with many of you in past lives and as you know I'm a tough teacher. I'm very demanding, I expect you to be perfect. But at the same time, I give people more than enough room to be themselves, because part of being perfect is being yourself. I have lots of things to teach you and offer you. Mostly light to transfer. But I can't transfer it to you if you don't like me. You see, if you have resistance it doesn't work. So you have to learn to like this ridiculous strange person who's your teacher.

I'm very eccentric. I'm the first to admit it. However, there's a madness to my method which brings you to liberation. But you have to want it badly. You have to want light more than anything. You have to want God more than anything. And yet at the same time you have to be willing to accept your physical life and enjoy it. To work, to make your own friends, to run your own life responsibly, to keep the checkbook balanced. To keep your house spotlessly clean.

All these things you must do yourself. And if you do them, and you do a good job, then when you come to work with me I can bring you into eternity. I have that power, or you might say it comes through me from the infinite. Although I can't distinguish myself from the infinite, anymore, to be honest. It's all the same.

I do love you very much. I worked very hard for you to get here, and you may not realize that. And I would like this very much to work for you. But you must work for it, and you must bring me your best. You must become pure, gentle, kind, open and luminous. That's what the study is for. I don't expect you to start out that way. But you must progress in that direction.

Be inspired. The world is filled with light. True, there are many problems in the world and much darkness, but there's also much light. Look at the light, not at the darkness. Have fun with your life, be free, but be sensible and balanced at the same time. Learn these arts, learn the art of your own immortality. Become eternity.

My favorite image of ecstasy, the ultimate Sufi, as far as I'm concerned, is Snoopy Dancing.[22] *There's an innocence and purity in that awareness that one must have. Along with the strength and clarity. Welcome to Lakshmi! Thank you.*

---

22 In the comic strip *Peanuts*, Charles Schulz created an iconic image of an ecstatic dancing beagle. The image is known as "Snoopy Dancing."

Samadhi is Loose in America

If I believed there was a physical, I could not do this. We walk upon the Grace of God. Nothing else exists except that. It's like gliding. You walk just above the physical. You only walk or live this way if you have a terrific love for Existence. If you have total faith and love then that which you love will help you. Then you can walk on anything.

- Rama

Atmananda planned a new set of public talks in the San Francisco Bay Area. He asked the helpers, "Who do you think we're going to run into?" Atmananda guessed the personalities and the number of new attendees and was usually correct.

Separate meetings for Bay Area people who enrolled to study with him—35 in the beginning, growing to several hundred—began at the Unitarian Church on Folsom Street. With vaulted ceilings and rows of wooden seats, the hall was warm and enticing. It had rich wood paneling and stained glass windows. Like the Neptunian Club, it held light and beauty.

Atmananda's relationship with the San Francisco students was different than the San Diego and Los Angeles student groups. According to the Northern Californians, he was gentler, always funny. The inside of the church filled with a pure golden light long before he arrived. He often sat on the floor in front of his chair, dangling his long legs over the stage. The students saw him change into an old Chinese man, a beautiful woman, an Indian monk. He accepted students like Terps, a female practitioner of asceticism, who crawled into the class on her hands and knees. Or Shanti, a street person clad in all white. Shanti was the only student, out of thousands over the years, who Atmananda allowed to perform "pranam" in front of him, which means to bow and touch his feet. Shanti once said to Atmananda, "They (the students) don't get who you are." And Atmananda agreed, the students did not get who he was.

In July, the students from Los Angeles, San Diego and San Francisco received an invitation to the first tri-center Lakshmi activity, a Saturday trip to Disneyland, to be followed the next day by a desert trip. One Mickey Mouse-related issue had to be dealt with: large groups weren't allowed in the park.

Atmananda said he would send lines of luminosity throughout the Magic Kingdom, so no one needed to cluster near him. Everyone was on their own. He provided an itinerary, starting with the Pirates of the Caribbean ride, going on to Space Mountain and It's a Small World, and ending after sunset with the Electronic Light Parade down Main Street.

An outing to the Disneyland theme park in Anaheim mystified some new students.

I shared that viewpoint. As a jaded adult visiting Disneyland for the first time since age 12, I was skeptical about the whole trip. Disneyland was plastic city! Fake! Of all the rides, there was one I knew I wanted to avoid—It's a Small World—which I viewed as a shallow, commercialized exploitation of the goodwill of children, prominently sponsored by a major toy manufacturer.

"But it's Atmananda's favorite ride," another student said. I was bewildered to hear this. How could I respect a teacher who liked It's a Small World? So I offered myself a deal: Try to have an open mind and attempt to tolerate a smarmy exhibition of wooden dolls chirping nonsense and drivel, and maybe it will be better than you think.

After going on the other rides, late in the afternoon, my Lakshmi student friends and I located the towering pink parapets of It's a Small World and filed to the back of a long line. Eventually, we climbed into a 20-person gondola moving along a shallow canal whose banks were lined with look-alike dolls, allegedly representing every country in the world. Each doll was garbed in a colorful native costume, designed before every kid on the globe wore jeans and T-shirts.

The first chorus line of singing kewpies appeared. I squashed any pleasurable response. The boat rounded the second corner. More dolls—different nationalities. Over and over again, one little figure after another warbled the same vapid refrain.

My shoulders felt tense and I tried to relax them. Why should escapist cheer make me so uncomfortable? I tried to still my mind. I searched the smiling faces of the many dolls. They did look happy, I admitted to myself.

Oddly, the admission acted like a wedge into my brain. Then something happened.

"It's a world of laughter, a world of tears."

I suddenly experienced it as an epiphany.

"There is just one moon and one golden sun."

That was TRUE.

"And a smile means friendship to everyone."

Truth!

"Though the mountains divide and the oceans are wide,
It's a small world after all."

I saw it. I felt a love that transcends all differences.

In this small, damp Disneyland cavern smelling of chlorine and a faint dash of mold, a spiritual doorway opened—I viewed the dolls in a state of wonder. The costumes' colors looked wildly vivid; the faces of the dolls appeared infinitely happy.

As we continued to wind through the ride, the emotion I felt—a sheer, overwhelming delight—was new. It reminded me of the only person I'd ever met in this incarnation who truly felt like that— Atmananda. I suddenly sensed his delight bouncing around the canals and the dolls. I realized that Atmananda, who had been on the ride about 20 minutes before me, had filled It's a Small World with mind-states of lightness and joy. Unprecedented blissful emotions entered my being in that Disneyland ride. It was how he taught; he threw your being into states of joy when your guard was down.

Atmananda on the Thunder Mountain ride in Disneyland

The next day, a number of the new San Francisco students joined the Southern California students for a desert trip. The San Francisco students went to the desert in a large touring bus which, when the hike was over, would drive them back to the Bay Area.

"There is a guy who lives in Los Angeles who walks on air," a Bay Area student said. "He did it last night in the Anza Borrego desert, and he didn't leave any footprints. He did it under a fullish moon, miles up a dry river gorge, at about three-thirty in the morning. There were 374 people watching. I was there. I'm an anthropologist and a lawyer, and I work at a large university psychiatric hospital. Part of my job is to know who's crazy and who's not. I'm not. But there's something going on, and it got me out of my home yesterday on a blistering summer's afternoon for a long drive to an all-night desert outing replete with scorpions, cacti, and an 'overnight low' of about 85 degrees.

"I went to the desert on a Grayline bus, feeling a bit like Charles Kuralt checking out a human interest story. The buses dropped their passengers, cars were parked and packs secured, and attendance was taken. The 374 names were checked off roll sheets as the crowd sat quietly in the moonlit gorge. Then the signal was given and the march began. The man from Los Angeles, Atmananda, walked in front with two companions, setting a brisk pace. The rest of us followed behind him, hiking through soft sand up the shining white expanse of the dry river gorge. The mountains looming on either side of the riverbed shimmered with reflections of the moon and stars. I felt like an extra in *Lawrence of Arabia*. I was one of hundreds of people, young and old, walking silently through the desert night.

"We were hiking to a sacred place, a place of power. Atmananda had told us that the gorge was a place where an older race of Indians had engaged in spiritual practices in previous ages. In the present day, the desert was certainly not part of our ordinary life. But the stillness and the night began to feel natural, like old friends, and we walked, wondering how we would share the sense of this night with our incredulous friends.

"It was a wonderful night. I won't attempt to describe it in full. I will say, rather, that wondrous things happened all night long, and that one thing seemed to me to be the heart of the experience. This man, this spiritual teacher named Atmananda, walked on air. I sat with hundreds of people in a semi-circle and watched as he walked on pads of golden light.

"He would lift a foot and drop it down with extraordinary grace and tenderness and care, and it would support his weight without ever touching the ground. Chills ran throughout my body as I watched him walk, and an indescribably sweet happiness flooded my mind. I don't know if everyone saw Atmananda walk on the pads of golden light. But everyone could see that Atmananda was moving across soft sand without leaving footprints. He walked down a steep sand ledge without causing any sand to slide down with the force of gravity. Everyone could hear the deep silence of the night, uninterrupted by the crunching of feet on sand."[23]

Another student, on the same desert trip, described a different experience. "After a lengthy discussion of the phenomena we were seeing," she said, "Atmananda asked us to lie down on our backs and observe the sky. I was expecting to see the 'usual miracles'—rearrangement of the star patterns and such. But something very different happened. As I lay there gazing at the star-spangled array, wave after wave of sparkling light began to explode across the sky. My whole being was inundated with

---

23   Alison. "Desert Experiences." *The Last Incarnation*. Los Angeles: Lakshmi Publications, 1983. PDF pp. 55-56.

each rush of light. Soon the entire sky was a swirling mass of colorful glittering light.

"The radiance was like none other I've ever perceived; it was alive, almost tangible. I was bathed in a profound feeling of all-encompassing peace and love. Then the whole sky disappeared and I felt that I was actually looking at God. I felt a quiet intimacy between myself and Atmananda, between myself and my Self. For a moment outside of time, the sky was alive. God was real."

This is a high spiritual art you're studying. When you're in the desert, what I show you is the transitory nature of all things, that everything that appears to be solid is actually liquid. That it's all a projection and if you know how, you can change the projection.

But there's one eternal Reality, with a capital R, out of which all things come, and that's your greatest interest. That Reality is in all the lesser realities. As the Tibetans say, the jewel is in the lotus. I'm interested in you not just knowing that in an intellectual sense but becoming that, you're having that awareness, which is when we say that you are enlightened and that awareness is there all the time.

The desert trip is an initiation. Whenever we're together it's an initiation into deeper and deeper levels of knowledge. Right now you're only seeing this much of it.

Atmananda held two fingers close together, indicating very little.

Tomorrow, this much, the next day, and so forth. It becomes more wondrous all the time. The edges become rounded. Everything becomes perfect.[24]

On July 5, 1982, at the San Diego center meeting, Atmananda announced that the San Diego Lakshmi center would close in August and the students from that area could join the L.A. student meetings going

24 Lenz, Frederick (Rama). Student meeting.
Los Angeles, CA, Jan. 6, 1982.

forward. After the meeting, Atmananda spoke earnestly with many of his old friends. It was the last time some students saw Atmananda as they opted out.

Mid-July, the Neptunian Club—a student asked a question. "My old way of life isn't working anymore and I haven't learned the new way yet. What am I doing wrong?"

"You're not doing anything wrong," Atmananda replied. "You're being too heavy. Your mind is telling you you're not happy. You're being a wimp. (Students laugh.) Why not lighten up a little and have some fun? Do you know what life is like?"

The student shook his head, smiling.

"Life is like a tomato! Did you know that a tomato is a fruit? Yes. They also were once believed to be poisonous. That's right, but they can't fool me. It's obvious that a tomato is a vegetable!"

The student was laughing now. "Sometimes I feel like I'm a prisoner in this body," the student continued. "Sometimes I just want to dissolve and be free."

"Yes, but you shouldn't worry about all that stuff. I never did. I just went for the love and service to others. Do you remember that line in *Blade Runner*?"

"'Wake up! It's time to die!'"

"No, that was just a flashy line. What was the main line?"

The student thought, then quoted the line, "'Too bad she won't live. But then again, who does?'"

"Right. Do you know what life is like?"

"I think I indulge myself too much," the student said.

Atmananda nodded vigorously with a broad grin.

"Maybe I should stop?"

Again the nod and the grin.

"During the conversation, and from the very beginning, Atmananda had not stopped meditating on me," the student said. "It was all power and dissolution. The evening had been incredible. There was a deeper connection between us because some kind of block in me had dissolved."

Friday, August 6th—Atmananda invited a student to join him at the movies. She drove to his house in Malibu to meet him at 7:00 p.m. "As I drove up to his closed gate and rang the bell," she said, "I had the impression that I was coming to the Mad Hatter's House for a crazy tea party. A funny voice came out of the box, 'Hallow! Hallow!' I answered, and the gate began to pull open. I coasted down the driveway and pulled up to his house. My consciousness went through some very quick transmutations as I got within a closer radius, and a crazy wild joy welled up for the occasion. I rang the doorbell, and the Mad Hatter came to the door.

"We saw Woody Allen's *A Midsummer's Night Sex Comedy*, which had opened several weeks earlier. It was humorous, and Allen had delved a bit into psychic phenomena and the unseen, which added a special touch. Leaving the theater, we were in a light consciousness and joked about life on earth. In the lobby of the theater, he turned to me and said:

"'The past few days, I have been existing in the outer fringes of consciousness. The worlds that I go to are formless, infinitely beautiful and perfect. There is absolutely no relation between these realities and this world we live in. When I get into these outer regions of consciousness, this world, as we know it, dissolves. I feel no need to come back to all this. I could very easily stay there and simply let this physical body fall away.'

"No, No, Atmananda, you don't want to do that," I said to him as we were leaving the theater. The light mood offset the rather serious tone of the conversation, and we ended up laughing.

"We walked out to the parking lot and its funny yellow lights lent a surreal glow to the scene. We spotted his burgundy Porsche in the distance and made our way over to it. As we reached the car, Atmananda said, 'When I find myself coming back to this world, I realize it's because of love. Love is the strongest force in the universe. You can travel to all the multifarious realities—infinite planes of awareness—merge with them and become them. Yet, if love is lacking, it will all remain flat. If love is lacking in your consciousness, your awareness will be dry. You will be empty. If you love enough, you can do anything.'"[25]

A few days later, it was business as usual at the Malibu house.

"About seven of us had been working in the office and art room at Atmananda's Malibu house," said Forge. "He came by the office and invited us to go for a hike in Charmlee Park in Malibu where we often went for spectacular meditations.

25 Lorraine. "Journeys." *The Last Incarnation*. Los Angeles: Lakshmi Publications, 1983. PDF p. 176.

"We drove up in three cars and hiked to a secluded spot high above the water. Atmananda sat facing us and I looked out at him and the horizon. We began to meditate. I had a realization of his love that was so far beyond any love I had felt or known in any lifetime. This was a higher form of love that I had never before experienced. He was so far beyond what we call 'love' in his level of heart. It was inspiring and beautiful. I aspired to feel that over and over and be in that space with him."

During the hot Malibu summer, another student recalled, "There was a pool at Goldie's. It was a weekend, quite a few people were there working on a set of audio tapes to be handed out at the public meetings. Atmananda asked us to gather around the pool. He was on one end and we were on the other. Atmananda said, 'We are going to meditate now. For the next hour I'm not going to breathe.' I was riveted, feeling and observing if he was breathing or not. As I focused on him, the whole area started undulating. I said to myself, 'he isn't breathing.' I saw it. WOW. It blew me away. It was a HIGH meditation. He would just do stuff like that."

At an L.A. student meeting in mid-August, Atmananda asked people to start writing their experiences with him for a new book he would publish, to be called *The Last Incarnation*. He said that the book would convey the truth of the students' experiences and would bring the moments back for future readers. Since everything the students would write about had happened outside of time, the moments would be accessible at any time in the future.

At the Malibu house, Atmananda described meeting with the public in San Francisco. He said a lot of people there already thought they knew a lot about spirituality, and he had to edge them along more slowly.

If I'm conducting a public meditation and 500 people come, and I'm meditating on all of them and trying to do my best for all of them, there may be five or ten people who have meditated a great deal in past lives or in this life who are very, very receptive. It's very easy for me—

because they have already let go of a lot of the weights—to move them into the superconscious. For some people who are just enshrouded in maya and they have nothing but weights, it's harder. You can give them a glimpse, but they won't see as much. So what you do as a teacher is you give them constant glimpses. You move them into the alternate realities constantly. Each time they advance, each time they let go of another weight, another attachment, another way of seeing things, you can take them a little further and show them the next step.[26]

On Wednesday nights after the San Francisco publics, Atmananda often spent the night in the Hyatt Regency Hotel, located in the downtown Embarcadero Center.

"One night, after a public meditation at the Moscone Center, we sat at the Hyatt bar," said a student. "I looked at Atmananda, and all I could see was bright golden light exploding in all directions. I could not even see his physical form."

"I felt that a few of the people at the meditation tonight were students of mine from my past lives in Tibet," Atmananda said. "I hope to have enough time in this life to meet my former students from Japan, Tibet, India and other places and awaken them to their true identities. Then, at a later time, they will be able to leave the cycle of their earthbound incarnations and join me in another plane of reality. We attempted this feat of power long ago and failed. We must not let ourselves fail again."[27]

On Thursday nights, after meeting with the San Francisco students, Atmananda raced to catch the last plane out of San Francisco.

"I remember being in the San Francisco airport with Atmananda and two other students, waiting for our flight back to L.A," a student said. "We had come from a Lakshmi meeting at the Unitarian Center and Atmananda was very high. As we stood in the boarding line, Atmananda began to smile, a huge ecstatic smile, and got all wobbly. He said, 'Oh no! Not here!' and started to dissolve into samadhi. He was leaning over and we grabbed him to help him walk down the ramp to

---

26 Lenz, Frederick (Rama). "Samadhi and the Supraconscious States." *The Lakshmi Series*. Los Angeles: Lakshmi Inc., 1982.

27 Laura. "Journeys." *The Last Incarnation*. Los Angeles: Lakshmi Publications, 1983. PDF pp. 166-167.

the plane. He was quietly laughing and beaming. Light was rolling off of him. I felt giddy.

"When we got to our seats he said that samadhi just takes him like that sometimes. He was still smiling and acting completely 'gone.' His carry-on bag was on his lap and he was pulling out stuff and looking at it like he had absolutely no idea what to do with any of it. He couldn't make conversation but occasionally uttered a comical word or two, like 'Frogs.'"

Atmananda explaining the process—

After 11 years of meditating, suddenly I started to go into samadhi every day, starting really in 1980. I had no choice. It was not something I could choose. I couldn't say, "Well, today I'm going to go into samadhi." It would just happen repeatedly. I'd sit down to meditate and I'd go into samadhi. In the evening I'd just be sitting at home and I'd go into samadhi.

Samadhi would never occur—it never does—at an inappropriate time. Eternity takes care of everything. If I needed to do something to function in the physical world, if I had to drive a car or talk to someone, it wouldn't occur. But it would occur again and again and I just watched myself dissolve and re-form again and again. I was a new person constantly, sometimes many times a day. As this happened over a period of years, there was less distance between the enlightenment that was within myself from past lives, we might say—this is a way, of course, of trying to describe something that's really impossible to describe— and that which I was in a waking state, so that now I'm always in a perpetual state of enlightenment. But for me the process hasn't ended as of the making of this tape on the 10th of September, 1982. Still, many of the powers that I developed from past lives, and just the integration of that enlightenment, is continuing so that each day there's less difference for me between the waking state and samadhi.

There really is almost no difference now, but any differences are gradually being wiped out.[28]

Atmananda invited all his students on a fall journey to the desert. After gathering at the Anza Borrego meeting place and hiking into the desert, he asked the students seated around him on the sand, "What do you really want tonight?"

Someone responded, "I want to know that you are the one true teacher for me."

"Ahh, a romantic," Atmananda shot back. "If you're still working on that one, what are you doing out here? There's only one true teacher and that's eternity. Everything is your true teacher. Nothing is your true teacher. That's what you have to see. You still have this idea that you will meet some person who is going to make everything wonderful. Some person who is your true teacher. You go on a picnic together and life will light up. It's not like that.

"The most you can do is find someone like me and see that I'm eternity. And that eternity is your true teacher. In other words, that's the true realization, that I am one with eternity—I can't be separated from it. If you see that I am eternity then not only do you see that 'I', that which you call Atmananda, am eternity, but you'll see that everything else is too. This gorge is your teacher, the moon is your teacher, the stars are your teachers, the scorpions are your teachers. Everything and everyone is your teacher.

"The only use that I have is that it's easier to use me as a doorway to see eternity through because as this world goes, I'm paper thin. ... When we're out here, what I am doing is showing you that I, Atmananda, whoever you say, am eternity. And that everything here, my friends who live in the gorge here who are very powerful beings, powerful warriors— that's why I bring you out here so the whole team—the wind, the sand, the brush—can work on you and help you simultaneously to see that the spirit of the desert itself is eternity."

Several weeks later, when Atmananda recorded "Samadhi and the Superconscious States" at his home office in Malibu, he included his samadhi progress report.

---

28 Lenz, Frederick (Rama). "Samadhi and the Supraconscious States." *The Lakshmi Series.* Los Angeles: Lakshmi Inc., 1982.

Now I'm always in a perpetual state of enlightenment. But for me the process hasn't ended as of the making of this tape. Still, many of the powers that I developed from past lives, and just the integration of that enlightenment, is continuing so that each day there's less difference for me between the waking state and samadhi. There really is almost no difference now, but any differences are gradually being wiped out.

In late September 1982, Atmananda invited Jenner to drive with him to the desert. They agreed to meet at the Malibu house, blastoff at 11:00 a.m. sharp. "Frogs," he greeted her as he opened the door with a big smile. "His eyes were incredibly shiny and clear," Jenner said.

In the sunlit kitchen, she prepared several thermoses of coffee. Before getting into the car, Atmananda walked out to his back yard. She followed him out to the back.

"Atmananda gazed up into the sky," she related, "and raised his hands above his head, breathing out sharply through his mouth, almost a soft whistle. Immediately, I saw two radiant beams of bright energy shoot into the sky from his hands. He then moved his arms down until they were horizontal, even with his shoulders, then brought both hands to his navel, breathing in. He repeated this sequence twice more, filling the entire area with light. The surface of my skin tingled and I felt the area in my temples open up and fill with energy. The whole back yard was now sparkling with energy and I was without one thought. I could distinctly see the aura of the ocean, a thick, luminous white band at the horizon. He glanced over at me and smiled."

"Ready? OK! Let's do it!"

Atmananda had given a meditation class the night before in San Francisco and had probably gone to sleep around 4 or 5 in the morning, Jenner said. After two hours of driving he asked her to take the wheel. They pulled into a gas station in Oceanside to switch places.

"I got into the car on the driver's side and adjusted all the apparatuses for my height," said Jenner. "As I adjusted the mirrors, he said, 'Now, when you drive, just take it easy. There's a little more energy in this car than you're used to.'

"He got a small pillow from the back and made himself comfortable on the passenger side. I pulled out, back on the road. I felt a little tense, but after about fifteen minutes I eased up and began to relax a little. I glanced to my right. Atmananda was sound asleep.

"As I drove, I found myself in a state of total quiet, without thoughts, without desires, without anything at all. But I noticed that I was filled with energy that flowed steadily up my back, causing a pleasantly cool burning sensation. Yes, there was a little more energy in the car than I was used to. There was a lot! This was the same car that he drove to all the meditations, driving back afterwards in deep states of samadhi, barely conscious of the physical world at all. The part of me that could still form thoughts realized that things were starting to become very different. I gazed down the road and nothing I saw, including the road, was solid.

"Escondido was the first major town. I slowed and drove through the main streets. In Escondido, the surroundings began to glow intensely and steadily. I could not have formed a concrete thought if I had wanted to. I kept driving.

"In the town of Ramona, the fields waved with light. In Julian, the mountains were melting, and still, Atmananda continued to sleep. Finally I turned down S2, connecting directly with the desert energy as I piloted the Porsche into the Anza Borrego. Overflow was achieved. The energy that had been flowing through my body and mind reached a threshold and kicked over to someplace I had never been before.

"It started in my hands. They began to tingle, and then gradually, they got numb. But not exactly numb. Numb still exists. My hands were dissolving, disappearing. I had a moment of panic. 'Oh my God,' I thought, 'I can't even feel the steering wheel!' It was then that I grasped, with semi-disbelief, that I could no longer feel my hands at all. The non-existence of my limbs seemed to be spreading quickly! Like a *dissolving* disease! Steadily, the non-sensation crept up my arms and they dissolved too, disappearing before my eyes.

"Then it hit my feet and legs. As I lost all feeling in my feet, the car continued to purr along the desert floor. But my feet weren't numb, they were simply gone! Was I still pressing down on the gas pedal? I guessed so as the car continued to cruise down the road at an even pace. Finally, the legs went. My body was completely dissolved in light! I was no longer conscious of driving the car, yet it continued to operate perfectly, clipping along at an even sixty miles an hour.

"This was really weird! My initial reaction was fear, which swiftly abated as I realized that everything for some reason was all right. I wondered how I would handle the turns without a body to turn the wheel. I knew that if Atmananda trusted me to drive, it would be all right, somehow, even if I couldn't feel the steering wheel or anything else.

"All the while, I was catapulting through a state of absolute bliss. My vision had long since changed, and everything appeared bright and translucent, as though it were very, very far away. When I saw a turn coming up in the distance, to make the turn, I willed what would have been my arms to turn the wheel, and even though I couldn't feel the wheel, the accelerator, the brake or the seat, the car turned perfectly.

"About half an hour before the meeting spot, Atmananda woke up. He took one look at me and began to laugh heartily.

"'So you're having a good time driving, I take it?'"

"I didn't say anything, couldn't really say anything. Atmananda saw that I couldn't physically function in this high a dimension of mind, and he started bringing me down, lowering me back to the earth with his will. Immediately the world began to solidify and I felt my hands pressing into the steering wheel. I was still pretty much in the outer ether though.

"'OK, that's enough for you. Pull over and I'll take it from here.'"

"He grinned at me as I pulled the car over to the side of the road and stopped on a dirt turnout. Opening the door, stepping onto semi-solid ground, I tentatively rounded the car to the passenger side, meeting Atmananda half way in front of the car.

"Atmananda, it was absolutely the most incredible thing I have ever experienced. I couldn't feel my body—nothing! But I kept driving anyway. It was so wild! Atmananda, how do you deal with it? It's too much!"

"'Well, you know, we all have our jobs,' he said, smiling, as he got into the driver's seat.

"The opening of the gorge loomed ahead and he slowed the car as he pulled up to a clearing off the side of the road. A few hundred yards away, two hundred students were there, waiting for him.

"'OK kid,' he said, 'heads up—it's showtime!'

"Gazing down the gorge, I just smiled. For me, the show already was well underway."

At the first Fall 1982 public workshops in San Francisco and Los Angeles, Atmananda handed out a new, hello-this-is-what-it's-about cassette tape, "Pathway to Enlightenment." He restated his teaching approach, with the intent of honing the listener's ability to get it.

Meditation is a radical practice, the most radical practice I know of. And in order to meditate, to really meditate, you have to be a revolutionary. A revolutionary in consciousness. The few people who have affected this world the most— Christ, Buddha, Krishna and others, were radicals. Each one of them was rebelling against a system that they felt was corrupt. And if you wish to reach high levels of awareness, if you want to have more fun with your life, then you have to take it in your own hands, and you have to be a little bit radical with the way you lead your life.

Meditation is a revolutionary practice because what you're doing is saying, 'I'm not interested in what anyone has told me or said that I am. I'm not really interested in what everyone says I should believe. I want to find out for myself what life is, and what I am. And then when I see that, if my own experiences show me that what others have said is true, then I'll know it's true, not because someone told me or programmed me when I was too young to know any better.' . . .

Who is Atmananda? Well, he's essentially, I suppose, a free spirit. Someone who's around to remind you that the spirit of life is wonderful and that you should dance with life. I'm essentially a radical, a revolutionary in my approach to self-discovery. Not necessarily revolutionary. I just think that I'm saying the same things that have been said for a long time, in a contemporary language. They're not my discoveries, they're yours.

The ever-evolving advertising campaign of an enlightened free spirit manifested as a full size newspaper with a color cover featuring a photo of a beautiful young blonde woman looking confidently and unflinchingly straight into the camera, as she sat in a full lotus position on a Porsche (Atmananda's). The back page of the Fall 1982 *Self Discovery* newspaper displayed Atmananda's past life resume. Advance stories of his students' mystical and miraculous experiences, soon to be published in *The Last Incarnation*, comprised the content.

Self Discovery

FALL
1982
ISSUE
FREE

Samadhi is
Loose in America

"If I believed there was a physical, I could not do this. We walk upon the Grace of God. Nothing else exists except that. It's like gliding. You walk just above the physical. You only walk or live this way if you have a terrific love for Existence. If you have total faith and love then that which you love will help you. Then you can walk on anything."

—Atmananda

How many buttons did this image push for non-revolutionary seekers?

> *No* to materialistic Porsche!
>
> *No* to attractive slim, young blonde woman!
>
> *No* to attractive woman looking independent and powerful!
>
> *No* to materialistic Porsche and attractive slim woman together in a spiritual context!
>
> *No* to a contemporary, wide-ranging collection of stories celebrating the miraculous and the mystical!
>
> *Noooo!*

Two hundred thousand copies were distributed. For the receptive, the cover photo, snapped by Atmananda, was a succinct statement: support for the power and sexual energy of women, the tantric path of the material and the spiritual, the possibility and actuality of mystical experience.

Atmananda said later that he had inundated the school teacher who sat on his Porsche with pure kundalini energy. As a result of the Fall 1982 *Self Discovery*, thousands of people attended Atmananda's talks. The newspaper's headline, "Samadhi is Loose in America," referred to Atmananda's iconic tale.

> *This weekend I went to Mount Palomar. I actually got three hours alone where I didn't have to do anything or meet with anybody, so I took off in my car for Mt. Palomar. I was listening to KROQ [a Los Angeles New Wave radio station]. I like New Wave. It's jnana. No 'love me baby.' It's more like 'screw off.' There's none of that mushy emotion in it. I like America. It's interesting. Though some of it is terribly ugly.*
>
> *So, I'm turning the radio dial and I'm driving. I'm totally out of the body. I'm feeling existence, feeling the vibrations of this and all other worlds. I realize I'm totally out of my mind. I like to listen to the lyrics of the songs on the radio. I mean that's poetry. That's the poetry of modern America. I like Country Western songs. That's human life. Heartache and misery.*

I get to Mount Palomar and I go into samadhi. I'm nothing. I don't exist. And yet I have to come back 'cause I have a meeting back in San Diego. And I'm seeing the birds and the trees and everything is so beautiful and I'm totally enraptured with the beauty. There's light everywhere. But I'm late for this meeting.

So I get in my car and I'm going back down the hill, back to San Diego. And I'm still back on Mount Palomar, I'm still back there in samadhi. And I'm setting some kind of land speed record in my car—I'm taking the turns down the hill really fast and there are waves of light shooting through me and I'm in all the other worlds at the same time. You have to realize that I pick up all the vibrations. Every time a car passes me I see into the inner beings and past lives of all the people in it.

I get to Escondido, which is some place you should never be anyway. I think, 'This is America. Pink neon hotels.' I'm not in America, but I'm in America. I stop at a JoJo's. This is always the best way to bring yourself down, JoJo's is great for that. But I'm totally out, you see, I'm still in samadhi back on Mount Palomar. I walk into JoJo's. I'm looking at everybody in the coffee shop and I can see their whole beings—all their pain and their misery and their futures. LSD is nothing compared to these states. I order coffee. I'm standing at the counter and I'm getting into the wrappers on the Trident gum. Wow! It's beautiful! I'm totally gone.

I go to the phone to call home and tell someone at the house that I'll be late for the meeting. There's someone in front of me and I have to wait and they're putting out awful energy and I'm just waiting there. I call the house and of course no one answers the phone. Very Zen. I hear, 'This is Atmananda. I'm not at home right now but if you'll wait for the beep you can leave a message.' I decide to leave a message but what will I say to myself?

You see, I'm still up on Mount Palomar, still in samadhi. I'm totally lost. A while ago I decided there was no such thing as lost because you're someplace, right? So I just drive. Here I was driving through Escondido. Looking at life. I'm in a place where the high school prom really MATTERS! I mean, you tune into life. A thought had been going through my mind—here I am in America. A self-realized person and here I am in my car in suburbia. I keep thinking, I could go anywhere and just knock on somebody's door and they'd open it and I'd just glow.

So when the telephone answering machine message ends and the thing beeps I say,

'Samadhi is loose in America.'

'Samadhi is loose in America.'

And then I hang up.

What's in a Name?

Throughout September 1982, a team of students reviewed over 500 stories of interactions and experiences with Atmananda for possible inclusion in *The Last Incarnation*. Acceptance criteria: accuracy, writing skill and energy. According to one team member. "Atmananda was so happy. We were going to blow people's minds."

One hundred sixty-six stories were selected, with Atmananda's final OK on each one. On October 20 at the Los Angeles Lakshmi center meeting, Atmananda announced a special desert trip for the 90-plus students whose stories would be published in the book. The trip was scheduled for the early evening, three days later, October 23.

The students gathered in the usual meeting place, a short distance from the road. Stories of what took place that evening were later added to *The Last Incarnation*:

"It was dark and windy the night of our journey to the desert. Fall temperatures had set in. Banks of clouds chased across the sky. The moon hid out somewhere behind a cloud. Only the stars shone as brightly as ever. We arrived at 7 p.m. and sat, meditating, in the sand. Atmananda joined our group at 10 p.m. I opened my eyes to see him walking towards us with his distinctive long-legged stride, his solar plexus seeming to lead the way and his upper body tilted slightly backwards, following the momentum of his legs and feet.

"He wore shorts, a sweatshirt and ankle-high hiking boots. A backpack was slung over his shoulders. He did not speak. He gestured for us to follow him and we rose as a group and started to walk.

"We hiked several miles into the desert and sat down on the sand, waiting for Atmananda to begin his play with the desert forces. Instead he just stood there silently. Suddenly his voice came out of the dark: 'I have to disappoint you,' he said. 'I am not who you think I am.'

"There was great puzzlement in the group. He went on: 'I don't really know how to tell you this. It's like breaking up with an old girlfriend, and I have never been good at that.' By now he had us all keyed up. I wondered what he was up to this time. Atmananda loved to surprise us with unexpected news, constantly unsettling people like myself who cling to old ways. Somehow I felt that what he was about to reveal to us went beyond his normal change of plans. My heart began to pound.

"He continued, 'You think I am a person, but I am not, although I used to think so too. I took myself for a spiritual seeker, for an English professor. During the years I spent meditating I felt my identities fade away one after the other. I was fighting the process tooth and nail, just like all of you are doing now, but in vain. I couldn't stop the dissolution of myself, and I finally had to realize that I was no longer a person.

"'After many years of studying with a spiritual teacher I was given the name of Atmananda. It is a beautiful name which means 'Bliss of the Soul,' or the 'Soul's Ecstasy.' I was very happy with that name until I began to feel that the being named Atmananda was dissolving.

"'I didn't understand what was happening. I felt the powers from my past lives come back to me with unbelievable speed. I became enlightened, then self-realized. The process hasn't stopped. I have no control over it.'

"He paused. The deep stillness of the desert made everything he said more real and visceral.

"'The molecular structure of my body has changed and keeps changing.' Atmananda slapped his arm several times. 'I'm not solid anymore.' He laughed heartily.

"'Time and again I asked myself who I was. As I watched myself being transformed into a vortex of energy, I kept wondering who all this was happening to. Here I was, this ridiculous being, cycling rapidly through a process that traditionally takes many years.

"'Then this morning I suddenly knew who I was. I woke up surrounded by a field of luminosity; a river of light was streaming through me. I suddenly understood. It was all so simple.'

"Atmananda became silent again, his arms folded across his chest. As I looked at his legs I noticed that they seemed to be rippling and the edges were hazy and undefined. A whitish light was emanating from them.

"'See the star up there, the one off by itself?' We looked in the sky, where his hand was pointing. One star stood apart from the others, shining brightly. 'Watch it closely.' Atmananda continued to point his hand at the star. It grew fuzzy, seemed to get bigger and then it disappeared.

"'Gone,' he said. 'I'll bring it back.' As we watched the sky, the star reappeared. 'I'll do it again.' The star disappeared and reappeared several more times.

"'Before I tell you who I am,' Atmananda said in a soft tone, 'I want to hear from you who you think I am.'

"No one spoke. 'Well, don't all answer at once.' A few chuckles.

"'I thought you were a man named Atmananda who meditated very well,' one student ventured.

"Atmananda shook his head, 'No.'

"'I don't care who you are, Atmananda, I'm just glad you're here,' another called out.

"'Please, no philosophy tonight.'

"Other students spoke out in the darkness, but no one seemed to have the answer to Atmananda's question.

"'A few days ago I stopped drinking Tab and started eating yogurt again. It was then I knew that something was happening.' We all laughed.

"'This morning when I woke up,' Atmananda continued, 'I looked at my body and there was nothing but light. I wasn't solid anymore. I was just streaming light.' He stopped pacing and looked out at us. 'My room is filled with golden light all the time now, even when I'm not there. Can you imagine how my friends feel when they come to my room to visit me? I'm not there, but the room is streaming with light.' Atmananda laughed.

"'Who am I?' Atmananda asked again.

"'You're Vishnu,' a student right behind me said.

"'Yes,' he answered, 'that's close.'

"'You're Rama,' the woman next to me said.

Deep silence.

"'Eternity has named me Rama,' Atmananda confirmed. 'Rama most clearly reflects that strand of luminosity of which I am a part.'

He eased the growing tension with a few jokes. Then his tone became more serious.

"'I want you to be very clear about what I just told you. I've had so many signs over the years, but I never put it together before.'

"'Then are you the Rama of the *Ramayana?*' a student asked.

"'No, I'm not the Rama of the Old Cycle. Eternity has named me Rama because it most clearly reflects the qualities that I express in this incarnation.' He sat down on his pack.

"'How are you doing out there?' Rama asked. 'What are you seeing?'

"'It looks like flashlights are going on and off all over the hillside behind you, Rama,' someone said.

"'Those are beings who have come to join us. There's really quite a crowd here with us tonight.'

"I had noticed tiny lights flashing for the last hour or so, a few on the hillside, a few right among our group. These flashes of light were quite different than when someone in the group turned on a flashlight and scanned the ground for scorpions.

Everyone was quiet.

"'I am not the Rama who was alive many years ago,' he emphasized. 'Rather I am an incarnation of that type of energy which in Hindu mythology is associated with Vishnu. Gods and goddesses are not what people think they are. Their names are terms with which we try to convey a certain experience, a state of consciousness.

"'You have to understand that everything is light. Human beings are light. There are different types or aspects of light. Rama is one particular aspect. You, too, are light. Do you understand? This is why I am sharing all of this with you.

"'Once, my teacher asked his assembled disciples who among them thought they would be God Realized in this lifetime. There I was, surrounded by all these saintly beings. And I used to sneak off to the movies on Friday nights, which was forbidden. I never thought

I was special. In fact, I figured I was pretty low vibe.' We couldn't help laughing with Rama.

"'There were hundreds of disciples in this auditorium and my teacher asked all who believed they would become Realized in this life to stand up.' Pause. 'Everyone in the room stood up except one other student and me. Then I knew I was low vibe.' More laughter.

"'But do you see my point? It can happen to anybody. Believe me, if it can happen to me, it can happen to you. Who I am is really not important. More importantly, who are you?

"'When you start to remember who you are, it will be very much like the stages of my own realization. It's an ongoing process. You don't just wake up one morning and *ZAP!* you're enlightened. Every day brings another change, the next step. And it can happen to you. This is what I want you to understand.'

"We were silent. His words rode on a powerful stream of energy.

"'Who are you?' Rama asked again. 'You're starting to remember. Now, watch this.'

"Rama stood up and started doing something very funny. He began walking around the open area in front of us, lifting each leg very high off the ground. As I watched this high-stepping I noticed that his legs seemed very rubbery. Sometimes he'd kick one out to the side or in front and it seemed to grow long and then become short. There was much chuckling while he continued to walk around in this strange way.

"Then as I watched I had the impression I was seeing his subtle body rise a few feet above the ground while his physical body pranced across the sand.

"'You're levitating,' someone said.

"'You're several feet off the ground now,' someone else added.

"Then his subtle body assumed the lotus posture and floated in mid-air. His physical body seemed to be elongating and rippling in unusual ways.

"'Whew,' Rama sighed comically. 'That's tiring.'

"The students' questions and Rama's answers went on through the night.

"'Rama?'

"'Yes, Esmond.'

"'What is the purpose of life, if one may ask such a question?'

"'Life is its own purpose. Life is divine play. Life is for the fun of it,' Rama replied.

"'How should we relate to you now?'

"'Just be yourselves, I always think that's the best.'

"At that moment a student spoke up from the rear of our group.

"'Rama, I've started to feel very sleepy. I'm having a hard time staying awake.'

"'Your body is saturated and it's closing down,' Rama answered. 'It's saying, I've had enough. No more of this tonight. It's at this time that a leap in awareness is possible. Sit up straight. Pull your shoulders back. When you think you've gone as far as you can, that's the time to push on. That's when quantum leaps in consciousness are made.'

"There was quite a bit of stirring among the students.

"'I want to make an important point now,' Rama said. 'It's critical that you understand that I am not special and that what's happening to me is not special. It just is. If you don't understand this very important point, then you'll be taken out by what I've told you and exaggerate its meaning out of all proportion. I am not a special person. I am no more or less important than the sand we're sitting on.'

Rama was silent for a few moments, then he continued.

"'I'm telling you about each stage of my process so that you'll realize that I'm really not any different than you are. Each stage I have gone through, you'll go through. And once the final stages begin, there's nothing you can do about it. The process went beyond my control long ago.

"'The people who have known me as Atmananda don't realize that he's gone. Atmananda has vanished, never to return. Erased by eternity forever.' Rama laughed. 'And in his place is Rama. A very different being.'

"The darkness dissolved into pale lavender light. The night was ending. Too soon we would leave this place and these moments.

"'I want you to understand that I'm not a special person; I'm not different from you. I had a pretty normal childhood. I played baseball. When I was about twelve a sort of return began. I was attracted to the books in my father's library on Buddhism. I didn't know why. I read them and didn't understand a word of it. Then puberty set in and my mind turned to other things.' We all laughed.

"It was first light. A few birds began to chirp. I looked up. The stars were gone, faded into the dawn.

"'The desert's waking up. It's time to go,' Rama said.

"We walked back in a long string of one's and two's and three's to the place where we had originally gathered. No one spoke.

"The sunrise was glorious. A crimson band stretched across the horizon. Streaks of red and gold extended through the cloud-filled sky. A pink hue spread over the mountains and the desert floor. I stopped from time to time just to watch the changing panorama of colored light as it ushered in the day. I wasn't tired at all.

"When we reached the gathering spot, we formed a large circle. Rama stood at its center and slowly rotated, looking at each one of us. He made three revolutions, gradually turning faster and faster. When he stopped, he addressed us a last time.

"'Try not to forget tonight. Try not to forget who I am. ... If you allow yourself to forget who I am, then you'll never remember who you are.'"[29]

Warrior

When a teacher gets a new spiritual name, it translates to the path of the students. Views and interactions with Rama changed because the name is like a mantra, a sound that manifests. The name and the person become a doorway to new realizations.

Outwardly, Rama continued the nonstop teaching activities. But now it was the warrior teaching, and the warrior needed a sidekick.

Rama had been searching for a particular dog for some time, an old friend. He already knew the breed—a Scottish Terrier. Scotties, Rama explained, are tough and have an esoteric nature that can deal with all kinds of energies in other dimensions. They are not like other dogs; they operate in a deep dimension and make great meditators. They are resonant and resilient with respect to high levels of energy and kundalini—they conduct that energy perfectly.

For an enlightened teacher, a Scottish Terrier would be a companion who, because of their esoteric nature, would understand what enlightenment is. The adopted Scottie would be a way for an enlightened teacher to safely show affection. He/she would be a fine example of a devotee.

"One evening in November," a student said, "I went over to Rama's house for a meeting. There were two adorable Scottish Terrier

---

29 Colleen and others. "The Last Incarnation." *The Last Incarnation*. Los Angeles: Lakshmi Publications, 1983. PDF pp. 189-194.

puppies in the living room. He explained that recently, he had seen an ad for Scotties in the newspaper and had been drawn to the breeder's house in Poway, near San Diego. The breeder brought eight Scottie puppies into the living room. Rama said he stood there and the whole group of them moved toward him and circled him. 'The vibe of those dogs! It was like a hum. They were really awesome.' He knew he had to get at least two of them.

"As we sat in the Lakshmi room, one of the puppies scampered around wildly. Rama looked at one of the students and said, 'That one's yours.' His puppy was much more still. Several weeks later, he named his dog Vayu, after the Hindu god of the wind. He said the puppy liked to sit on the bluff in back of the house, look out at the ocean and feel the wind blow. He built a pen for Vayu that he kept in the kitchen, while Rama was teaching him to be house-trained. He said he had been feeling this dog for a long time. He said they had been together in many previous lives."

Vayu often accompanied Rama during long periods of meditation, and Rama added long walks with Vayu to his Malibu life.

A student recalled, "One time I came over to the Malibu house. It was a time when Rama was encouraging those of us who had moved up from San Diego to dress in more of a chic manner, more L.A.-style than earthmom-San Diego. I had just purchased a new, hot pair of shoes. Vayu had recently come into Rama's life, and Rama warned us not to leave our shoes on the floor in the entryway, as we had always done. But I forgot. I entered the house, leaving my new chic shoes on the ground. When it came time to leave, Rama and I were heading out the door, and I bent down to pick up my shoes. I couldn't believe it! All that was left of them was wet globs of shredded leather—they were as thoroughly chewed up as any leather dog toy would be. Rama knew his priorities. He laughed and said, 'Your beautiful new Italian shoes are no more. Fair game!'"

The week before Thanksgiving, at the conclusion of a public meditation intensive at the Miramar Hotel in Santa Monica, over one hundred people walked up to the front of the ballroom to apply to be a student. Rama interacted briefly with each person. A similar scenario had taken place several times during 1982, but as this was the last set of new students for the year, Rama felt the interactions had special significance.

The next night at the Miramar, speaking to a student-only gathering, Rama shared his views on the new wave of applicants.

"The other evening, I sat down with 140 persons who are tentatively applying to join a spiritual organization that they don't know much about, with a teacher they've seen a few times. …

"So I looked at their applications, looking at their past lives and peeking through their beings, you know, I had to do this in microseconds. And it was a very magical moment; it was just really nice. I mean, if the moment never went any further, if I never saw them again, I'd be just as happy. We build very hard for moments of beauty, and I find moments of beauty in the building, too. They're apogees, moments of height that we reach, these little epiphanies.

"It was a really smooth, really lovely moment that, as far as I'm concerned, made everything that all of us have gone through—the *Self Discoverys*, the stories you wrote and working at the tables and selling tickets and just absorbing all sorts of strange energies from strange people who come by to see strange spiritual teachers—going through this whole grand process. Which is why I like you to get involved in it to some extent because it makes you part of it. You begin to learn about the nurturing of consciousness because for me, this has always been what it's all about.

"In other words, bringing people to enlightenment is fascinating, it's an art in itself. But yet, where I'm concerned, when I was teaching Mr. Sanchez his ABC's, when he 'got' his first written sentence, to see the light in his face at the moment of breakthrough after 63 years of always feeling bad because when he walked into an employment place he had to make an "X" when he couldn't write his name, when finally he could write his name, that moment for me was as important or as valuable as seeing a person enter into samadhi for the first time. I don't see that they're essentially different, which is why I do what I do. I've been doing it for a long time. It's called 'education.'"

On November 24, Rama met with the Los Angeles students at Lincoln Junior High School in Santa Monica, a temporary holding place until larger facilities could be found. "We started the year with approximately 225 students, and it was our intention in our spring series to double, which we did," he announced. "We went up to about 450. The intention of this season was to double again, to 900. I wanted to have a lot of quantum growth this year because it's a very special year.

We'll have about 400 students in San Francisco and 500 in Los Angeles. Next year, it's my intention not to grow as much.

"Tomorrow in our chemical experiment, we're going to add 200 persons, almost all of whom have energy that is a little bit different. Almost every one of the applications indicated that they have studied meditation before, which is neither good nor bad, it's just another interesting factor to watch. In other words, the Center will never be like this again. This is the last night. It's going to be radically different not in terms of what I do but in the general consciousness. Also, you'll find that the meditations will be getting stronger because there are more people and they pull more light as a group. (In his whimpering comic student voice) 'Oh no!'"

"With all the new people, it seems like the teaching itself has become less personal," a student commented.

"That's because I've been changing," Rama replied. "I would be using the same style if there were only 50 people. That really isn't because of numbers, it's because I've been cycling to higher and higher levels of consciousness or whatever you want to call it and it's just becoming much stronger, much more powerful, much cleaner.

"By and large there are very few people in the Center who I spend much time with any more, and that's because no one really wants to spend time with me. Because if they did, I would. You see, everything is intentional. Some people like to blame circumstances, life, their health for what they do in life, but everything is set up from a part of ourselves within ourselves. Whenever a person has wanted to have more personal contact with me, it's always happened, if that's what they wanted. Their mind may have said 'Oh yes I'd like that,' but another part of their self might have said, 'no,' more strongly.

"You have to understand—personal contact means faster change, and most people don't want faster change. While a part of a person wants more contact, a large part of them isn't ready, they don't really want that yet. When I look at a person, I don't just look at the parts they see themselves. As you know, I see you all very differently than you may see yourselves. For me there is no unconscious or subconscious, I see you as one unified being. And it's always very clear to me when someone is ready to move closer in terms of physical circumstances."

Someone in the audience pressed the point, asking, "How can we change to encourage more personal interactions with you?" Rama's answer was even and firm. "I don't make any personal decisions because

I like a person. If I like a person, the reason is because they show spiritual potential, not because of their personality. That's what I mean by liking people. When you get to the point where I am, you don't like people any more or dislike people any more for the same reasons you did before. If you see someone who has more light in them, or that light is trying to come out, or they're constantly working at it, you're more drawn to them. That's why I moved to Los Angeles from San Diego. I moved to L.A. because I was drawn here, I didn't choose it. I didn't particularly want to move to Los Angeles. But I was compelled to move here because there were more people here than in San Diego who were aspiring.

"What I'm most interested in with the expansion of the Center at this point is not the addition of the 200 new people, not my effect on them, not your effect on them. As you know, I'm always backwards in the way I look at things. What I'm interested in is their effect on you. Basically what I'm ending up with is two new centers next week in L.A. and San Francisco. It's a great opportunity for all of you to advance even faster, that's what I'm trying to get across.

"It's going to be pretty neat. It came out OK, all the work was worthwhile. It would have been worthwhile even if it didn't come out OK, but I'm really happy with the whole thing." Rama humorously pretended to cry.

Then Rama asked, "What do you suppose this is all leading up to?"

No one in the audience responded.

Rama answered his own question. "What language have I been speaking? Mysticism. Remember, what's 1983? The year of? Mysticism, right! We're almost there, right? Right. You know what mysticism is—lots of humor, lots of fun, lots of adventure, your life totally upside down all the time. Terrible!

"For the first time next year in maybe eleven years or twelve years of giving talks, I'm putting very little attention towards meeting new people, which means that I'm going to be putting it somewhere else. The other part's going to be where?"

"On us," someone called out.

"Yeah. In other words, you're gonna learn. Whether you like it or not, it's irrelevant. If you stay here you will grow by leaps and bounds."

"It was early morning, the day before Christmas," a student recalled. "I was on my way to work, driving over one of the canyon roads that leads in and out of Malibu. It was very misty and the winding road was wet and frosty. I rounded a curve and my car started to slide. It slid into the oncoming lane and someone hit me head on. The impact was so strong that it pushed me out of my seat and my head went through the windshield, shattering the glass. I could have been killed and should have been unconscious, but I was able to stand up and walk around until an ambulance came. That was the first miracle.

"While I was in the hospital, I was lifted into the highest state of awareness. I could feel Rama healing me. But when I got out of the hospital I was still sensitive and weak. I could barely walk. I had a hole in my knee, half my scalp was torn by glass. I was bruised all over. After several days, I went to Rama's house to work in the office. There was a beautiful Christmas tree in the living room. I was so sensitive that I couldn't talk to people.

"I was sitting in a chair in the corner of the living room when Rama walked up behind me. He placed his hands on my shoulders. As I sat there, an intense kundalini energy rush started going up and down my body, as if I were plugged into a wall socket. It felt funny and crackly. Tremendous energy started moving powerfully through me at what felt like a cellular level. Other people were present in the room while this was happening.

"While his hands were on my shoulders, Rama spoke very sweetly to the group. He was using the moment of moving me into a state of non-solid energy to take everyone in the room through a transit with me. I looked out at their faces as if they were the audience. He addressed the effect of the crash as he moved pure light through me and the group. He took everyone through a huge doorway that the accident had created. I saw him dissolving everyone in light—actively dancing with us all in eternity in this everyday moment.

"As I sat there, the kundalini went into everything—it burned me head to toe. It was the kind of burning that happens when a wound is healing, only it consumed my entire body. What he did with the kundalini was a miracle. I was spinning, unloosened from my life, my fixations, my illusions. I was in a state of utter dissolution. Then, he did something that was quite shocking. It was an act of such tenderness and compassion and was the final undoing. He bent over and kissed my cheek. This simple gesture had so many profound and moving results.

"First, the surprise of it brought me back to the physical in a gentle, kindly way. Second, it allowed me to surrender to the transmutation that was occurring, to let go of my insecurity that I had done something wrong, or was 'bad', and to simply trust his love and compassion. Third, it got everybody in the room to drop any judgments and to experience his compassion with him. When he removed his hands, I was able to walk, to move, I was laughing.

"Later in the night, he addressed the issues that had been present in my consciousness that had made me vulnerable to the accident. It was truth time. He exposed the problematic emotions that had been driving me, and then he blew them out. I saw how I had been gripped in a set of illusions that were blocking me from my own highest truth. Shining the light on them was painful, but the exposure allowed them to be dispersed. A deep healing had occurred in my heart and soul. He used this experience to bring love and compassion to everyone present. It was a group transformation that had a deep and profound effect.

"The day after Christmas, I went to the doctor's office. Three doctors looked me and all said, 'What?!?' They could not believe it. They kept poking at my knee and head to make sure they were actually seeing what they saw. They told me that normally it would take at least three to four weeks to heal my serious and deep wounds, if they would heal at all.

"Not only did Rama heal me completely, he used the opportunity to transform other people as well. When I told him about what happened in the doctor's office, he just shrugged. It was all part of a day's work."[30]

---

30   Leah M. "A Christmas Gift." www.RamaTribute.org > Healings

8

1983 - MODULAR MYSTICISM

Mysticism is an eclectic mixture of various forms of self-discovery that's primarily experiential. When we speak of a mystic, rather than a philosophical, understanding of a higher truth, we're speaking of someone who is more involved with direct meditative experience, where they're perceiving truth, they're having visions, moving into other strata of awareness. - Rama

Modular Mysticism

Rama announced it—the wheel of dharma landed on mysticism. Not the whoohoo, pot-stirring, rabbit-in-hat mysticism that one might conjure, but a very precise, practical and artful way of being.

In the Tantric Buddhism of Tibet, mysticism is often referred to as the "Secret Doctrine." Rama pointed out that these doctrines are secret not because they are hidden or restricted to a few individuals, but because understanding them requires more than an intellectual understanding. Mystical doctrines are not the words, but rather the direct experiences of enlightenment and the superconscious, what in Zen Buddhism is called "the direct transmission outside the scriptures."

Rama's description of mysticism drew not only from Vedanta and Tibetan Buddhism but also the American mystic teachings described by Carlos Castaneda. He often referenced the vocabulary employed by Castaneda's teachers, the Yaqui Indian mystics don Juan and don Genaro. Rama assigned two of Castaneda's books, *Journey to Ixtlan* and *Tales of Power,* as student reading. He found parallels between the teachings of don Juan and don Genaro and classical Buddhism.

Don Juan describes two key aspects of each individual—the tonal (also referred to as the first attention) and the nagual (also referred to as the second attention). The first attention is one's physical life, everything about a person that can be talked about—where they live, where they work, what they believe, what they eat, their clothes, their relationships, their family, their car. The second attention is what is beyond the power of words to define—it is the magic and mystery of life, the mystical experience. Beyond the tonal and the nagual is nirvana. The totality of the self is nirvana.

Rama explained that a student's ability to move into the second attention or superconscious is limited by how tight their first attention is. The stronger a student's tonal, the further they will be able to travel into the nagual and the higher ranges of light. In 1983, the year of foundational teachings on mysticism, Rama devoted considerable time to teaching students how to order and structure the first attention.

> When we meet here, when we talk, answer questions, I'm addressing your tonal. I'm teaching you a way or a series of ways of dealing with the world. It's very physically oriented. We spend a great deal of time talking about careers, relationships, economics, in other words the structure, the nitty-gritty of your life and what you do with your time because it's necessary for you to work out a way of living that's very strong, very tight and grounded and very powerful, otherwise you will not be able to deal with the unknown.

> In the study of mysticism, you become the most sane person on earth, the most rational, the most orderly, the most capable and the most logical. At the same time, you have excursions into the unknown that would defy the imaginations of the most imaginative thinkers on earth.

> The Buddha spent all of his time talking about what? The eightfold path. Well, what's the eightfold path if not ordering the island of the tonal completely?[31]

---

31   The Eightfold Path: Right view, Right intention, Right speech, Right action, Right livelihood, Right effort, Right mindfulness, Right concentration.

Rama also emphasized that the path of mysticism was not cold, but rather is based deeply in compassion, as are all of the spiritual pathways.

> *That's why there's always a tear in the eye of the Buddha, that no one sees, for the pain and suffering of others. Without a requisite knowledge of that pain and suffering, you're limited, you're mortal. You only become immortal when you feel the suffering of others and are one with it, as you feel the joy of others and are one with it, yet step beyond both into immortality itself and dissolve in eternity.*

To help his students discern a practical, grounded, orderly way of living, Rama spoke of mysticism as the study of power—learning to gain power, to stop losing power, to store power, and eventually to share power with others.

"In the practice of mysticism," Rama said, "it's necessary first to gain power. We gain power so that we can walk through that doorway that leads to enlightenment, to become conscious, to become what you really are.

"The first thing you need to do is to increase your personal power," he stated. "You have to make a list of the things that cause you to gain power. To do this accurately, you need to take a piece of paper out when you're home and write down all of the things in your life that have ever caused you to change in an affirmative way. For example, places, experiences, helping others, reading, writing, a hobby, career, an attitude, exercise, a type of diet, a type of food, music. You have to trace back all of the moments in your life when you have gone through a major transit or change and recall the things that worked."

The students called out examples—physical things—getting a new car, landing a promotion at work, winning a tennis game, scuba diving in the Caribbean. Laughing more. Getting a higher belt in martial arts. Buying new shoes. Bright moments in life.

"Then," Rama said, "on a separate piece of paper, you need to assess and make a list of the opposite, of those things and people in your life that have caused you to lose power. No blame is necessary, it just happens. Habits could cause you to lose power, places, attitudes, ideas. Try to be as physical in your perceptions as possible. Very often the things that cause you to lose and gain power are not necessarily all that profound, they're rather simple. It's good to make a list because you bring these things into your conscious field of attention and as you focus on it, you begin to work with it."

The student examples: long commutes, getting poor grades at school, too much TV, lack of exercise, bad diet, unfulfilling or boring job, angry or wrong partners/kids/parents/spouses. As many students cited bad relationships, Rama agreed—many people lose power in relationships.

"About 75 to 95 percent of all attention in this world, so says Don Juan and I think he's right, is devoted to romance. And it's such a waste, it's incredible, because you get almost no return on your investment—it's power lost. I think you need to look at yourself a little bit and assess how much of your energy you're putting in that direction. I have no argument with romance or with love but if you're fixating on it too much, you'll find that you're losing a tremendous amount of energy. If that's the way you look at life, then you're an amateur from a spiritual point of view."

Summarizing the mysticism list-making evening—

It is necessary for you to focus your attention upon your physical being—your body and its strength, upon your mind and its clarity, upon the place you live, the manner in which you live, the way you dress, the way you walk, the way you speak, the way you laugh, the way you think, the concerns that you have, the depth and level of your emotions, your attachments, your career, your interactions with those around you, how and where you spend your time—all of the subjects of your daily life, be they in the waking hours or ultimately in the dreamtime, but for now in the waking hours.

Why is one person enlightened and another not? Why is one person able to see the lines of the world or see the different vortexes? Why does one person go into samadhi and another not? Because they have learned to stop losing power, to maximize and gain power, and to increase the power they have.

Rama advised his students to become aware of the effect of locations on their state of mind. One can gain or lose power in a location. He explained that energy shifts in a location can happen on a block to block basis. Why is one part of town well kept, filled with nice houses and lovely gardens; and half a mile away is a neighborhood that is run down, the homes and streets in disrepair? It's because the energy or power lines in the land are different. Wealthy people are intuitively drawn to nicer neighborhoods not only for their beauty but because they sense how their minds will feel there, and they that will make more money in a powerful location.

The Lakshmi locations moved to stronger power lines. Having outgrown most auditoriums and smaller venues, starting in 1983, Rama began holding both public lectures and student meetings in two Los Angeles landmarks. The first and most frequently used assemblage spot was the Warner Beverly Theatre on Wilshire Boulevard in Beverly Hills. Built in 1931 in ornate art deco style and impeccably maintained, the Beverly retained a lush sense of show business beauty. The stage was swathed in red velvet. Elaborate chandeliers dropped majestically from the gilded, five-story high ceiling. The walls of the theater were covered with layers of symmetrical, sculpted patterns, all painted shiny gold, punctuated with gleaming wood faux columns. The 1,500 seats were velvet, soft and reassuringly comfortable.

Several miles further east in the Los Feliz area of town, the Wilshire Ebell Theater, built in 1927, evoked a different feeling. Orchestras and ballet companies played there. The stage was wider, the foyer larger and lined with elegant dark wood. Although the deep blue velvet stage curtains and wide auditorium seating were designed to express luxury, the hall was somewhat colder than its red hot Beverly Hills cousin.

Whenever he used either theater, Rama generally entered via stage doors on the side of the theaters. A small dressing room was readied for his arrival with flowers, fruit and water. He rarely drove on his own to the public talks but instead hired a driver to take him to and from Malibu because at the end of the evening classes, he often was too immersed in samadhi to drive. He frequently arrived ahead of time to make sure the sound checks were right and the evening's paperwork in place. The stage set consisted of a freshly cleaned Asian rug, an Asian screen as a backdrop and a simple, modern dark wood dining chair. Next to the chair was a side table for water and electronics.

According to David Silver, who managed the sound systems, Rama always wanted to use his own sound system, not the theater's, and the system was always whatever was the best on the market. Rama would not start a class for students or the public until the sound was right. He always meditated long before the lecture began and often meditated backstage until the energy in the auditorium was right. Paying close attention to the details was a central tenet of mysticism.

Rama suggested to his students that they should not scrimp on rent—or home ownership—because the energetic quality of where you live and sleep at night is critical for the practitioner of mysticism.

Another tech of mysticism concerned storing power, the mystic's way. Rama taught that one of the most effective ways to store power is writing about moments of power. "Whenever you write about a moment of power, if you write about a desert trip that we go on or a meditation that you have, or whatever it might be, when you write it down you are pressurizing it, you're compacting it. You're taking all the force and energy of that experience and you're squeezing it into a few words. In the moments that you are sitting there struggling to do that, you are compressing power, you're storing it. You're taking something that's very large and making it very small. Later you will be able to come back to it when you need it and make it very large again. This is an occult practice, a mystical practice. At the same time you are creating an identification with something specific."

Now began a new challenge, as the students regularly journaled the experiences they had with Rama. These journals were not to be measured for writing prowess. They were for the writer, the person distilling bright mystical experiences into words.

"You can compress power with spoken words, too," he taught. "When you go to a power place, if you speak very powerful words, it does the same thing. When I bring you to power places you'll notice that very often I give you a hard time if you say things that don't mean anything, that don't have heart and feeling because you're doing the opposite. You're losing power. Someone who can see and actually says something with feeling, even if it's very simple, is compressing power in that moment. That power will always be there if they think about that place. Then if you write it down afterwards, you compress it again. This is how you store power."

Other ways to store power: "Moments of self-giving compress power. Some people give but they don't pick the right moment or they don't pick the right way, so there's very little power in it. But when done in the right spirit, you compress power. Sometimes sharing power with others increases power and compresses it. That's what I do constantly. You also store power through love. Whenever you love, you compress time. Time stops. The world stops and you step outside of it."

Rama spoke of dressing well to gain and store power. Dressing well as a mystical teaching? Yes, and for many reasons. In this overcrowded planet, you constantly interact with people whom you do not know but who judge you by your appearance. They can instantly slam you, which means using their second attention to slap you down; or they can instantly respect you, or judge you to be successful, stylish, neat, competent. The latter makes the mystic's path easier.

"Let's begin with clothing," Rama said. "It doesn't really matter where we start because the rule will apply to everything we discuss. We could discuss the orderliness of your room or your house, your career. But let us begin with clothing because once you understand the principle, you can apply it to any aspect of your life.

"The way you dress is extremely important. If you don't think it's important, then you're failing to see that everything matters along the warrior's way. It's very important because it demonstrates the impeccability of your spirit. It's the guise through which the world evaluates and views you and the way people treat you in a world in which the description of clothing is essentially more important than what a person is. In other words, all the visible sensory details determine how they see you and how they react to you. ...

"The rule of thumb for the warrior is to be conservative in outer appearance, to find a very clean image and to use that image as a gateway into another world."

For his 900 students, Rama set a physical example by constantly raising the bar on his own clothing tonal. The white sweaters and the tan corduroy pants vanished. In their place—impeccably detailed clothing that offered clues to his past life resume. Rama came to student gatherings, public talks and appeared in print media wearing clothing that appeared Asian, or American mystic, or American Indian. The outfits were meticulously prepared and tailored.

Rama held spontaneous fashion shows, accompanied by rounds of laughter, in which students went on stage and Rama would comment on their attire. He advised Leah Antignes, one of his younger students, to look more sophisticated. He critiqued some of his software developer students for lacking style and suggested they upgrade their wardrobe. He advised his women students to peruse *Vogue Magazine*, not to purchase ultra-expensive haute couture but to be aware of what such garments looked and felt like. (Many years later, Rama joked that the one thing he had succeeded in doing was getting his students to dress well.)

Break your routines, Rama advised. If you have been doing the same thing for years, sitting in the same easy chair, living in the same place, listening to the same music, wearing the same hairstyle, you are losing energy. By changing and experimenting with new elements of your life, you build energy.

Another key teaching for the aspiring mystic—understand that many of your thoughts are not your own. Everyone is psychic. People pick up others' thoughts and feelings and think they are their own. The only way to experience your true self is to meditate well and to spend time alone in nature where the thoughts of others can literally be washed away. In our overcrowded planet with billions of people and extreme media/information overload, experiencing your own thoughts and feelings is essential but increasingly difficult. The modern mystic recognizes the challenge and takes steps to buffer the input and find their own pathway to self-knowledge.

"It's necessary to bring about a tremendous refinement in your being," Rama said. "That refinement begins from the ground up, and it is the focus of the daylight hours of your study."

Why Don't More Women Attain Enlightenment?

Another mystical teaching: Misunderstandings about the innate qualities of women and men create significant energy loss for both genders.

Rama stated that the main focus of his teaching in this life was the enlightenment of women. He said he had tried teaching this topic in past lives and always had his ass kicked to the ground. He said he had paid heavily for trying to help women. Now he saw a window—it might be a short one—where women could take the lead and experience full enlightenment.

Rama's first public talk for women in 1983 was held at the Beverly Theatre. A line of attendees, primarily female, wound around Wilshire Boulevard and down a side street to get in. On the theater marquee, block letters read, "Rama - Why Don't More Women Attain Enlightenment?"

That night, when Rama walked onto the theater's rose-toned stage, I sensed more than the usual audience disconnects. He was dressed simply, in all black. His curly hair formed a large circle around his head. His body language was unassuming and supple. But—issue! He was tall, nice looking, confident in his right to speak. I felt some women were nervous about that. He sat on the couch and sorted through the contents of a folder left on the small table next to his chair. As he did that, I felt him taking the temperature of the audience.

He greeted everyone evenly then posited questions. Why are most of the enlightened teachers that people have heard of, men? Is there something wrong with a woman's physiology that makes it harder for her to make leaps and do cartwheels of light on the spiritual path? Why are women behind men in positions of authority and power?

He then explained that the reason more women don't attain enlightenment, and are held back and repressed, and do not comprehend how powerful they are, even a little bit—is cultural. It has to do with recent history (the last few thousand years) and mental programming.

Women exemplify, from a spiritual point of view, power. The power of the kundalini energy, the energy of life, flows through them in a very different way than it does through a man, innately. In a fallen world, in a world of fear and darkness, men have reacted very negatively to the power that is inherent in women. Rather than realizing that that power is also indigenous to themselves, that they have the same power, only it manifests in other ways, they have rejected that power and sought to convince women of the exact opposite, that they are powerless. They have done this through sexual repression, economic repression, political repression, social repression, ideological repression and spiritual repression. Women have been given a description of the world that they are taught from childhood, which they believe is true, as are men. We are taught by our societies, by our parents, by the examples of those we see. ...

There is really no such thing as a woman or a man. There is a physical body, a subtle physical body, a soul. But there is no such thing as a woman or a man. What we consider to be a woman is an idea. This idea has been formed through history, culture, politics, art, religion—the same is true of a man. These ideas are out of balance.

Rama described a woman's energy body as fluid and able to conduct kundalini or life force more readily and rapidly than a man's. A woman has a stronger second attention. But in the repressive environment of the last several millennia, women had to use that powerful second attention not to achieve enlightenment but to manipulate men to feel attracted and sexually aroused—because marriage to the "best" man was the sole ticket to a decent life. The consciousness of manipulation, however justified, causes a person to lose power and prevents enlightenment.

Men, over the past millennia, have dominated and felt superior to women. A consciousness of domination and superiority is a lower state of mind, causing a person to lose power. Enlightenment will not take place.

The primary reason why more women don't attain enlightenment is that they have a misunderstanding of their purpose as women. Women have a preconceived notion of what it means to be a woman, and this notion is incorrect. Everything is reversed in this age. Men appear to be more powerful than women, while the opposite is really true. What appears to be light is dark, and what appears to be dark is light. ...

In response to a question, Rama explained his stance on homosexuality. Sexual preference, he stated, has no bearing whatsoever on a person's ability to attain higher states of awareness and enlightenment. Have consenting sex with whomever you want. In some cases, when a person's sexual preference is same-sex, it means that they had many prior incarnations in a different gender. For example, a woman sexually attracted at an early age to women may have had many previous lives as a man. Sexual attraction is a samskara, or tendency, he said. It did not necessarily switch from lifetime to lifetime. Bottom line—sexual preference whether heterosexual or homosexual was a non-issue. The issue is finding nice people to spend time with.

One student, Zoe Nicholson, a feminist and active proponent of women's rights since the 1960s, wrote about the evening this way:

"The room was filled to capacity with women of every educational and economic background. There were women in business suits, women in Birkenstocks, women in tie-dye. There were feminists, lesbians, radicals, mainstream, older, younger, married, single, simply hundreds of women, as diverse as women are. It was a dream come true: Rama empowering any and all women who came to hear him speak. He walked out on stage and sat down on a white couch.

"Rama began to talk about women and power. He explained that women are naturally more powerful than men because of a fundamental difference in the structure of a woman's subtle body that allows women to conduct kundalini faster and more easily than men. He explained further that the imbalance of the sexes in the world today is actually an inversion. Essentially, women are the source of power.

"Rama said that for women to realize their true nature, they would have to tap into their raw power. This would require nothing less than a total revolution in how women think about men and about themselves. It was certainly not going to happen if things are left in the hands of men, since women have been culturally, economically, religiously, politically and educationally repressed since the dawn of recorded history. 'They have suffered to have their identities destroyed, their sisterhood splintered, their spirituality denied and then been placed into an endless slavery to the men of this world.'

"Rama said that men's thoughts of domination and superiority make it clear to a woman that her primary purpose in life is to bear children and/or produce sexual pleasure for someone else. 'Sexual slavery is the ability to push the right buttons to receive the desired response when the individual who is being manipulated is either unaware that they are being manipulated or they are unable to defend themselves. Men manage to perpetuate sexual slavery by making it seem that there is no other alternative, and by using social pressure, guilt, rejection and other controlling mechanisms when a woman tries to buck the system.'

"Rama spoke of using make-up, hairstyles, clothing and high heels in a particular manner, not to look attractive to men but to make a woman's appearance more powerful. By looking more assertive and in control, this would help protect her from men's thoughts that she is an object put on earth for their observation, domination and exploitation. ...

"After presenting a short lesson on meditation and meditating with everyone, Rama offered to answer questions. Dozens of hands shot up. Rama called on a woman and she stood up. I recognized her from the clinic where I worked. She was a marriage and family therapist who was accruing volunteer hours that were required by the state for her license. 'Doesn't a successful career give a woman power?'

"Rama explained to her that the successes women are able to achieve are controlled by men. These accomplishments are highly regulated. Although it may appear that a woman's opinion is valued and her integrity admired, she is still viewed as a commodity. Rama went on to caution her that an education, a successful career and a 'new white Mazda' did not really begin to equal a woman's true potential for power.

"I immediately remembered that just that morning she had driven to the clinic and shown everyone her brand new white Mazda! I laughed aloud at how deeply that must have affected her.

"Suddenly a woman in the third row stood up and began to shout, 'How dare you talk about the oppression of women! You are a man and you know nothing about being a woman. You have never been raped. You don't know what it is like to be a woman!' She was shaking and very upset. It was evident that she was not just having a difficult time with all of the information or that she was hearing it from a man, but she was expressing a lifetime of anger.

"Rama stood up from the couch, walked to the edge of the stage and knelt down. He sat back on his heels and looked tenderly at this woman. He listened at length to all of her pain and anger. He agreed with her every word and confirmed the profoundness of her grief.

"As the two of them continued to talk, I began to notice great swirls of energy moving throughout the room. Currents of energy were swelling and shifting, running in a circular motion from the left to the right. They were filled with pain, grief, loneliness and frustration. As I sat in my chair in the Beverly Theatre, I saw something I will never forget. Rama began to pull all of this energy into himself. He sat on the edge of the stage in quiet conversation with a woman in pain, while transmuting the energy of each and every woman in the theater. From his left side, he took all of our emotions, our karmas, our sadness into his aura, and to the right he sent out beautiful clear, radiant crystal light.

"Probably most of the women did not see this miracle of compassion and transformation, at least not with their eyes. But, I am certain that it changed their lives. It changed mine forever."[32]

Rama's feminist teachings ranged from broad teachings to individual and specific guidance about covert sexism. One of the students who helped out at the Malibu office recalls listening to some rock and roll music on her drive to the house. She felt confused and discouraged when she got there. She saw Rama soon after she arrived and mentioned that she felt insecure, that she suddenly could not get anything right. Rama asked her to describe what happened as she drove to his home. She said she had been listening to the radio and mentioned the all-male band that was featured. "The men in that band don't like women," Rama said. "They projected that feeling into you. You just picked up their feelings about women." After the conversation, her self-esteem and energy returned, higher than before.

Another woman student recalls visiting Rama at his Old Field house in New York several years later and playing the Nintendo game, Super Mario Brothers. "It was a new release and he had never played the game before," she said. "We alternated turns. When it was his turn to play, he jumped level after level. After about two or three levels, he turned to me and said, 'I feel that the developers of this game are angry at women.' I felt startled because I thought of Super Mario as a cute kids' game.

"'All energy affects your awareness, including energy from software,' he continued. He made it to the top of the game while I tried to figure out the traps on the early levels."

---

32 Nicholson, Zoe Ann. *The Passionate Heart*. Newport Beach, CA: Lune Soleil Press, 2003.

How to Have a Mystical Experience or Realize that All Experiences Are[33]

On February 9, 1983, Rama turned 33. He invited his 900 students from the three Lakshmi centers to a party at the Wilshire Ebell. Each person brought their own vase of flowers. I shopped for a small crystal vase and filled it with tubular stalks of yellow, white and lavender freesias. That night, hundreds of flower vases stretched across the stage and along the aisles, warming the dispassionate hall with exotic scents, shapes and colors. In honor of the occasion, Rama wore a white Chinese-style silk jacket embroidered in gold. He was funny, loving and light.

In the midst of the festivities, Rama announced that at the end of the summer, all current students would be asked to re-apply. He said that this would give all the current students time to evaluate their intent and interest in the study. Some students would not be accepted going forward. Everyone was so lit up that the import of his words did not sink in. They didn't sink in for me. It just sounded like more paperwork. Plus, Rama already had built a history of forgiving every student transgression. He seemed to accept that his students had their up and down days and behaviors.

At this moment, he said, he didn't see "little Lakshmis" all over the world; he did plan on touring the U.S. next year—Boston, Chicago, Phoenix, Washington—because of the energetic power lines in these cities and the seekers he saw there.

A few nights later, a one-evening Lakshmi "Saturday Night Live", with entertainment by students and extreme humor and kundalini supplied by Rama, opened on the raised stage of the main ballroom at the Miramar Sheraton Hotel in Santa Monica. Several weeks earlier, Rama had approached one of his students, studio musician Steve Kaplan, to take part in the show. Rama loved music and said he had been a composer and musician in past lives. One of Rama's favorite electronic musical groups was the synthesizer-driven band, Tangerine Dream, and Kaplan was an expert synthesizer player.

Rama's interaction with Kaplan exemplifies how he worked with students on the path of mysticism.

---

33   Lenz, Frederick (Rama). "Tibetan Yoga and Secret Doctrine." *Insights: Talks on the Nature of Existence.* Los Angeles: Lakshmi Inc., 1983.

Kaplan recalled, "I had been a student of Rama's for about a year and a half. I had been a musician for almost all of my twenty-four years, having started piano lessons when I was five years old. Just before I met Rama I had begun to feel that my potential for making music was not being fully exploited. I felt that an important part of my being was lying dormant and was not being used in a productive way. One of the first things I felt upon meeting Rama was that he could awaken this deeper self that I couldn't seem to get in touch with.

"One evening, Rama approached me at one of the weekly Center meetings in Los Angeles and invited me to take part in a project. He was planning a special evening that would include entertainment to be supplied by some of his students. Rama wanted me to play synthesizer music during the evening's meditations. He told me, 'You supply the music, and I'll supply the meditation. It should be fun.'"

"This sounded like an interesting idea to me. Rama had a yen for synthesizer music, and he often played tapes of synthesized music during meditations. But since I had been around he had never had any live music at a meditation. I was pleased and excited that he wanted to work with me in this way.

"I began to think about suitable material to play for the upcoming 'performance,' but I was very busy at the time with studio recording work, and it was difficult to make time to work on this project. Rama had suggested that I make a tape of the music I was planning to play so that he could screen it before the performance. I had every intention of doing this, but things were so hectic in my life that ten days from the date of the program I hadn't even started recording the tape. As a matter of fact, the idea of making a tape had slipped my mind completely.

"Apparently Rama had a sense of what was going on, and at the Center meeting a week before the performance he greeted me by saying, 'What's happening with the music? We've got a gig coming up, you know.' I told him that I wasn't quite sure what to prepare, and that I was glad we were talking about it. He then said, 'I like synthesizers, so bring your Jupiter (Rama's favorite synthesizer was the Jupiter, and he had recommended it to me when I was synthesizer-shopping a few months earlier). You can play classical music if you like, or anything for that matter, as long as it has a high vibration. I want you to try and stay away from rock music.'

"Then he continued, 'I had hoped that you would make me a tape of what you planned to play, so that I could select which music would work best. We could avoid some very embarrassing moments that way. But we still have a week and a half before the gig. Make me a tape this week and bring it to the next Center meeting. I'll listen to it before the performance and let you know what I think, O.K.? Good, thank you.' We said goodbye and Rama went on to other business.

"That night as I drove home, I realized clearly the pattern of my life. I have a tendency to wait until just before a deadline to get to work, and as a result, my preparation is always rushed and a bit haphazard. I had always gotten by with these sloppy work habits in school, music, and virtually every part of my life. In a way, I was attempting to get by again on this particular project. I had conveniently forgotten about the tape I was supposed to make and figured sub-consciously that it wouldn't make any difference. But Rama was having none of this from me. I felt that he was using this project to force me to get my act together. While we were talking, it didn't seem like anything extraordinary was happening, we were just people having a conversation. But afterwards, I began to realize the implications of what he was communicating below the surface, and I was blown away.

"All of a sudden I was embarrassed and disgusted with myself for allowing my habit of procrastination to go on for so many years. I resolved to get to work immediately. I was never so productive as I was in that following week. I recorded the tape for Rama, ran all over town buying electronic equipment for the performance, hardly slept at all (but felt great anyway), and still had just enough time to take care of my usual worldly obligations.

"The week flew by and the big night was upon us. I arrived at the hall about two hours early to set up my equipment and rehearse to get a sound level on the music. Some of the other students were rehearsing the plays that were to be performed that evening, and there was a lot of hustling and bustling about to get everything ready before the people started to arrive. During this rehearsal period I could feel the energy level in the room rising. Soon, students from Rama's centers in San Francisco, San Diego and Los Angeles began to arrive, and after a while the room was filled with 425 excited spiritual seekers.

"Usually before performing a concert, I find that I experience a certain degree of nervousness and excitement. On this night I was excited, but in a different way. I wasn't nervous, but rather calm and collected. Rama took the stage after a few minutes and talked for about a half hour, discussing the things we would be studying in the coming months, the desert trip we were taking the following day, and generally preparing us for the ensuing evening. While he talked I got really high and felt extremely clear, with few thoughts in my mind. I saw the room fill with golden light as Rama spoke and had almost forgotten that I was going to play in a few minutes.

"Then Rama finished his talk and introduced me to his students as a studio musician who would be playing during the meditations that evening. I walked to the front of the room and took my position behind the keyboards. He looked over at me and motioned for me to begin. I was amazed at the degree of clarity I was experiencing in my mind. I guess being in the presence of so much light and luminosity brought a tremendous level of clarity to the music (and everything else). The sounds from the synthesizers were jumping out at me as if I had never heard them before. I felt a wonderful sense of discovery as I played, and I found myself inundated by a flood of spontaneous, original ideas.

"Soon I found myself experimenting with some new concepts that I had not rehearsed. They were such logical ideas that I just found myself playing them automatically. I realized I was in a flow of inspiration. I was in another world for a time; everyone in the room disappeared and it was just me, my keyboards and the music. I felt that instead of creating the music I was merely a channel for the music to flow through. The clearer I became, the purer the music became. After about twenty minutes, I finished playing and looked up at Rama who was absorbed in samadhi as usual. He came out of samadhi, looked over at me and smiled, and then began to introduce the first play of the evening. I got up and returned to my seat in the audience.

"Later on that evening, after all the other entertainers were finished, Rama had me play for another meditation. This time I got up to play with no preconceived idea of what I was going to do. I just began playing and once again found myself in a flow. While I played I had the strange sensation of being out of my body. I would be playing in my usual manner when suddenly I would have the sensation of watching someone else's hands on the keyboard. I seemed to be looking in from another world, a world where everything sounded absolutely crystal clear. I heard myself creating effects in the music that I have never been able to achieve as well as I did that night. The most beautiful part of it all was that there was practically no effort involved on my part. The music seemed to flow and evolve of its own free will, while I casually observed it taking place.

"I played for about twenty minutes, and when I finished I looked up and noticed that Rama was in samadhi again. I had been so engrossed in the music that when I finished playing I noticed my body was in a state of excitation, with my heart pounding away at a quick rate. Then I saw Rama turn and focus on me. Almost immediately an extreme sense of calm enveloped my being, and I felt my heartbeat ease and slow down, becoming much less intense. The room became thick with golden light, especially around Rama, who seemed to be in a constant state of dissolution. Soon after that, Rama bade everyone good night."[34]

During the "Saturday Night Live", the quality of the meditation combined with the soaring effects of the synthesizer reminded me of something long forgotten—a way to teach advanced awareness through music, to convey complex states of mind that were impossible to talk about in words. Rama could create a legacy of teaching by working with musicians such as Steve. I recognized it. This role of music felt familiar in a profound and moving way.

Rama had brought the Scottie dog, Vayu, into his life, and the small group of students who worked at the house in Malibu were aware of Vayu's place in Rama's heart. But the larger group was unaware of the new canine catechism.

In late March, seated with 400 students in the majestic desert, Rama suggested that they get dogs as a part of their mystical path. He said he was introducing dogs because the students should love them the way they were supposed to love him. The puppies brought perfect, pure unconditional love, that state of no mind, of constant innocence, the ability to be open to exuberant, perfect love. They would become part of

---

34   Steve Kaplan (Phil). "Center Meetings." *The Last Incarnation*. Los
     Angeles: Lakshmi Publications, 1983. PDF pp. 125-127.

the sadhana. The students' beings would open up to eternity at another level, with the ability to exercise that love.

In the dogs, the students could see that there's only this moment. The dogs would be little shards of Rama. He suggested terrier breeds because he could infuse them with light. The breeds he suggested would hold his light and bring it through into the students' lives. He also advised waiting to get a dog until a student could take care of it impeccably.

Many students started planning to get their own forever friend, the Scottie dog. I, however, had lodged the term "terrier" in my mind, rather than the word "Scottie." As soon as I got home from the desert trip, I bought a breed book on terriers and began looking at ads. Several weeks later, an ad for a Lakeland Terrier caught my eye. A Lakeland is a dog in the 17-pound range with orange or beige curly hair. They are like small Airedales.

I drove about 90 minutes northeast of Los Angeles to a little town called Palmdale and there, as I sat amidst a litter of seven pups, was selected by my first and foremost canine companion, Murphy. She was the one who walked over to me and nudged me with her little nose with an attitude of, "You'll do." I brought her home several weeks later, and she lived with me until she was 16. I loved her more fiercely than I could have imagined. Murphy was a fighter, literally and figuratively. Our mutual unconditional love helped me stretch the boundaries of love and understand my warrior nature, as well as learn more about how to love Rama.

Late March, 1983, marked the publication of *The Last Incarnation,* the book of student stories about their adventures with Rama in a variety of settings. The miracles, magic, healings, movie run-ins, grocery store revelations—it was all there. The marketing plan consisted of distribution to New Age bookstores and mentions in Rama's full-page advertising. The goal: millions of people would buy the book and become inspired to embark on the path of self-discovery.

THE LAST
INCARNATION

LAKSHMI
PUBLICATIONS
$8.95

In the L.A. student meeting, Rama read aloud the epilogue, written by a student named Gerry, telling of his departure from San Diego to move to Los Angeles. Rama commented how he had reached that point of departure and cutting the past many times along his journey—a poignant moment when great transformation can occur.

"... And for a while I just watched the scenery. The sun was close to the horizon now. A group of about twenty seagulls flew by below me. The wind had calmed to a slight breeze from the west. A few surfers were still in the water, catching the last waves before dark.

"My whole life had been in San Diego. I was born there, went to grammar school and high school there. Even when I was overseas in the Navy I knew I would be coming back. I had met the woman I married there. I was going to college there. I had met my spiritual teacher there. Now he was leaving and I was going with him. Now it was time to say goodbye.

"I had said goodbye to every person I could remember in my life. Faces long forgotten came to mind and I wished them all well. I said goodbye to my parents, my ex-wife, to the women I had loved, to my best friends, my childhood friends, my high school and Navy friends. I said goodbye to people I had known for only a few hours or met for a moment in passing. I said goodbye and wished them well. And I felt true love for all of them.

"I said goodbye to San Diego and to all the places I had lived there, all the experiences I had there. I said goodbye to my life and to everyone and everything in it. Then I said goodbye to myself and to all the different people I had been over the years.

"I watched the sun go down and said goodbye to it and to the day. I said goodbye to this place I had come to so often, and to the waves I knew so well. I said goodbye to the moment and got up to leave.

"There were still two surfers in the water, though it was almost too dark to see. One of them was paddling hard to catch a wave. He stood up as it broke just behind him. He slid to the base of the wave and snapped into a sharp left turn. As the wall of water formed in front of him, he moved forward on his board to gain speed.

"I turned around and walked toward my car."[35]

When Rama finished reading, silence permeated the theater. Soft gold light rippled lightly across the hall, like gentle waves touching the sand. Rama thanked everyone who had submitted a story and complimented the students, the book and all whose stories were

---

35 Gerry. "Epilogue." *The Last Incarnation*. Los Angeles: Lakshmi Publications, 1983. PDF pp. 202-203.

published. He said he would initially place the book in several New Age bookstores and gauge the response.

Towards the end of April, at a public seminar, version three of Rama's "Pathway to Enlightenment" cassette tape offered a guideline to all who attended. Every time he re-did this tape, I noticed, he refined it with new hooks, based on what the last group didn't quite get. Or likely, what I was not quite getting.

> *I teach a graduate course in self-discovery. While many of the people I work with have never even meditated in this life before until I met them—in other lives they've done quite a bit. They don't know that though.*

> *The process of self-discovery turns you inside and out, backward and forward and around again. It's not just learning to meditate. It's passing through hundreds of selves, taking what you might have done in a thousand lifetimes and doing it in one. Shifting levels of attention constantly, in ways that I can't possibly describe. That's what it's like to work with an Enlightened teacher, and it doesn't make sense.*

On May 1, Rama invited the students to Disneyland. Five hundred people managed to meander happily through the park without looking like a group. The cherry on the icing of the mystic cake—at the end of the evening, just before the park closed—the electric light parade. The students who still lingered in the park lined up along the fence where the parade would pass.

I stood about ten feet from Rama. As the lit-up floats went by, I saw him very unobtrusively raising his hands and zapping the floats with light, adding lights that weren't there. The last float was an eagle saluting America. A bright, luminous red light hovered several feet above the eagle. We followed the eagle float all the way down Main Street. All of us, Rama and the students, bounced around to the music, dancing through the streets. There it was again in my brain and being—joy.

At the end of May, Rama introduced a serious topic. In a soft yet penetrating tone, he spoke about hostility and hate, how bad it is for seekers to feel these emotions, especially towards another spiritual seeker. He said these feelings bounce back to you with an amplified effect. He said it was very important to leave Lakshmi if you have those feelings towards him or anyone else there.

He explained that over time, a student gets to a point where they see truth, whether it be truth in existence or truth about themselves. At that point, either a person has to make inner changes or—if it is not the right time to consider changing—drop out and leave the center. There is no blame in leaving for that reason—you are doing the right thing in the right way. The wrong way to leave is to blame others and become hostile.

The next night, Rama invited students who had moved to Malibu to a potluck dinner and a meditation. Instead of 500 in a theater, about 125 people joined him for festivities at the more intimate Neptunian Club in Manhattan Beach.

During the break, a student recalled, she saw Rama walking around in his stocking feet on the Neptunian's linoleum floors. "I asked if we could talk," she said. "He was exceptionally gracious and suggested that we sit down. I asked him some of my questions, and he gave me his impressions. Then Rama began to describe some of the changes he'd been going through.

"Rama explained that he wanted to distance himself from the human world. 'I just don't want anything to do with it anymore.' His tone was very gentle, but also very firm. 'If that's the world that people want, then I'll just wave and say hi.' He gestured, showing me how he would smile and wave and even ask how things were going but remain detached. While we sat there, a few people actually did walk by and Rama spoke to them just as he had shown me. I watched his manner and his eyes and was struck by the internal changes he was referring to. I thought to myself, 'He says he'll help his students no matter what level we're at. But there are infinite wonders we'll never see unless we meditate more deeply and start to access more light.'"[36]

Several days after the potluck, Rama pulled *The Last Incarnation* from bookstores. For the two months it had been in circulation,

---

36   Carolyn. "You Could Have Had Anything." *Self Discovery.* Los Angeles: Lakshmi Publications, Fall 1983.

while some readers found the stories of mysticism, miracles and transformation uplifting, others responded with anger and fear. Rama told the students that the time was not right for the book, and it was never made available to the public again.[37]

In mid-June, Rama drove across town to the Harry Langdon Studio. Langdon, a well-known Hollywood celebrity photographer, had been recommended to Rama by one of his Malibu neighbors. By selecting Harry, Rama opted for photos that would be clear, beautiful yet startling—ways to both open and still the mind. For the right person, the photos would become a doorway, an invitation to reconnect (or have the opposite effect). Rama already had a set of head shots, but for Los Angelenos and the cities he was about to tour, he wanted more powerful tools.

According to Langdon, "By the time Dr. Lenz came into the studio, he knew I was aware of the spiritual world and kundalini techniques. He and I had a wonderful camaraderie—we had similar knowledge.

"Dr. Lenz was all business. He brought several changes of clothing. He used my stylist for makeup and hair. In front of the camera, he would go into a zone—he imparted energy. I always visualize in my mind how I want a client to perform in front of the camera and quite often they will do that without my having to physically direct them. Dr. Lenz and I were working on that level. He would come out and I would say, stand there or sit there. He would go into a lotus position or move his hands in the form of mudras.

"I talk with everyone about a subject that we both understand. Dr. Lenz had that knowing in his eyes, that awareness, that we both understood, that lit up his eyes. In every photo, I tuned into his eyes.

"We are all an equal balance between masculine and feminine. Some of us want to reveal more of one side than the other. The feminine side is very sensitive and more intuitive. I expected that from him. All the men I have known who have done meditative work have been more

---

37 The book was not republished during Rama's lifetime. It is available online today, at www.RamaMeditationSociety.org

androgynous appearing because of a great balance. The same is true of women who are leaders—they have more of a balance as well."

The Langdon photos—Rama selected several dozen from hundreds taken that day—were both provocative and polarizing. Over the next six years, Rama returned to the studio several more times to use Langdon's shots in full page print ads in large-circulation newspapers and magazines across the United States.

When the full page ads first appeared in the *Los Angeles Times*, the men in my PR office found the images sneer-worthy. Yes, there were many teachers offering meditation. But none took full page ads in a range of costumes. I told Rama about the response, and he simply did not care. It was like telling an elephant about a gnat. The message in the photos was exactly what he intended to convey. He would not compromise. The photos were koans, power moments between himself and another old soul. Not for my office-mates.

Simmering on the back burner—student re-applications. Many of us hoped he would forget about it. But no. During the Los Angeles center meeting of June 22, Rama serenely announced that a lot of people who had been his students for years would be leaving soon. He gave reasons for such departures. Perhaps people were attached to how things used to be, or were attention seekers, or were people who fixated on wanting to spend more time with him. Perhaps they hadn't changed and must change, or would feel uncomfortable in the upcoming teaching environment. Rama explained that it was natural for students to come and go. It is the dharma, the way it should be.

Rama described a tradition in Tibetan monasteries. From time to time, the abbot would ask all of the monks to reapply. It was a chance to reevaluate one's dedication, to look deeply inside and renew one's direction. The abbot would examine the applications and possibly release some of the community members, recommending a life in the world. But mostly, it was a process for the applicants to reevaluate their direction and commitments.

During July, Rama said, every student could change if that's what they wanted. The change would be deep, vibrational. To effect change, he suggested chanting aloud the mantra "sring" 108 times at least once a day, ideally before meditation and sleep. Sring is the mantra of Lakshmi. Mantras are doorways to higher planes of awareness.

'Lakshmi represents beauty, harmony and abundance,' I thought. 'Can't be so bad.' I went to the local new age bookstore and bought a sandalwood mala (string of 108 beads) to count the repetitions. For the next two months, I sat on my bed in the evenings and chanted this mantra aloud, elongating the iiiing—"sriiiiiiiiiiing"—as I moved my fingers along the necklace, one bead at a time, each time I completed the sound. By only the third repetition, I would feel a soft, full vibration in my mind. Sometimes a soft luminosity would fill my room.

Rama did not recommend the use of mantras for meditating with eyes closed. He said they only take you a certain way and then you get stuck. But for general practice, he recommended chanting them aloud approximately seven times before and after meditation. He often suggested and demonstrated using the mantra, "AUM."

On July 3, I drove alone in my new, black Jeep along the freeways and winding roads that led to our meeting spot in the Anza Borrego desert. On my car seat, music from Tangerine Dream blared from an audio cassette player. As soon as I turned off the main highway, the rugged landscape of rocks and hills filled my mind with appreciation and beauty. To be in the desert with Rama—the sense of incredible good fortune lodged in my heart.

In the long hours of summer daylight, we started our hike in at around 8 p.m. At midnight, in the deep, intense stillness of the Anza Borrego desert, the temperature still hovering at 90 degrees, Rama led a Fourth of July birthday song to celebrate America. Several hundred voices rang out amidst the rock strewn sand and resilient shrubs—

> *"Happy birthday to you, happy birthday to you,*
>
> *Happy birthday, dear America, happy birthday to you!"*

A student wrote:

"I watched in easy wonder as Rama, reaching into silence, called out 'Whoash! Whoash!' As each note shocked the desert stillness, the earth shook, a violent tremor fiercely rippling through the ground. Looking at my friend, inquiring with a shaken tone, I asked, 'Did you feel that? Did you feel the earthquake?' Before my friend could reply, Rama gazed at him, saying softly, 'That wasn't an earthquake.'

"Sliding to the circle's center, Rama lifted his hands into the air. From the center of his palms multi-colored lights shot out, with electric intensity. Urgent but informal in its patterns, the light struck the distant cliffs before careening back to its source. Sitting in the light's path, I felt the power hit and pierce my body before returning home to Rama's palms.

"In time Rama instructed us to commence meditating. I closed my eyes as Rama exhaled loudly, again that strange command, 'Whoash!' With a sudden snap my meditation intensified and I became aware of an all pervasive scent of roses, voluptuous sweetness on the edge of ken.

"Finally, Rama had everyone gather their belongings in preparation for departing from the canyon. Feeling the heat abating only slightly in the passage of the night, we walked halfway, perhaps a measure less, to the road before breaking for a rest. Rama walking up on a partial rise prior to a cliff, said with a slight smile, 'Let's cool things off.' Lifting his arms, Rama again interrupted the desert with that same sound, 'Whoash!' Suddenly a great wind drove in behind us, creating clouds of sand and dust as it swept towards Rama's spot. Its power exponential in growth, the wind abruptly stopped after a few minutes, returning calmness to the desert.

"The sound of vehicles rumbling along the sand startled the quietness. Suddenly, five off-road trucks appeared, heading straight towards our circle, bright headlights shining ghostly white. This had never happened before on a desert trip! I looked over at Rama. He was calm and smiling. The vehicles stopped, and I saw that each four-wheeler was driven by a student. The lift-gates were lowered, and big tubs of ice cream, frozen solid from a long journey packed in dry ice, were set on each gate. Soon, scoops of delicious ice cream had been dispensed to everyone. We were truly cooled off."

On August 1 at the Wilshire Ebell Theater during a "Special Intensive in Meditation," Rama spoke of feeling badly. He said he had been going through a tough time. A lot of people were throwing hatred at him. They were students, yet held critical viewpoints. They were focusing on him and his body. He sounded discouraged. He said, "Do you think I would choose this?" He gestured to his body from top to bottom. "If I had a choice about what body I entered into?"

"I started massaging him a lot more," said a student/nurse/friend, commenting on the repercussions of having 1,000 enrolled students. "He was in a lot more pain. He told me, 'I not only deal with each person who comes individually but I deal with everyone they're connected to inwardly, as well.' He was absorbing a lot of karma for people and was starting to see the effects on his physical body. It was muscle cramping more than anything. This was not something he could control, as long as he was committed to helping so many people closely. He did what he could to cope, but his release from pain happened when he meditated and went into samadhi."

On August 8th, at a public lecture at the Beverly Theatre, Rama sat as always with a tall, erect spine on his small white couch. He spoke of Tibet. He wore a dark pink silk shirt. A person in the audience recalled, "After a few minutes, I noticed that he had changed. Sitting on stage was an Asian man. His eyes were piercing. I knew they could cut right through illusion and find truth. I saw we were no longer in the Beverly Theatre. We seemed to be in a temple or monastery.

"A few moments later, we were back at the Beverly, and Rama was sitting up front again. He scanned the room, formally meditating on the audience. I saw him filling the room with golden light. Everyone in front of me was dissolved in an ocean of golden pulsating energy. For a moment, I felt myself let go. I felt myself soaring into light. I became completely charged with energy. I felt ecstatic. Energy was surging through me at what seemed to be over 100 miles per hour. Then everything disappeared. I lost all awareness of my thoughts and my body. I was caught up in a whirlwind of light. It gradually stilled. I felt I was floating, weightless, as if I were in outer space. I was at peace.

"The room began to take form again. Rama had just finished meditating and was bowing. He was surrounded by red and gold light. He was so dissolved in clear light, I could see right through him to the curtains behind. He began to get up (quite a feat—the thought of even moving my arm seemed like an impossibility to me). He flipped on a cassette tape.

"Rama's smile grew wide and mischievous. He winked to the audience and half walked, half danced off stage as Donna Summer's disco tune, "She Works Hard for the Money," blared over the speakers. I laughed uproariously. So did about 600 other people."[38]

In mid-August, the deadline struck—student re-application time. I still was not quite sure what Rama sought in a student, but I felt inwardly that I wanted to keep studying with him. I felt such a strong inner connection, yet at the same time I was one of those people who always noticed with whom he spent time, who got the helper jobs. I

---

38 Joanne. "Donna Summer and the Tibetan Master." *Self Discovery*. Los Angeles: Lakshmi Publications, Fall 1983.

wanted his attention, and at the same time I "got" that this wanting was based on old, junior high-level status habits and ego.

A questionnaire was distributed. The re-application asked what one hoped to gain from the study, what one might be able to change and shift in their own life in order to gain more. Rama earnestly told people that if their application were not accepted, they would no longer be eligible to attend his talks and events.

I loved attending Rama's talks and events. My life had become exciting and open-ended in ways I never could have dreamed. Rama's lectures made me laugh, reflect and glow for days afterwards. I put a lot of thought into my re-application, filled it out carefully and sent it to a Malibu P.O. box. Whatever would be, would be.

August 31 was the last center meeting of the trimester. All the student re-applications had been submitted. "No matter what happens," Rama said, "life will be good." Yes, I knew life would be good, I was working away in a public relations office with great success, but the love of my life was my adventurous meditation practice and my spiritual teacher.

Two weeks later, in mid-September, close to 1,000 people received a letter from Rama. It arrived in a plain blue envelope with a Lakshmi return address. I wrestled with opening my envelope, but after putting it on my dining room table and circling it a number of times, doing some grocery shopping and going out to dinner, I decided to tear it open. There it was in the first sentence.

You have been accepted to continue your study at Lakshmi. I feel that our destiny is to travel the road together.

I don't remember what else was in the letter. It had details about a next meeting. It was signed by Rama. I remember feeling a blast of warm air shooting through my being, white light flooding my forehead, a deep sense of gratitude towards Rama for sensing the being I would become, not the person I was at that time. I remember feeling fortunate to be given a chance to change and grow in this study. I felt glad to continue on our wild and wonderful path.

Five hundred people were let go. For those people, the letter assured them that although Rama felt he was not their teacher, they would have a wonderful life. Rama suggested that they pursue the path with other teachers. In some cases, he recommended a specific teacher.

The evening that most students received their letters, some of the remaining students gathered at one of their homes in Malibu. Rama dropped by. One of the students said, "Rama came into the house, quieter than usual. He did not seem to be his usual perky self but instead seemed sad but resolved. He had lost some weight, probably due to fasting, and his skin was paler than usual. He wore jeans and a T-shirt, and I felt he'd been spending a lot of time by himself. I could see the seriousness and dedication he felt towards all of us in doing what was right.

"He said he looked over all the applications more carefully than we could have ever dreamt. He talked about how we've always wanted a small center, to get closer to him. Now we would have it, and he's going to get to know every one of us, and we have to change. No choice. He said this moment is a new beginning, we have to live it, be alive, make our path our life and practice selfless giving. If we inspire one person, we have done what is right. He said to stay in a high consciousness and have fun with it. His words were upbeat but somehow solemn, as if he had reached a new turning point."

Rama closed the San Francisco Center at the end of September. Many of the remaining Northern California students moved to Los Angeles. The ship sailed ahead, Rama's intense teaching focus and humor in full force.

> *I'll do anything to blow someone's concepts. Just when you think you've set me up with limitations and you think, 'Oh, he won't do that,' that's when I push it. I'll do anything that breaks your description of the world. I can see what does it for you, so that's what I'll use. I push it just past your limits—then you change.*[39]

---

39 Williams, D. G. Student journal. Public lecture. Los Angeles, CA, Oct. 17, 1983.

I made such a fool out of myself last night! It's so great! People must get awfully frustrated. They expect, I don't know what, from a spiritual teacher, to wear robes and jewels and speak like an Indian guru breathing enlightenment. Instead, they get this ridiculous being—I love it. I have a good time.[40]

It amazes me that people can come to our meetings and not understand what holds the whole center together, why we all give everything and never hold back. It's because we love madly and wildly, the few of us who do that. We give everything for the study because there's nothing else, because when you love, you love completely. You can't hold back. That's why we're free.[41]

November 14, 1983—Rama's restatement of a core Buddhist teaching:

At the border of nirvana, there's a crossing. And when you reach the border of nirvana, someone will come up to you and inform you that if you enter into nirvana, everything that you've ever loved will be lost. You will be alone. There will be the most terrible aloneness that you can imagine. You will be alienated from everything, including yourself, forever. A sense of drifting in a cold, irresolute space forever.

At that moment, O nobly born, all the images from all of your lives will come forward and will demand your attention. They will say, "Don't cross over there; you will lose us and you will be sorrowful and empty and void."

40 Williams, D. G. Student journal. Student meeting. Los Angeles, CA, Oct. 18, 1983.
41 Lenz, Frederick (Rama). "Love, the Fourth Level of Ecstasy." *Insights: Talks on the Nature of Existence.* Los Angeles: Lakshmi Inc., 1983.

If you listen to what that fellow at the border tells you, then you won't cross over. You'll go back to all of the things that you've always loved and all of the things that have bound you and limited you also. You'll go back to both because in the world of duality you have the pairs of opposites.

If you listen to me, which no one does, fortunately, I would suggest that it's not like that at all. That when that fellow comes up to you and warns you against crossing the border, you'll say, "Listen, several lifetimes ago I went to one of Rama's talks and while he very rarely says anything of any value whatsoever, there was one point he made which I put on a three-by-five file card which I happen to have in my back pocket, and I was going to review it because he said I would run into you. I didn't necessarily believe him at the time, but now that I've run into you, I just happen to have this file card tucked away here, and I'd like to examine it for a moment, if you don't mind."

And of course he'll say, "We don't have time. The worlds are turning, existence is manifesting—" And you'll say, "Just a minute!" You'll take out your faded three-by-five file card, it's a few lifetimes old—actually it would be better if you had a plastic one which you had laser engraved, because as we all know plastic lasts forever—and it says,

DON'T LISTEN

Hopefully, it will be in the right language.

Don't listen because in nirvana it's not like that. It's not empty or cold or barren. You don't remember that the ecstasy and the completion of absorption in God is so fantastic that you can't possibly have lost anything because all of the things that you've always loved and always experienced came forth from there and exist there and are always there.[42]

---

42   Lenz, Frederick (Rama). "Tibetan Yoga and Secret Doctrine." *Insights: Talks on the Nature of Existence.* Los Angeles: Lakshmi Inc., 1983.

In late November, during a public meditation at the Miramar Sheraton Hotel in Santa Monica, Rama discussed forgiveness—how to give it and how to get it. He spoke of the obvious methods, such as simply apologizing and asking for forgiveness. For the injured party, the path was the realization that human beings are flawed and letting the transgression go. He discussed more complex cases and pointed out that some of the world's major religions, most obviously Roman Catholicism, had made confession and forgiveness central to their faiths.

He tried to keep the mood light and slightly humorous to keep the audience from reverting to a western "Mea Culpa" mind-set. He discussed other circumstances, such as when you have injured someone in the past, perhaps to the point where they will no longer speak to you. Rama recommended that in situations like that you should write that person a letter.

"You should explain that you were in a confused state of mind, and that you are sorry that you hurt them. It is not necessary that they ever respond, it is only required that you send them the letter for your attention to be shifted, and for you to make peace with yourself." He used some absurd and fairly lewd examples of what we might have done to require that such a letter be written, and the audience was laughing pretty hard.

There was a man, perhaps in his late thirties, sitting in the first row, and he was not laughing. He was hunched over with his hands clasped together in his lap, and his breathing seemed labored. I was near the front myself, sitting off to one side, and I had a good view of him.

As usual, Rama asked if there were any questions. The man raised his hand and tried to talk. His voice was so soft that Rama had to ask him to speak up a couple of times. The man took a deep breath and finally managed to say that he understood the purpose of writing such a letter, and he was happy it might help others. But he said that it couldn't work for him, and would Rama please suggest some alternative.

Rama's mood instantly matched the somberness of the moment. The man was absolutely serious and in immense pain. Rama asked him what the problem was, and the man replied, "I cannot write to them because the people I hurt are dead. I killed them, I killed people in Vietnam, they're dead because of me and I never knew their names. So who could I possibly write to?"

The light in the room became a soft, soft, gold. Rama said, "Look at me, look at me," and the man raised his head. Rama went on. "Of course it will work for you. Just write them the letter, and say what you have to say. I will make sure that they get it."

I watched as all the contracted agony drained out of his body. He finally began to cry, almost uncontrollably. As his tears flowed, you could see that he had finally found a way of atonement. He managed to sit up straighter, and the vise of pain that had gripped his being slowly gave way to an expression of peace.

Christmas, 1983. For sale on several long tables in the Wilshire Ebell lobby were Rama's recorded talks: the 28-talk *Lakshmi Series*, "the basics that everyone should know," and the 13-talk *Insights: Talks on the Nature of Existence* series, the core teachings of 1983's modular mysticism. The talks were housed on audio cassettes, the latest technology! Now people could listen to Rama's lectures at home.

Next to the array of tape sets stood another long table filled with every variety of cheesecake known to foodies, to be consumed during the halftime break.

"That evening," said Nevil Blanke, "Rama walked up to me as I stood, plastic fork in hand, nibbling at my dessert on a white paper plate.

"'I've got to have just one bite!' Rama exclaimed, gazing at my slice of cheesecake.

"I am an admirer of food," said Nevil. "Not just any food. I have conducted a never-ending search for the most exotic and appealing tastes that can be found. This cheesecake was good, but I wasn't particularly impressed by it. It was just a cheesecake.

"I handed Rama the plate and the fork. He took a bite and closed his eyes for a second. He looked at me and smiled.

"'Have a bite,' he said, 'and I will show you something.'

"I took a bite and couldn't believe that this was the same cheesecake that I had been eating a few moments ago. The taste was exquisite beyond anything I had so far experienced in this life. Food always tastes better around Rama, but this was bliss in edible form. As I experienced this, Rama spoke—

"'You can see everything in this cheesecake. It is possible to see the myriad worlds of existence in it. You can see the birth, life and ultimate transformation of the multiple universes. Spinning worlds coming into being and then dissolving—all in this cheesecake.'

"As he spoke, I actually saw these things—the cheesecake became eternity, infinity, nirvana and samsara. I closed and reopened my eyes and was astounded to find myself still in the theater foyer. I turned to Rama, who was smiling at me.

"That was ecstasy," I told him.

"'One day, Nevil, when you become enlightened,' he replied, 'You will be able to eat this way all of the time!'"[43]

---

43 Nevil. "The Case of the Enlightened Cheesecake." *Self Discovery.* Los Angeles: Lakshmi Publications, Fall 1983.

9

1984 - COMPUTER MIND

Tantric mysticism is, if I can use a computer analogy, spiritual systems analysis and networking. And at the same time to just know that all there is to know is what we know at the present time. Does that make sense? I'm not sure. It's not always necessary to make sense. That's a difficult one for some people. In other words, you don't have to understand life. You can't, it's impossible to understand life. You can become fully conscious of it, merge with it, be it and go beyond it, but you can't understand it. That's what makes it exciting. But you should never stop trying. That's tantric mysticism. - Rama

Jeff Richards, a recent graduate of UCLA, recalled his entrance into the non-ashram ashram as a new Rama student in January of 1984. "I had attended a number of Rama's talks at UCLA," he said. "They were often held in the chemistry lab with the periodic table in the back of the room. It was stadium seating, he'd sit on a desk with the Bunsen burners. Every time I went, he would blast energy into the room, his face changed into images of teachers from other lifetimes. It was the world of enlightened magic, and I wanted to be part of it.

"When I joined, there were a few main themes. The first was the enlightenment of women. As a person of color, when I was growing up I was always surrounded by strong women, but their strength was somewhat buried by habits and cultural expectations. Once, during a student meeting, I asked Rama, 'What is the difference between men and women?' He answered, 'Women have more power.' And once he said that, I began to notice it everywhere. Over time, it helped me accept myself as I am and to feel comfortable with women in a new way. It was life-changing.

"Another theme was 'etiquette.' Rama spoke a lot about the etiquette of being around an enlightened teacher and the students of an enlightened teacher. The unspoken rule was, don't fawn over Rama or push your way into his awareness. You will interact with him at the just right time. The students had been to the desert countless times with Rama, they joked about movies, they seemed to know the latest music, which I later found out Rama had played for them. They were adventurous and funny, like their teacher. The M.O. was to interact with lots of students at a break but not try to push your way into their space. It was about fun and lightness and non-attachment.

"I also remember dressing up to go to the talks," said Richards. "Attire was business casual, and it was fun to learn how to do that. Of course, a dominant theme was computer science. I decided to enroll in a local technology trade school, Computer Learning Center (CLC), because I wanted to change my life. And my life did change—computer science became my lifelong profession."

Richards' choice to go to CLC in the beginning of 1984 aligned with Rama's amped-up focus on computer science. With 1983's emphasis on the core tenets of mysticism, in 1984 Rama introduced advanced mysticism, the path of Vajrayana Buddhism. Rama spoke of the training given to monks in Tibetan monasteries—mathematics, astrology, detailed visualizations. The monks practiced numerous techniques to strengthen their minds and gain the focus and precision needed to meditate. Advanced mysticism could not be taught without a precise mental grounding.

Similarly, a focused, grounded mind is required in a technical profession. Thus 1984, the year of advanced mysticism, meant increasing the students' mental strength which, for most students, meant studying and embarking on a career in computer science. Technology was the fast path for the modern monk ("monk," in Rama's view, meaning not celibate, not male or female, not married or unmarried, but someone who meditated regularly and aspired to gain higher awareness). If someone could not ultimately achieve mental focus and a mentally challenging career, they were not right for the Lakshmi program.

Rama increasingly introduced computers into his conversations on various topics and generally made nerd-ness seem sexy and alluring.

As you may know, I have a favorite profession, and that's computer science. I feel that the computer world is a fine place for spiritual seekers to be. Because the mind-set that it takes to use computer technology is the Zen mind. It's very similar. In other words, as you meditate, your mind changes in specific ways, and those ways are perfect for people who program computers and work in the computer field. It's very similar. ...

There are few more challenging or fun experiences than to create a program, because you use your total mind. It's very Jnana Yoga, it's marvelous. And also, within not many years, in the primary grades, every child will be learning programming.

I think that computer programming for a person who lives and works in the world is ideal. Or, many other professions. Medicine, law, whatever you prefer. It helps you develop your mind in a way that's very similar to the way that we develop the mind in meditation. Clear and precise logic. It's a fascinating field for many reasons.

As Rama spoke, seated straight-backed and cross-legged on his small teaching couch, his enthusiasm and vision for the topic was palpable and persuasive. Suddenly, if you weren't yet in computer science, you wanted to be.

He laid out a career program for beginners—learn to type, learn word processing. Earn more money and become comfortable with it.

Take some courses. Begin to find out what it's all about. Now, you may be at a point where the last thing you need to do is get involved with computers. I'm not suggesting that everyone should go do that. But what I'm saying is, if your life is in a state of change, and you're at the point where you are considering a career for many, many years, I think from a spiritual point of view it's a very interesting career to examine. Or whatever suits you. You follow your own heart in the matter. That's always the best. But I see something spiritually, is what I'm trying to say about this particular field. It also allows you to make a tremendous amount of money with which you can buy space around yourself.

You see, in the world, as the society and the population gets denser and denser and it gets darker out there, which it's definitely doing—money buys you space. It buys you protection in a world gone mad. So you need to find something that will give you enough money to make you independent. If you have an old car and it breaks down on the freeway in the middle of the night and you never know who's going to come along, you don't want that sort of thing to happen. We live in the world of violence, there's an astounding crime rate, and you need to be able to buy a little space around yourself so you can lead a more refined life and keep yourself in good shape so you can then do more for others.

What I'm suggesting is that life is like a giant computer. The computer is nothing without the software. The computer is just a big piece of metal, tubes, transistors, chips, diodes, and it sits there and it doesn't do much. What gives the computer life is the software, the programs that we run on the computer. Now, there is no such thing as a program. A program is a dream. We dream a context in an alphanumeric sense. We create a reality through designing a program. This is why I think computer programming is so fascinating and such a good art for a person who practices meditation, because it's advanced dreaming. When you write a program, you are practicing dreaming.[44]

When Rama asked the students to master the basics in their lives so they could move on to more interesting studies in self-realization, the analogy was to computer programming.

Spend some time, get your physical together, and just get it running and forget about it. Once we set up the software program, we'll let it run. Once in a while we make modifications in it. Initially we have to write a program. We have a new computer and now we have to write the program which will run on the computer. The program will

44   Lenz, Frederick (Rama). "Dreaming." *The Lakshmi Series.* Los Angeles: Lakshmi Inc., 1982.

*determine how we're going to process data—how we're going
to store it, subdivisions, categories, different functions. So
we take the time and we do a systems analysis.*

*We determine what it is we want. We write the program
and then we start to run it. Once we start to run any
program there are going to be a lot of bugs in it. We're going
to find that it's not going to go exactly as we planned. But if
we work on it, we can work out the bugs in the system and
just let it run.*

When Rama spoke about mental conditioning, the analogy was
to computers.

*Conditioning is responsible for what our life is. The totality
of your life at this time is dependent upon what's happened
to you. We are reflections of reflections of reflections. These
images are literally programmed into us from the time we
were born. A number of different interlocking programs
were written, and gradually you were given a description
of the world, a way of seeing.*

*There are alternate descriptions of the world, and what
I try to do is provide not simply one other description,
but a number of different descriptions that you can use.
We can think of the description as computer languages.
The very basic languages or the most basic languages—
machine code, assembler—are the description of the world
most people have. It's an operable description that really
only deals with very simple operations, and its code is the
language of duality: male, female, dark, light, up, down,
in, out.*

*Then, of course, just as in computers, there are more
sophisticated languages, other descriptions that are useful
for you. I have handed you initially four basic descriptions
and one overriding description. The four basic descriptions,
of course, are love, self-giving, knowledge and mysticism.
Each has a language all its own. They are all united by
something we call Tantric Mysticism. Tantric Mysticism*

is the glue that binds together not one description, but all descriptions of existence.[45]

Computer science careers supported the practice of advanced Tantric Mysticism—using everything in your life to grow, whether it be selecting a place to live, practicing a mentally challenging profession or shopping in a particular location.

Rama, for example, liked certain shopping centers. For him, they were multi-dimensional bardos of human existence. One favorite place, a monolithic eight-story structure located at the edge of Beverly Hills and West Hollywood, was the Beverly Center. Opened in 1982, it featured 14 movie theaters and 160 stores. Exterior escalators resembled the entrance to Disneyland's Space Mountain ride, with strobe-lights along the sides and ceilings.

"I lived two blocks away from the Beverly Center," said Deborah Brandeis, a student who had recently been accepted into the MBA program at UCLA. "One day in April, I had a strong feeling to go there. I was walking down the hall to the escalators when guess who was coming up the escalator next to the blue strobe lights—the curly hair, the tall body perched on the metal step—floated up. I waited for him at the top of the escalator. He came over to me and said, 'It's about time you got here!'

"I fell into step with him. We walked directly to the floor with over 50 women's clothing stores. Together, we walked into many of these stores. He would have me observe various people in the shops. Then we would walk out of the store and he asked me what I saw. We would talk about who they were and what their auras looked like. In the little boutiques, there often would be young, bright women. You could see exactly what was going on in their minds without ever speaking to them. We'd talk about someone who had just walked past. It was an amazing education in looking at the state of a person's aura or subtle physical body.

"Rama showed me how to trace back from what something looked like in their aura, to an understanding of why it looked that way. It was easy to see how the bright young women had been programmed not to see themselves as powerful. I emerged from that day of teaching

---

45 Lenz, Frederick (Rama). "Modular Mysticism - Seeing." *Insights: Talks on the Nature of Existence.* Los Angeles: Lakshmi Inc., 1983.

realizing how important it was for me to view myself as powerful, in spite of any previous mental programming."

In 1984, I was one of those few students for whom another career had opened up. As Rama continued in his quest to find his past life students and work with his enrolled students in several cities, I continued to learn the tracks of public relations. For me, tantric mysticism was using public relations to grow.

In 1984, the TV talk show host Johnny Carson launched a new production company. His company quickly assembled a lineup of media projects. On behalf of Carson Productions, I handled publicity for a bittersweet romance drama starring Joanne Woodward (her husband, Paul Newman, always deferential and polite, used to visit the large, rented Brentwood home used as a set). I started prep work for a new TV series, "Partners in Crime," starring the actresses Lynda Carter and Loni Anderson.

On behalf of my PR firm, I wrote a new business proposal for a potential large client and, to the owner of the firm's great surprise, landed the contract. Soon I was on a plane to the Caribbean island of Curacao, where Faberge, a large beauty product manufacturer, launched a new product line. Cary Grant had signed on as a spokesperson and I accompanied him (shy, embarrassed to be there, clearly for the $) and his wife on jaunts around the island.

I held a different perspective on my work. Interacting with anyone famous was interesting, but did it compare to the multi-life epiphany of being on a desert trip with Rama? No. Did it compare to an evening class with Rama with the blasts of stillness and gold light? No. Primarily, the profession helped me to hone my tonal and observe Rama's teachings on fame.

Rama taught that everyone is psychic. The thoughts and feelings of other people are like radio wave transmissions that can easily be picked up by your own psychic mind, and you mistakenly think they are your own. This happens to everyone all the time. But the more fame you have, then the more other people think about you, and if you are not aware of this radio wave effect, you can become like a cut-rate bargain counter of other people's thoughts and emotions. Whenever I met a famous person for the first time, I always could tell whether or not they lived a grounded, practical life by the number of other people's thoughts I felt around them.

Public relations was good, but computer programming was the paradigm.

At the start of one student meeting, Rama stood by one of the wide doors that led into the Beverly Theatre's main hall, his tall frame leaning against a door jam. He grinned ear to ear. Prominently placed on one of the reception tables next to him sat three comical and outlandish little stuffed animal critters, one yellow and two blue, each about eight inches tall, with soft plush fur and mops of white, fluffy hair. He called them *blisses*. A predecessor bliss had once been featured on the 7th and final issue of *WOOF!* Magazine, back in 1981. Now, Rama had ordered 1,000 blisses to give out to his students. As every student entered, he directed their attention to a bliss. "That's how happy you should be!"

On stage, just before the break, Rama talked about the blisses. He explained they have awareness. Everything has energy, including blisses. Blisses are pure innocence and fun. Blisses are a reminder that you can let yourself be silly. As he spoke, Rama waved a bliss hand puppet through the air, opening and closing its mouth. The puppets were configured to smile ecstatically with every movement.

Rama shared the etiquette of blisses: feed them with the scent of flowers, don't give them to children because they shouldn't be abused, and be careful of their noses. Blisses are a reminder that the path of self-discovery is not heavy or ponderous.

In the audience, I suddenly felt ridiculously happy. One of the craziest by-products of spiritual seeking is becoming self-absorbed and heavy. You get so wrapped up in your internal process that you forget about light and ecstasy. Most of the people with whom you interact throughout the day are not in states of buoyant joy. But here was a bliss, a fuzzy nine-inch puppet, a flagrant happiness role model, and Rama was about to hand them out to each student!

At the end of the evening, one by one, the students walked up to Rama as he stood at the front of the stage. Rama reached into a box full of blisses and lightly tapped each bliss's large round nose before giving it away. My Rama-irradiated bliss wore bright green. I named him Newbie. He sits on my desk today, perched underneath some flowers.

When I put my hand inside his puppet casings and open his mouth, nothing has changed. He exudes wild, playful silliness.

Three blisses on a bridge

Blisses are icons of study with Rama. They are humble, funny, innocent and delightful. Advanced tantric mysticism.

In the fall, Rama taught a series of public seminars in Phoenix, Arizona. "Soon after he returned, he held a student meeting at the Beverly Theatre," Forge said. "He was on stage meditating. I could tell he was going through an intensive enlightenment process. He was getting so inebriated with the light of the infinite that he had a very difficult time walking. His samadhis were changing and deepening in such a way they manifested in his having a more difficult time being in the physical body.

"That night it was a long meditation, he was extremely brilliant. At first the light was blue then it shifted to pure gold. I saw giant gold Buddhas on the stage behind him. Then he turned into this giant gold Buddha. I realized his lineage and where he came from. This vision was magnificent. I was completely overtaken by it and sat there, stunned and extremely high.

"At the end of the evening, he pointed to the crowd. He said, 'Kathy, come here, I need your help.' I walked to the side of the stage, the guys were helping him to the edge of the stage. I saw what was happening and I came running up the stairs to the stage and held his body as best as I could. He was so gone. I said, 'Let's just sit down.' We both sat down. The suit he was wearing didn't matter, all that mattered was getting him to the point where he could stand up.

"We sat side by side in silence on the scuffed, wood stage floor for several minutes. Then he turned to me and said, 'Thank you, you were shining so bright.' I told him of my seeing of the golden Buddhas. He said, 'Aren't they wonderful?' His eyes shone like an innocent child.

"'OK,' I said, "'I can tell you're not much in your body. Make sure someone drives you home.' Rama stood up slowly, carefully. I and one of the guys brought him to the car."

A milestone movie in the fall of 1984—*The Terminator*. Arnold Schwarzenegger got all the buzz for the film, but the person that interested Rama as a teaching point was an actress, Linda Hamilton playing Sarah Connor. During the course of the movie, as Sarah Connor battles a cyborg (Schwarzenegger), she transforms from giggly, airheaded Barbie doll to self-confident, centered warrior. It was the transformation that Rama sought for all his women students, and he continually found ways to help them gain confidence in the face of adversity.

"I was in MBA school," said Brandeis. "Rama was glad I was making the leap towards an MBA, and he invited me to go to the movies with him. Rama wore this cool, all-black L.A. outfit, and I was trying my best to look chic. After seeing a film that starred Milla Jovovich, we went to a café in West Hollywood, a late night hip-ish diner. They served stuff like fried zucchini with blue cheese dressing. Crowded, bright lighting but I liked the food. We had food not alcohol—it wasn't an alcohol place.

"We were seated at a small table for two with very little room between us and the next table. It so happened that seated at that next table was the only guy in my MBA class who had ever given me a hard time. He was one of those people who thought it was funny to put me down every time I said anything in class.

"It was almost impossible for either table to not hear the conversation at the next. Rama and I started talking about the movie. We liked Milla and the fact there was a female heroine. I thought the story line was weak. Suddenly, this guy from my class leaned towards our table and started making sarcastic comments about my observations regarding the movie. Before I could say anything, Rama responded with several lightning sharp and pointed comments and to my delight, completely shut the a-hole down. I could feel how stunned my classmate felt. He and the friend he was with left after several minutes.

"Later, Rama said that the guy would now respect me after seeing me with someone like him. It was like having an occultly badass big brother. The guy in my class never gave me a hard time again."

During a public lecture, Rama said that his real work would start in 1985. He said that seekers of light use times of change to grow and make rapid change in their own life. 1985 would start a challenging thirty-year cycle but it would be easier to change with the new energy. The energy would be neither good nor bad, but it would be intense. If you used it correctly, it could help you change more rapidly. It could be a time of new beginnings.

I experienced new beginnings. The TV series, "Partners in Crime" was in pre-production. The series featured two prominent TV actresses, but to launch the first episode, Carson Productions decided to include a third prominent starlet. One of the executives called me to say he was worried about "a catfight," and could I please go to Vancouver to keep things calm on the set. I assured him there would be no fighting, and in fact shooting of the first episode went smoothly.

When I got back to L.A., I received a call from the same executive. "Congratulations, Liz," he exulted. "It was a MIRACLE you kept those women away from each other. You deserve a promotion." I assured him I had done nothing at all, but pressure was put on my boss, and about a week after my return I became the first female Vice President of Mahoney/Wasserman Public Relations.

At the next student meeting at the Beverly Theatre, I came up to Rama during the break. I managed to get within a few feet of Rama and caught his attention. I told him about the promotion. I had only been in the PR profession for three years, and already I was a Vice President. I was working with national media and mainstream famous folks. How amazing! I felt he had supercharged my career path.

Rama was pleased and startled to hear the news. At that moment, out of all the years I interacted with him, something happened that was most unusual. A tremor passed through Rama's entire body, as if the news of my promotion pinged at something deep in his inner being. I know now (did not know then) that it was the prediction—of his being a great teacher for the West who would help millions of people. I know my promotion deeply affected him. But for me, the new title was kind of an inner joke—it had been gained based on a complete misunderstanding of the power of women.

In mid-October at the student meeting, Rama announced he was going away to the Rocky Mountains, either Denver or Boulder. He spoke quietly. He said he was exhausted, his subtle body was wearing down and aging. He said he was taking 20 people with him who also needed renewal. He was moving out of the Malibu house and would be getting an apartment in Laguna Beach, an oceanfront town about sixty miles south of Los Angeles. For the first time in five years of teaching, he changed the schedule of student meetings from twice a week to every other week.

Two nights later, when Rama left the theater after a long night of speaking, answering questions and chatting with individual students, Rama slowly walked out of the Ebell Theater and headed for a waiting car. He was driven to Malibu where his fully-packed, dark blue SUV awaited him. In the back seat of the car was a cozy dog bed for Vayu. Rama changed his clothes from suit to denims and a sweatshirt. He then drove to a nearby student's apartment where 20 students, also with cars packed for travel, awaited him. It was after 1 a.m. when they set off in a 14-car caravan for the 1,046-mile journey to Boulder or Denver, with many stops planned in between.

As soon as they left the confines of L.A., heading northeast to Las Vegas, the impact of the journey kicked in. On the road!

"The trip was intended to look for places to move, not only for the students on the trip but for all the students," said David Silver. "The goal was to find a pure place to practice meditation and set up a computer company. He felt that the energy in L.A. was too dreamy and would take us out.

"Our first stop was Las Vegas and we stayed there several days. Las Vegas is built on strong desert power lines, and Rama wanted us to see and feel if it was an appropriate place to live. We all had fun. Rama would pick a slot machine and usually hit a jackpot in a few minutes. He played blackjack, and we watched him beat the house. After he had won a moderate amount at a table, he would get up and walk around.

"We could feel the high energy of the desert, but we did not think it was right for business or meditation so we continued on. But we were open-minded. The whole trip was like that. It was a sense of freedom and feeling the right thing to do. It was a trip of seeing, a sort of walkabout[46] in a car. We called it a driveabout."

After Las Vegas, the group headed to Utah, meeting along the road for conversations at Denny's restaurants. Every evening, reservations at roadside three-star Best Western hotels were made in advance so everyone knew where to meet up again. In Utah, the group headed off I-70 East to explore Canyonland and Arches National Park.

At Arches, Rama and fellow adventurers hiked along a trail that led away from the road to less visited stone arches, pinnacles and astounding red rock formations. They stopped to meditate in the late afternoon. "Since we had meditated so many times with Rama in the Anza Borrego desert," said Morrell, "I was able to discern an entirely different energy at Arches. It was like being in the front room of a different dynasty of desert beings. After we meditated, we hiked back to the cars under a tomato red sunset. Rama gave us the name of a Mexican restaurant he knew about in a nearby town, and we all met there for dinner. We sat at three large tables. Rama went from table to table and asked about our impressions of the places we drove through or visited."

---

46   A walkabout is the Australian term for the aboriginal custom of walking through the desert as a rite of passage.

The group drove to Santa Fe and Albuquerque, stopping first for a short visit in Four Corners, New Mexico, where Rama purchased some finely crafted Navajo jewelry. Santa Fe seemed promising, but Rama felt it was similar to Los Angeles, with a dream-like quality that would be difficult for both business and meditation.

They then motored to Aspen, Colorado for two days of exploration before driving to Boulder, their anticipated destination. After several days in Boulder, Rama and the students felt that the energy lines were good for both business and meditation. A number of apartments were rented and the students moved in, unpacked and began looking for computer jobs as everyone on the trip had been trained as a computer programmer, and many had already been working in the field. A few people found work immediately.

Two weeks later, Rama—following his own adage, "Things can change in a second"—determined that the Denver/Boulder axis was not an ideal spot. Throughout the meandering driveabout, Rama observed the effect that the locations they visited had on his students' awareness level. The students were happy to settle down in Boulder, but once the nesting began, Rama saw their awareness drop. Rama pointed out that in the future, the power lines of the area might change. But for now—time to move on.

The group re-packed their cars and headed east, as far as North Platte, Nebraska. When they emerged from their cars in the late afternoon at an I-80 rest area, they found the energy surprisingly pure, clear and still. The Great Plains, the land of buffalo, Sioux Indians, the American dream of open space, stretched for miles out to the horizon. The area felt surprisingly creative and nurturing. The blue-jean and sweatshirt clad journeyers formed a circle. Rama asked them the question that he had asked in previous spots on the driveabout—was this the place for seekers of enlightenment to live and work? It seemed unlikely.

One of the students on the journey had been insistent that Boston was the right place to meditate and form a software company. Rama was open to the idea of continuing east on the driveabout. At the rest stop in North Platte, however, he asked David Silver for his opinion—should they go to Boston or go back to Laguna Beach? Silver said he thought it was time to go back.

Done. The group returned to their cars and, at the next highway exit, turned back towards the West Coast. They circled the Southwest one more time to see if any place had been missed. Ultimately, in early December, they returned to Laguna Beach.

Throughout the driveabout, Rama flew back and forth to Los Angeles to continue teaching his enrolled students. He also flew on his own to explore Boston.

I've been traveling around talking Zen to people in Denny's. You tend to think of eternity as something quite large but maybe it's something quite small.

The three-person band Zazen, which over the next decade would produce 16 albums with Rama, first got together during the time of the driveabout.

According to guitarist and Zazen musician Joaquin Lievano, he and Andy West, bass player for Zazen, had attended Rama's seminars in San Francisco. Both were respected and experienced musicians for well-known fusion bands (Andy—Dixie Dregs, Joaquin—Jean-Luc Ponty), and they decided to form their own band in the Bay Area. When Rama closed the San Francisco Center in 1984, Andy decided to move to L.A. Their new band was now in limbo.

"In November of 1984," said Lievano, "we were at a seminar with Rama at the Beverly Theatre and Andy just happened to walk up to Rama. Andy asked Rama if he knew a keyboard player. Rama said, 'I know just the guy.' He hooked us up with another one of his students named Steve Kaplan. Then Rama came up with this idea that the three of us should play together in the public seminar of January 1985 at the Beverly Theatre. The only instruction he gave us was, 'Don't play any blues.' Later when we got together, the three of us looked at each other. Rock music is based on blues! So in the short time we had to prepare, we listened to a lot of Tangerine Dream, as we knew Rama liked their music, and we tried to make the music our own in a matter of weeks.

"We wrote and rehearsed out of Steve's apartment in Malibu. We worked up some tunes. We didn't know if we were doing anything right. We did not know if Rama was extremely nice to work with or not. We figured we'd find out."

On December 31, Rama held a Gong Show at the Wilshire Ebell. Students in frog costumes hopped about the stage on pogo sticks. Other students performed send-ups of the year's hot films—*Ghostbusters, Star Trek, Gremlins, The Karate Kid*. The funniest part of the night was Rama, speaking in the rolling accent of an Irish priest.

Rama launched into New Year's Eve analytics—

- Most students in the room had an average of 20,000 to 30,000 lifetimes, and it takes about 84,000 to reach enlightenment.
- He expects about 10% return on his investment from his students so try to think at least 10% positive thoughts.
- We only access about 2% of what he has to offer.
- We need to put in another 25% extra effort than we have been, to get an A out of life instead of a C.
- 99% of the thoughts we think are not our own.

He likes us for the being that he sees can emerge after our layers are peeled back. He does not expect us to be holy, just honest.

Everyone at the Gong Show received a handout:

Flamingo Island

There was once a king and a queen who had a daughter who was stolen out of her crib by a roving band of flamingos. The flamingos took her to a small island and raised her. They taught her secret flamingo arts and she walked around thinking she was a flamingo.

One day as fate would have it, a great spiritual sage was traveling through the astral planes and saw the little island of flamingos where the young girl lived. Seeing a delightful opportunity to confuse everyone, he manifested himself on the island in the form of a flamingo, naturally, because she would only listen to flamingos since she only spoke flamingese.

The sage approached her and explained that she was the daughter of a great king and queen and that she came from another kingdom. She listened and the light of knowledge dawned and she left with the sage, they married and lived happily after.

No. What actually happened was that she went back to the kingdom and discovered that her parents had died and she had inherited a lot of money, and she lived flagrantly but happily ever after.

No. I'll get the story right. What happened was that she realized she was not who she thought she was. So she decided to walk on two feet and give up flying.

Anyway, someday when you run into your spiritual teacher, you'll realize that you're not a flamingo. That's my point. You will change.

The sleeper inside you will begin to awaken and you will find you are far different from the person you supposed yourself to be.

I read the handout in my Brentwood apartment on the first day of the New Year. According to Rama's statistics, while I had certainly run into my spiritual teacher, I was still 98 percent flaminga.

10

1985 – ON THE ROAD WITH RAMA

No one can do it for you. You have to take what you learn from the teacher and go out and live it. You have to fight your battles of power. You have to overcome your own conditioning. You have to change your life. - Rama

On New Year's Day, I drove east along Wilshire Boulevard, a road that stretches from East Los Angeles to the cliffs of Santa Monica. About one mile east of Westwood, a ten block stretch of high-rise apartment buildings line both sides of the busy thoroughfare, providing a brief hint of the walled canyons of New York City. This section of Wilshire Boulevard begins and ends abruptly and is book-ended by traditional two-story units and dwellings.

As I entered this part of the road, suddenly my awareness flipped into limitless awareness—in the form of skyscrapers. I became aware of NO separation between my surroundings and my being. There was no difference. I was my surroundings. I drove through my Self, eternity—a tall urban canyon.

Merging with no time, no-self, eternal high-rises continued until I emerged from the stretch of tall buildings. As I headed towards Beverly Hills, I suddenly flipped back into "me" within the confines of a body. One millisecond earlier, I had been an eternal fortress of steel and glass. Now I was braking for a red light. I kept my hands on the steering wheel.

Rama's words, casually spoken a few days earlier, popped into my mind: "I was driving down Wilshire Boulevard and realized I was driving through my own mind."

My momentary, riveting slice into Rama's awareness ricocheted around the sky-rises.

At the first public seminar in January, the three musicians played their compositions. "We were OK," Lievano said. "We weren't great but we showed our intention to work together." Shortly thereafter, Rama (unaware that there was already a garage band in Aberdeen, Washington with the same name) selected "Nirvana" as the band's name and gave the musicians more direction.

"He knew a lot about electronic music," Lievano said. "He wanted more looping sequences. He said he wanted to continue to work with us. He told us he was going to do some public seminars in Boston and asked us to play there. We rearranged the music to be more suitable for meditation and put in more looping sequences. It was a good start but we knew we had a long way to go."

In Rama's fifth year as a solo spiritual teacher, his mission— to find past life or appropriate students and help to bring them to enlightenment—had not changed. He would do whatever it took, follow and teach whatever pathway worked to make that happen, and he observed his students' progress closely.

But something structural needed to change. After four years of empowerments, teaching essential self-discovery and the tech of mysticism, not just in words but in mind-states, the students had reached, but not retained, high levels of awareness. Students stepped back and observed—but did not become—luminous awareness. Or as Rama frequently quipped, his teaching of enlightenment for the West went "in one chakra and out the other."

At the beginning of January, he announced that everyone would be different at the end of the trimester than when they started.

On February 6th, when Rama visited the Continental Divide in Colorado, he recorded the first of a series of audio tapes, *On the Road with Rama*. Anticipating the challenges that lay ahead, each talk was a specific roadmap to bring the listener back to a still point in the turning worlds.

Seated in a rental car at 9,000 feet, surrounded by snow and pulled off the highway, Rama recorded "Neutral Density," a term used in photography for a filter that reduces or modifies intensity of all wavelengths or colors of light equally, giving no changes in hue or color.

"The neutral density of perpetual being is the acceptance of your own immortality, your awareness of awareness, being awareness without being aware of yourself," he recorded. "The Continental Divide is the point where the energies of East and West in the United States meet. It's like two rivers merging; at the point of merging there's a great deal of activity. The sunset and the sunrise, when it's neither dark nor light, are the moments of transition. And moments of transition are a time when the ring of our awareness falls away for a moment and we can see eternity more clearly."

A transition opportunity was presented on February 19th at the Beverly Theatre. With most of the students now living back in Southern California, Rama asked them to consider why moving to Boston would be a good idea. In a back-and-forth with the audience, it became evident that many of the students were not inspired by the suggestion.

The next night, February 20th, Rama stated that he was starting a Boston center and that students could relocate there to study with him, if they would like. He spoke about the clear energy lines of Boston and said that he felt many of his students would enjoy living there. He described the Back Bay and the university environment. The seeds of desire were planted.

Two weeks later, when the next student meeting took place, the big B(oston) moment became actionable as each student walked into the Beverly Theatre and was handed a blank sheet of light blue paper.

During the first part of the evening the sheet remained blank as Rama talked about the rough, dreamlike energy of Los Angeles. He then spoke of the smoother, crisper energy of Boston. He said he had already decided to live in Boston and was enjoying hikes around Walden Pond. He spoke again of the mental sharpness of M.I.T., Harvard, the beauty of the Charles River. He felt it was time to make a shift. The point of the move to Boston, said Rama, was to make his students happier, as most of the students were not feeling too frosty in Los Angeles. He said that getting away from L.A. had helped him feel stronger.

Each of the 400 students present was asked to meditate for several minutes, then write on the front of the blank blue paper their choice—either Boston or Los Angeles—regarding where they would be living and attending his meditation classes as of June that year. On the flip side of the page, the students were asked to write the number of people they saw would select Boston. Also on the back of the page, he asked the students to write down something they wanted his help with—something getting in the way of their spiritual progress. He said it was important to work on whatever they wrote down on the piece of paper with all their heart.

Tension rippled through the hall as each person sorted through their decision—stay or leave? What do I need help with?

I sat quietly in the psychic stew. I had a job and an apartment. I had spent many years of my life in Los Angeles. I had never lived on the East Coast. I owned no winter clothes. I opted to stay. I wrote that I needed help with meditation—all the years of meditating with my understanding that thoughts during meditation signified release of stress (which, alas, is not true—thoughts during meditation just mean you are a beginner) had taken a toll on my meditative prowess.

The light blue sheets of paper were collected and responses tallied. That evening, one student guessed the exact number of people who said they would go to Boston—163. He received a spiritual name.

That night, I left the hall feeling unsettled. Rama's offer had raised the "cons" side of my current place of employment. At work, I sat jammed in a small, poorly ventilated, alley-facing room with four men, including the boss's youngest son, whose idea of fun banter was putting down their girlfriends, female actresses, the female office manager and her daughters, probably me when I wasn't there. (This was before sensitivity training regarding gender issues had been invented.) The show I represented, "Partners in Crime," had not been renewed for another TV season, and my upcoming workload seemed bleak. Plus, Rama spoke so glowingly of computer science. Was I just in the wrong profession? The inner debate began.

After the seminar, while his students churned over next steps, Rama flew to Lake Tahoe in Northern California to renew and refresh. There he recorded what he felt his students needed next in their lives. "Magic," he spoke into his handheld mic, seated in his car in a scenic view spot overlooking the lake, "begins just beyond the realm of thought, in that perpetual silence of the void, where there are all the forms that have ever been or will ever be, kind of in a huge bank, a flux. They float there—everything, all eternities, all possibilities—just float there, in a perfect sea of awareness. The art of magic is the transformation of the self. It's the ability to go into that flux, the totality. To enter into it consciously, and when you've entered into it consciously, you reorder."

March 17th, St. Patrick's Day, brought Rama's wild Irish upbringing back to the fore. Ever since he was a boy, Rama said, his father used to wake him early on the morning of St. Patrick's Day to sing Irish songs with a booming Irish tenor. The tradition had persisted to this day, and no matter where he was, his father would find him, phone him and wake him up to belt out the old chestnut Irish tunes. Rama said he was certain that his father did not have his current phone number, but he was wrong. That morning, he'd been awakened by a phone call and the sound of his father's voice loudly caroling Irish melodies. Rama then proceeded to sing a sweet Irish lullaby with a full Irish brogue for his students.

We students felt soft as marshmallows and warm as kittens.

Into this sea of contentment came another bolt of light blue—the blank piece of light blue paper. Rama cheerfully asked everyone to reconsider their relocation decision. He felt that some people had selected L.A. who should have chosen Boston. This time, the meditation was longer, and the papers were once again written upon, collected and counted.

That was when I shocked myself. I wrote "Boston" on the front of the paper. I would move to Boston, take advantage of the brainy climate to enroll in a computer programming trade school and begin life anew in a new land. Suddenly, when I handed in the paper, I felt my life hitting a restart button. It was scary but exciting. Rama announced that the exodus to Boston would begin in the middle of May.

In the meantime, to reduce the number of people on desert trips, Rama started taking people to the desert by astrology sign. On March 24, Taurus, Aries, Gemini, Cancer, Pisces and Aquarius went on a nighttime journey to the Anza Borrego desert.

During the night, Rama lightly touched each student in the middle of their forehead to make it easier for them to see and to learn more about making decisions. He explained that the students who chose Boston saw that was the correct choice for someone who was more serious about their spiritual aspirations. Those who did not select Boston still had other priorities. He said either decision was fine. If people chose to come to Boston later, that would be their moment of power.

Someone commented on the ancient feeling of the desert. He said the land is old but what the students feel as ancient is actually something else. Boston is also an ancient place. He said his students came from a vast variety of worlds and dimensions. As a teacher, it's more interesting for him that way.

Rama recorded "Unity" on March 30th. "It's around 5:00 in the afternoon. I'm on the Big Island of Hawaii, and I'm pulled off to the side of the road at around three thousand feet. I'm going to roll up the window here 'cause it's getting a little loud.

"There's a lot of traffic on this particular road, but it's a power place. Beneath me I see the island stretching out. The sun will probably be setting in about an hour. I'm facing the direction of the volcano Mauna Kea. It's obscured by a heavy cloud cover. Behind me is Mauna Loa—the twin peaks of the Big Island. And today I'd like to talk to you about making yourself available to energy, to power.

"You've decided to look for power, to look for light, to look for truth. So now you've started on your journey. But there are some things that you need to consider. The first is to be strategic. The second is to be earnest, and the third is not to give a damn. They really all go together."[47]

On April 6th, 24-year-old student and aspiring businessman Davide Khalen recollected, "There was a postering meeting that took place in Laguna Beach, where the bliss was intense, and Rama gave his delicate satsang[48] for hours that evening, the night of Easter, when Christ rose from the dead. He talked about how some people are karmically designed to spend their life cloistered in retreat and others the reverse, in the world, and various mixes in between, different phases in life.

"Into this he wove a dream of our one day having a place, or a few places perhaps, that would be the mother ship, our lineage's holdings, the great monastic university of enlightenment that would have a retreat center in Hawaii, in the desert, in Nevada, some holdings of other land in power spots.

---

47   Lenz, Frederick (Rama). "Unity." *On the Road with Rama.* Los Angeles: Lakshmi Inc., 1985.

48   Satsang is a Sanskrit term meaning, in the company of the highest truth.

"Funnily, this meeting would later coincide with his death, as I reflect—just 14 years later. As he spoke, I felt such acceptance for those spiritual types who wanted no more experience, but I had much yet to learn. This was a postering meeting, and we were doing his dharma by helping him to get the word out to future students whom he was looking to engage and assist.

"I mean 'assist,' as that's what it was. Rama was a benevolent Buddha, it was a privilege to sit in that golden room. And at one point in the meeting Rama held his hand out commenting that we couldn't handle the kundalini he was processing. He grabbed an imaginary dial in the air, like an oven knob, and he turned it until I was so on fire with energy I could not move. I was immobilized by the kundalini, and this went for perhaps 10 seconds until he dialed it back and released us from the bondage of the light.

"Then there was a moment when he held his Scottie dog Vayu and scratched his back saying, 'Watch this, he hates this,' and scratching him on the back and Vayu would snap at the air with his teeth at being teased by Rama's playfulness. All I recall of the evening, the deepest significant part, was the love and the river of tears down my cheeks, it was so deeply beautiful to be embraced by that spiritual trust of Rama's refuge."

In mid-April, Rama spoke and the three musicians (still calling themselves Nirvana) played at several three-night public lecture series in Boston and Los Angeles. In all the venues, Rama danced—a balletic, meditative, multi-dimensional Zen meditation to live music.

In Los Angeles, a student wrote: "When I saw Rama dance for the first time, it was beautiful and poignant. The dance evoked ecstasy and compassion. Rama later said that his dancing was the way he had broken through timidity. It would have been easier for him to never get up and dance.

"Rama then spoke of love. He said the reason many of us have a strange love for him that we don't understand is that we sense his willingness to take on our pain to help us."

The next evening, Rama described his experience with the band.

I'm remembering more about dancing. We're all remembering things, so it'll be interesting to see it in a couple of years. It's the same with the guys with their music.

You know, they're not very good yet. They're good inside, but they haven't remembered enough. They've all been musicians in other lives. Also they don't practice much. We hope for better things in the future. But - you can see the potential there. You can see the evolutionary jump they've made. They haven't really worked together a lot but their consciousness is evolving, and as your attention evolves, if you work at whatever it is—music, computers, dancing, anything—the leaps you can make are amazing. It's attention that does it. Intention and attention.

I really didn't notice the people much last night, I was too far away. But I noticed the music, I liked the music a lot, that was fun for me to meditate. I think the guys did a good job. They're better this time in the sense that I didn't notice "them" as personalities as much. I noticed music more and I didn't feel "them." You know, I'm so sensitive up here, and I didn't feel their egos as much, which was very nice for me. I almost didn't even know they were here. That was good, and it reflected in the music they played—a higher vibe music, I thought. That was nice.

At the end of the meeting, he asked the students, "Consider when your life is over, will you feel good about your dance? Will it have been a dance of power or Cream of Wheat timidity?"

For future Bostonians, the last meeting at the Beverly Theatre took place on April 17. For most of the meeting, Rama spoke of projects and pre-Boston preparations. Moving van space estimates were distributed. Details were hassled.

As far as the Boston thing is concerned, you see, my idea is that—I don't like living in one place too long. I like to move around, because I figure we only have so many years on the planet. And so I find it intriguing to live in different places. I find I change more that way myself. It breaks up my routines, it causes me to rise to new and different challenges. But not everybody feels that way, and you remember the maxim is, "If it works, don't fix it." If a place is working well for you, then that's a good thing.

But I expect that I will always be living in a place for a couple of years, two years, three years, whatever, and then moving someplace else. And some people like that idea, they're excited by that. They feel very comfortable with that. For them that's a very good thing. So the idea then, of moving to Boston is exciting, and then, probably after about two years they'll be looking at me getting bored, saying, "Where do we go next?" And since most of the people are in computers, it's very easy to do that. There's no problem because we can hop to any major city and everybody can get jobs quickly, particularly as they evolve and get better and better at what they do.

Rama suggested driving rather than flying across the country and gave some attitude guidance.

I do feel driving will be fun for you because it'll give you a chance to watch the energy as you go along to Boston. It's a great adventure. You should see America if you haven't done it lately.

A word about Boston. And then I want to get this microphone and be a roving reporter for a few minutes and talk to you about a few things. I just want to clarify it one more time, because I've received a few sort of frantic letters from people saying, "God, I'm not moving to Boston, am I doing the wrong thing?" And, certainly not. You see, life is a series of adventures. This is the Lakshmi philosophy, if there is one. Life is a series of adventures. When you have an adventure, you're alive.

Most people are bored to tears by their lives. They're so bored that they sit around and watch TV, not because they like what's on but because there's nothing else happening in their lives. They have lots of affairs. Not because they're excited or madly in love with anyone, but because there's nothing going on. They eat too much. Not because they really like what they're eating, or even taste it, but because there's nothing else going on. They go to the movies too much, because there's nothing going on. Life for most people is a pretty dull experience, sometimes very painful.

At Lakshmi we look at it in a different way. Life is an adventure. You have to make everything into an adventure. That's mysticism. But there are different adventures. And you have to feel out what is the best adventure for you. All of you have been in Lakshmi for this trimester. And just looking at this trimester I think you will see as I promised you on the first evening, that you would be different at the end of the trimester than when you started, yes? I have fulfilled my promise, I think, yes? [Audience responds, "Yes."] Yes. So, I kept my part of the bargain. And the trimester is, needless to say, not over. [Audience laughs.] It won't be over until we make that circle in the desert, OK? So there's a ways to go yet friends, there's a ways to go.

On May 1, Rama flew to Boston for a public lecture and "Music from Nirvana" concert held at a theater in the Back Bay. James Dorje, an economics student at New York University, attended the meeting. He described the evening as "contextually beyond." According to Dorje, "The musicians jammed at the highest level of the greatest groups. Rama's dancing started out slow and elegant, then the rhythms and tempos became fast. He performed thousands of mudras—graceful, emotional, powerful. His range of mobility was acrobatic. The music was intense, jazzy and profound and had its own sound.

"That was the night I asked Rama my first question, before the dancing. I said, 'Rama, I feel I worship you too much and that interferes with my meditation.' Golden light poured out of his body. I thought, 'Oh my God, he's enlightened.' Most of the audience did not know what that implied. He gave me this long answer. The essence was—I don't like people worshiping me but you can love me."

Lievano also recalled the "Music from Nirvana" concert. "Afterwards," he said, "Rama met with us. He was totally psyched about the music. It was something he really wanted to do. He said I had something special but it hadn't blossomed yet. He said I was much better than Edward Froese of Tangerine Dream. He told me the band was going to get really interesting."

Rama returned to the West Coast and supervised the packing of his home and office. On May 4, Rama embarked on the drive east across the country in a new chariot, a black Turbo Porsche, accompanied by several students in their cars. Jeffrey Sutter, a student, also was asked to join the caravan, much to Jeffrey's surprise.

"In late April on my twenty-ninth birthday, I had decided to share my 'special' energy with Rama by sending him a card," said Sutter. "At a recent seminar I'd attended, Rama had discussed some astrological concepts, mentioning how the planetary and star maps at the time of birth formed the basic chart for astrology readings and projections. A birthday was a special time in the sense that it astrologically documented the energetic moment an individual chose to incarnate into the physical universe.

"I sought an appropriate card but finally decided to create my own. The idea I had in mind was to depict a normal working day in a bright colorful way and to express some gratitude in the form of a happy depiction of my current condition. I purchased from a nearby drugstore many sheets of stickers that refracted and reflected light. I decided that glitter and sparkling effects would be the most apropos.

"For about a week at breakfast on the kitchen table, I experimented with various designs of humorous or silly themes. My effort to formulate a happy design and encapsulate what-I-do, and why-I-do-it into a shiny bright card, plus pondering Rama's reaction, radically shifted my awareness. Relentless giggles were produced and joyous bursts of sporadic laughter resounded as I came up with silly ideas and continued to wonder about my design for Rama. By the time I headed out the door to commute, I'd left tears of joy on the green linoleum and drunk ecstatic tears that had rolled from my cheeks to the milk in my cereal.

"I attended the next seminar at Lincoln Junior High School in Los Angeles and left the card with attendance. Two weeks later, Rama invited me to join his road trip across America to Boston. His dog Vayu and four other students made up the caravan.

"'So you wanna ride up front, fwaz?' Rama asked me as we walked Vayu at a rest area on I-40. He suggested I grab my thermos flask and join him. As his passenger riding through the Nevada desert towards Las Vegas, Rama pointed out some beautiful rock formations. 'Even the physical beauty is gorgeous,' he remarked as he gestured to some tall rocks. After a while he asked me, 'Do you know why I invited you on this trip?' I sat there embarrassed.

"I'm sorry Rama, really I don't," I quietly replied.

"'That's okay, I know you don't know,' he said, and was quiet for a while. Then he said, 'It was the card that you sent me.'

"I'd forgotten about the card, and when he mentioned it, I remembered. The honest truth of that moment is that I just couldn't believe the card was the reason. How could a birthday card warrant a road trip across America with Rama? I didn't know what to say and remained quiet, I felt so uncomfortable with the thoughts I had. How could I not believe Rama? All the magic of the desert, the hundred foot halos of shimmering electric green, purple and gold light in the Unitarian Church when he meditated—and now he's sitting right there, driving me to Las Vegas!"

"'Don't you think I can feel that?' Rama gently questioned and interrupted the chaos of my thoughts.

"What do you. ... I'm not sure. ..." I mumbled.

"'Don't you think I could feel what you were feeling when you wrote me that card?' Rama asked.

"The concept shocked me as I thought to myself, 'Rama was feeling what I felt when I was working on my card for him?!'

"'So that's why I invited you on the trip,' Rama added. 'So how about you pour us some coffee, here, use my flask. I know you're not comfortable around me but you can learn, this trip will help you to learn.'

"I poured our coffee and petted Vayu on my lap; the twinkling lights of Las Vegas appeared on the horizon."

I attached a small U-Haul to the back of my car and packed up my goods. I set out for Boston on May 9, planning to meet up with a friend at an off-road inn just past the Nevada/Utah border. The tension of packing and moving coursed through my body until I crossed the state line into Nevada. I pulled off to the side of the road, and it hit me. I was off to a wild adventure with friends I liked and a teacher I respected and loved, even if he had the gall to tell me the truth. The tension poured out of my body and elation rolled in. Boston bound!

I met my friend in Utah, and we soon ran into several other students. We formed a caravan. It was the first time ever I had driven across the country. In the rugged southwest, I was entranced by the scenery. All the way to Nebraska, America the beautiful radiated a colorful patchwork of impressions. Iowa and parts East? The best part of Iowa and the highways leading east to Boston was this—you don't think. You just drive through rural and urban monotony and notice the miles passing and the placement of the sun in the sky. Burger Kings become your friends. Only when we crossed into New York State did I notice a difference. There was a mental perkiness I did not feel in Los Angeles, like mental synapses firing more quickly.

In Boston, I found a house to share with several other students and began to attend classes in computer programming at the Boston Computer Learning Center (CLC.) About 18 other Rama students also enrolled at CLC.

Vishnu Systems

When Rama arrived in Boston on May 14, he did not yet have a house of his own so bunked at the rental house of four of his male students in Lincoln, Massachusetts. The students had all been working in software development for five to eight years.

As they sat in a circle in the sparsely furnished living room of the Lincoln house, Rama shared a vision. He explained that he sought a business structure that would help and protect 200 of his students who were engaged in computer science. The company would produce great technical products while insulating his students from the world. The people in the company would be just those students who really wanted to work the computer line.

Boston, with its combination of brains and technology, seemed like the ideal place to accomplish this dream.

He and the four students named the new dream Vishnu Systems. He appointed one of the four students in the Lincoln house to head up the project.

Each day in Lincoln, Rama meditated for long hours, sitting in the living room. As a seer, Rama's approach to problem-solving was to go into samadhi. He said he was not getting the answer regarding the direction of Vishnu Systems. He was being told inwardly (not in words, but as an intuition) to wait. When not meditating, he played Frisbee with the guys or went with them for walks around Walden Pond. "We're just settling in," he remarked cheerfully.

Rama asked one of his women students to find a house for him. As was known among the students, when Rama gave a task, he gave an empowerment to accomplish the task. The woman, Mary Doore, found a sunlit, spacious guest house, and Rama was pleased that she had found the right place. She, however, rented it for herself and the search continued.

At the end of May, Rama took the car ferry to Nantucket Island and resumed the "On the Road" recordings. As he sat in his Porsche in the parking lot of a popular beach, his topic was "Electronic Tribe."

> There are different networks that work the galaxies, the universes. I am part of a particular net: enlightenment. The network of enlightenment. There are other nets; they're not connected. In this great chaos that is existence, this redolent, wonderful disorder that is life, each network cruises, endlessly moving, with no apparent motion, through all of the worlds.

> We are the electronic tribe, bound together by secrets that exist in other worlds. ... A tribe is not a loose collaboration of beings who just get together in a powwow, who live together or work together. A nation is not a tribe. A family is not a tribe. A racial or ethnic group is not a tribe. Ancestry does not create a tribe, at least not bloodline. What creates a tribe is a bond, a sharing of secrets. Not a secret that could ever be told in any words, but a secret that's much too wonderful for that—a secret that can only be told by the unfolding of one's life, specifically, your life.

> A tribe is mobile, it doesn't stay in one place. It moves from one locale to another—from one, I suppose, hunting ground to another. The only thing is, we hunt power instead of animals. We hunt light. We hunt perfection. We hunt oneness. We are that.

> The tribe unites, it joins. And as the tribe moves into a higher level of attention, there's less internal disagreement within the tribe. The tribe and the leader of the tribe are

not separate, they're one. The members of the tribe get
along. There's no jealousy. There's no fear. There's a common
purpose that unites us.

Days later, a recently constructed house in Needham, Massachusetts was found and rented for Rama. He moved in at the beginning of June. Except for books and thangkas, Rama had not brought his Malibu furnishings to Boston. The house was outfitted with a new office, simple but elegant furniture and a computer with office software.

Compared to the beauty and magic of the Malibu house, the Needham home, although spacious and open, was plain, rather "Bostonian," according to Lois Harrison, a student (dancer turned computer scientist) who visited several times. It featured a number of bedrooms used as offices and a kitchen with a blond hardwood floor. The living room was long and narrow, with one wall of large paneled windows, a wood floor covered with white flokati rugs and a white leather chair where Rama sat and meditated. Inside the house, huge potted plants flourished in the bright light. Vayu the Scottie padded happily around the rooms.

One visitor's view of the house was less than sanguine. "It had just been built. Rama was dealing with lots of things the builder did not finish. There were problems, pushing to get stuff done. All the new houses in the neighborhood had cookie cutter plans. The neighborhood had no character. It was shiny only because it was new.

"Neighbors complained because there were so many cars around the house. He was on the neighbors' radar. He needed lots of land and no human aura coming in on him. In the Del Mar castle and at Goldie's house in Malibu, the wind would blow and you would hear the chimes. You were above the human aura. In the Needham house, you sucked it."

Even so, the house was a hub of activity, with students coming and going throughout the day to discuss various tasks. The latest musical sound system was installed so that Rama and friends could savor the sounds from the musicians Rama liked for their creativity, vision, talent, chutzpah, or all four. The three musicians from Zazen often came by to discuss and play their latest work.

With the home base established, the next task was the creation of Vishnu Systems. In the weeks that followed, the Vishnu Systems team was able to secure a small technical consulting contract for six students.

It was not a company but it was a start. Rama took it as a positive omen and an affirmation of a new teaching direction.

For the first time in his teaching career and his life, Rama decided to move his focus completely to the creation of a software company.

On June 17, when the students who had traveled cross-country met with Rama in a small church near Copley Hall, Rama delivered the news. He walked on stage, knelt down near the edge and sat back on his heels. "I have something important to tell you. I have decided to step back for a while from spiritual teaching."

I had a mind-splattered-on-the-ceiling moment. All I could think was that I had hauled my ass across the country to a new land, was barely settling in and would soon be starting computer school. Now it was all going to happen without regular interactions with Rama. I was stunned. I'm sure others in the room felt the same way.

And yet, in another way, I was not surprised. I felt that the move was not going that well for me or many students. I felt we had shown up in Boston in a sluggish mind-state. Instead of feeling *Wow, I can make this happen!* it was more like, *Rama, make this happen for me!* And that was not how he taught.

Rama explained that he needed to build something completely different.

In previous incarnations, in other cultures, other countries, Rama said, he had worked with people who naturally had a deep sense of tradition and etiquette. Eastern families and societies understood and respected communities seeking enlightenment. Here, in the United States, people simply did not understand. This was his first incarnation in the West and he said that he had not been accustomed to teaching Westerners. The type of teaching he had been doing was not working. We were not advancing.

A community dedicated to meditation and enlightenment needs to be insulated from the violence and anger of the U.S. and the world. Had we been in India or Tibet, we would have been carrying forward centuries of tradition and been born to families who not only knew but accepted that we were different. The advancement of women was particularly difficult because in both East and West, women are held back. Women did not have a chance anywhere on the earth to fully realize their potential.

Rama explained that it had taken him some time in his own cycle to fully understand what was happening. Methods that would have been appropriate and far more successful in the East were not working here.

In the United States, Rama said, men and women seeking light have to take responsibility for their own lives, their own well-being, their own livelihood. Career and meditation have to be perfectly melded. For Americans, the study of self-discovery must include economic advancement.

"To move to higher states of attention and to meditate perfectly, you must have fully integrated lives. To go beyond the states you are currently traversing, you will need to collect and store more personal power than your present lives could ever create."

And so Rama announced that he would be closing Lakshmi at the end of August. He said he would spend the entire summer recapitulating everything he had ever taught and defining what was ahead. This would be done in monthly meetings during July and August on both coasts.

He explained that in several months, he would start a new program—Vishnu Systems. This was not going to be a center devoted exclusively to the study of meditation. Vishnu Systems would be a complete program for American women and men who seek enlightenment. It would include economic advancement, martial arts, career seminars and, of course, meditation.[49]

Several days later, Rama flew to Los Angeles. He presented a similar message to the L.A. students, with an even stronger spin. A student wrote in her journal: "Rama announced he is closing Lakshmi. He is tired of being a spiritual teacher. Politically the climate is an accident waiting to happen for meditation groups. He's closing both the L.A. and the Boston centers. Instead he is starting a computer company called Vishnu Systems. He is going to be a corporate president instead of a spiritual teacher.

"He said a lot of his former students had been in monasteries and needed a form of karma yoga (work as a core practice in spiritual development). Rama said he would continue to teach a series of public seminars—four seminars four times a year in L.A. and Boston. He gave

---

49   Nicholson, Zoe Ann. *The Passionate Heart*. Newport Beach, CA: Lune Soleil Press, 2003. pp. 144–145.

dates—October, January, April and May. One each season. This way, he would not have to put so much time into running the organization.

"The changes are a Zen koan. We have three possible responses. One, we will attend seminars. Two, we will apply to work at Vishnu Systems. Three, we will decide not to continue. All choices are fine. Rama said that people in Vishnu Systems should work well in a group, meditate well so their mind would be clear, and should either know how to program or plan to learn right away.

"He is not unhappy with his students, he just does not want the responsibility of teaching anymore because he is tired of pushing people and having to tell them to shape up. With the seminar approach, we can go at our own pace. Whenever anyone is genuinely interested in enlightenment, he's available inwardly. He said the seminars would be more than enough for people to keep progressing."

After the L.A. meeting, Rama flew back to his new home—Boston—where Vishnu Systems was to begin in earnest.

During the hot Boston summer, Rama held meetings and logged many hours with a twelve-member Vishnu Systems team to come up with products.

"Rama used amazing empowerments and coaching to get us to grow into this role, but honestly, we didn't know what to do," said Randy Rochte, a team member and future Vishnu Systems manager. "I used to meet with one of the other team members. We were both good technologists, but neither of us had business experience. We were around an incubator—Rama—who was more formless than formed. I woke up every morning, trying to figure it out. What product would we make? Who would be in Vishnu Systems? What role would they play?

"We wanted to become an instant Microsoft. That idea probably got us stuck. We were two software nerds, and we were struggling. It never occurred to us to get outside advice. We tried to come up with a profitable business structure, but we didn't realize we were missing basic entrepreneurial knowledge."

Rama often stopped by the Lincoln house and invited the roommates to movies in nearby Acton. During the drive, he would ask questions and give pointers. "My awareness would fill with light," said Rochte, "but in hindsight, I thought like a consultant, not an MBA-trained head of a company."

During the day, Rama also worked with one of his students, Richard Hammon, an accountant. "I spent most waking hours in the summer of 1985 at his house in Needham," Hammon said. "I did some financial work for him—helping him prepare for an IRS audit.

"My first day at the house, I inadvertently used an upstairs bathroom that apparently was exclusively reserved for Rama. As I exited the hall bathroom, someone in his office became enraged, literally screaming at me, "How dare you use Rama's bathroom! Don't you have any sense of etiquette?" As I followed her down the stairs, I responded, "I don't understand your fucking etiquette! How am I supposed to know what bathroom I'm not supposed to use!"

At the base of the stairs, Hammon recalled, Rama sat on a couch, listening to the exchange, roaring with laughter at his rejoinder. (After the audit, Rama hired the accounting firm of Ernst & Young to manage his finances).

"Around 3 a.m. one night at the Needham house," Hammon recollected, "Rama had drifted asleep on a couch maybe 15 feet away from where I was sitting, typing on my 'portable' Compaq computer that weighed in at 35 pounds. He had one arm on the back of the couch, the other on the arm of the couch, his head leaning against the back cushion and rolled to the side. He had simply nodded off, but was also apparently deep in samadhi. As I continued to work, wave after wave after wave of gold light flooded out from him—sweeping across the room—wave after wave after wave—frikking unbelievable."

A few days later, when an unseasonable storm swept through the Needham suburbs, David Silver visited the house and found trees and power lines down. Chain saw in hand, Rama was cutting up a tree that had fallen in the back yard. "I helped him stack the wood neatly on the side of the house," said Silver. "Even though I'd come over to talk about sound systems, he was focused on cutting the wood and stacking it perfectly—it was all done in silence and with complete focus."

In the middle of the summer, Rama invited the people working on various projects, including the Nirvana musicians, to meet with him for a retreat at The Hawk Resort. A caravan of six cars drove to Rochester, Vermont off Route 107. Rama rented his own villa, and the students shared the others. Meetings were held in Rama's living room. The topics were Vishnu Systems and music. The musicians had their own bungalow.

"Rama was in intense kundalini samadhi the whole time," said a Vishnu Systems programmer. "The whole perimeter of the landscape that you could see through the windows behind him was molten. The mountains would undulate. We continued to weigh and discuss ideas for Vishnu Systems, but no single plan emerged."

During August, Rama recorded the final three talks of his *On the Road with Rama* series—"Kundalini Yoga" at the Haleakala Volcano National Park in Maui, Hawaii, "Power" at the Continental Divide in Colorado and "Transcendentalism" at Walden Pond. The series sign off:

> *It's hard sometimes to understand why we do what we do. It's hard sometimes to understand why we feel what we feel. But if you would try to become less attached to the doings and feelings in your life and instead consider the world around you more—an essential step in becoming a good reflector is in Zen what they call polishing the mirror. In order to reflect well, the mirror has to be clearly polished— there can't be any dust on the mirror. Transcendentalism has a lot to do with clearing the mirror of the self. And if the mirror is spotless, we will reflect diverse forms of eternity, which is what we call enlightenment. ...*

> *Transcendentalism is the spirit of eternity. It's the spirit of well wishing, of seeing beyond the surface. Henry Thoreau came out here to look in Walden Pond and he saw the stars like dust reflected in it. Yet Walden had its own depths, and he saw the depths of his own soul to some extent out here— in this beautiful power place, on this wonderful planet, in this fantastic galaxy, in this endless creation. So seek more deeply. Meditate more quietly. And walk in the woods. Get out there and hike a little bit and look at eternity and let it look at you. And maybe life will work out pretty well. You won't know till you get out here what you're missing.*

During the summer, Rama held separate, monthly meetings with the larger group of Boston and L.A. students. He acquired an apartment in Westwood to serve as lodgings when he came to town. Prior to the final Lakshmi seminar meeting in Los Angeles, he joined his band Nirvana at a music studio in West Hollywood to record some music they'd been working on.

"Rama had asked Steve to find a studio, and Steve selected Chick Corea's studio, called Mad Hatter," Lievano recalled. "Rama subsidized the studio rental. When we got there, there were some musicians ahead of us. While we sat in the waiting room, Rama was looking at all of Chick Corea's awards on the wall. He said, 'Someday you guys will have these too.' When it came time to move our equipment into the studio, I picked up my large pedal board. He said, 'Here, let me help you.' I was shocked, I couldn't believe it. He picked it up and we both carried it inside.

"I'm not sure if Rama had been in a studio before. The three of us were experienced in recording but there was some friction. As the night went on, it got worse and worse between the three of us, and there was some nastiness going back and forth. Rama was just sitting and watching us. He did make some suggestions about the arrangements of a few pieces that were not that easy to make—we were using computers to write the music which was new, at least to me. We had to write new code to implement his suggestions and there was some inner pushback. Finally, we got to the end of the session. Rama walked over to us and said, 'You guys were just awful. Just terrible. That's it, I'm done. It's over. The ways you guys treated each other is awful.'

"I didn't think it was that awful because I'd been in bands that had fistfights in the studio. Then he softened it a bit and added, 'Let's take some time off and maybe get together in six months.' He said keep writing, just work by yourself."

Two nights later, at the end of August, Rama met and spoke with the Los Angeles students. The meeting ended when he stood up from his couch and walked to the front of the stage. He bowed and said, "I'm sorry, I can't serve you."

In this manner, the five-year old Lakshmi center ended.

In mid-September, the formal launch of Vishnu Systems, Inc. took place at the Lincoln House. Prior to the launch, Rama and one of the programmers threw a Frisbee eighty yards back and forth in a long grassy space between two rows of trees. When the meeting started, Rama spoke to the full VSI team—twelve men and eight women.

He again shared his vision of a company that would employ many students and give them a nice environment to work in. He joked about hiring a receptionist from New York. "Hello!" he said with a thick Brooklyn accent, "This is Vishnu Systems. No, they are *not* in the office. No, they are *not* in the lobby. They are out on the holy mountain."

Rama asked Rochte and another programmer to put together a business plan. He did not appear concerned that the pair had not been able to come up with a viable business strategy over the summer. According to Rochte, he and the other programmer met frequently and talked, but still, nothing gelled.

"Rama relied on us to figure it out and we didn't," said Rochte. "We never had a clear vision—no specific deliverables, no financials, never pulled it together. Rama was so innocent and optimistic that he did not see this.

"The emphasis in VSI was on camaraderie and the input was Buddhist—keep your ego out of it," said Rochte. "Be receptive to higher ideas and structures. It was like how he worked with the three musicians in Nirvana. Rama would bring music from another dimension and find someone who knew the musical structures. The humble individual is supposed to receive the waves of knowledge and then use the classical structures to implement them. But if your ego gets too big, the energy doesn't manifest."

In spite of the non-start of the business start-up, the group remaining in Boston enjoyed quality time with Rama. On Halloween, they gathered at Rama's house to watch five horror movies in a row. "We laughed so hard we barely saw the movies," said Rochte. "At Thanksgiving we had a bounteous potluck."

By the end of November, however, as the temperature plummeted in Boston, so too did the perception about what Vishnu Systems could become or achieve within a short time frame.

The night before Christmas, the team met in the living room in the Needham house, and Rama sat in his chair wearing a big white sweater with 30 multi-colored bliss puppets around the chair. He said he had been traveling. He closed his eyes to meditate.

"I had been feeling guilty about Vishnu Systems," said Rochte. "As we sat with Rama, I went into a very deep meditation. Everything dissolved in gold light. He cleared my emotions. He cleared my mind. Everything was gone.

"Eventually, he came out of samadhi. I felt the deep unity of our team. Everything else didn't matter. We sat in silence around Rama. After several minutes, Rama gently explained that he would soon be ending Vishnu Systems."

Rochte and others began preparing for a move.

"Around Rama," Rochte said, "there were no rules, just an awful lot of etiquette."

Endings, Beginnings

Rama returned to Los Angeles in mid-December to hold a "Four Evening Intensive Seminar in Psychic Development" for the public, and for any former students who cared to attend.

I attended this seminar. I had just completed my intensive six-month course in computer programming and flew back to L.A. with a hard-earned Certificate in Computer Programming. I was not a tech genius but I wasn't a total washout either. I had learned the basics of computer science and gained a fearless technology mind-set. I had lived in a new city, gone through an early winter, survived Boston traffic and felt much stronger than the person who had left L.A. six months earlier. But I was not sure if I should go for programming work or return to public relations.

As I stood in the long line to get into the meeting room in the Wilshire Ebell, Rama walked by. He stopped right in front of me. "Are you thinking of going into computer science or returning to PR?" he asked. The gray-blue eyes stared into mine. I had the usual moment of total disorientation—the curly hair, the cool black outfit, the eternity in the eyes. Enlightened teacher?!?

I answered spontaneously, "I'm thinking about public relations." He stood in front of me for a few moments, quiet, his arms folded. I felt him taking a multi-dimensional scan and look-see. Then he commented, "I think that's a good idea." He continued walking towards the auditorium.

Within a week I juggled two job offers—one for Vice President of Publicity and Marketing at Carson Productions, the other for Vice President of Publicity, Advertising and Promotion at Tri-Star Television, a new branch of a then-burgeoning film studio. I chose the latter.

Later, Rama told a group of Los Angeles students that the reason the Boston venture had not worked out was because he was living in the wrong house.

11

1986 - RAMA SEMINARS

Zen is the way of splitting the self *again and again, until there is nothing left.* - Rama

The small group of Vishnu Systems technologists packed up the Needham house and joined Rama in a line of moving cars for a cross-country return to the West Coast. They left on New Year's Day. It was a relaxed, slow odyssey. Rama called it a pilgrimage. The cars en caravan used CB radios to communicate. Groups of people traveled together and then met up with Rama as they pulled off the highway into the night's lodging. He held teaching meetings along the way.

"As we drove cross country, we took a more southern route as it was winter," said Hammon. "We drove through New Mexico and stopped at his favorite Indian jewelry store in Santa Fe, Ortega's. As we were about to embark, Rama walked out into the street, looked up at a sunny blue sky with a few white clouds and said, 'Not yet!' We stood around our cars and chatted. Ten minutes later, a freak snow storm pelted the city with thick snow flurries. We ran for cover in our respective parked vehicles. The storm lasted for about 20 minutes. Moments after the last snow flake fell, Rama broadcast via CB radio, 'Time to go!' And off we went."

Lois Harrison recalled pulling into a roadside motel at the end of a long day's drive and feeling inspired to buy ice cream for Rama. She was surprised to discover an ice cream store that sold high quality, hand-packed ice cream right next to the motel. She purchased several containers.

"I normally would never try to visit Rama without an invitation, but I felt I had to deliver the gift right away," Harrison said. Among over seventy identical rooms, she had no idea which one was Rama's. Harrison found herself walking directly to a particular brown door. She knocked on it. Jackpot! Rama opened the door immediately. Harrison offered to share the ice cream.

"I entered the room," she said. "It was a standard roadside room. He had brightened it up with a white flokati rug and Tibetan thangkas. Another person from our team was with him, and they had been talking.

"'Oh,' he said, accepting my gift of ice cream, 'A good host will always accept a gift from his guest. A student brought me a gift and it's the right thing to accept and enjoy it.' He found some little brown plastic cups next to an ancient coffee maker and two small motel room water glasses. Using the wooden spoons I had brought, he scooped the ice cream into the cups and glasses.

"We sat on the droopy, queen-sized beds and had a little party. Rama often said that a bit of sugar when your energy is low will perk up your awarenesss. Rama had been working with us inwardly and outwardly all day. In his room, we laughed and talked about how delicious the ice cream was. I felt ecstatic when I left the room because I had been able to do something for Rama, I trusted my intuition and he was so gracious."

As the group drove further west, with snow falling in the moonlight, they pulled off the road and simply savored the beauty of the moment.

"I remember feeling in Rama's presence how important it was to have a good time," said Harrison. "We shared big jokes. We were making a conscious effort to have fun, and it worked. We would eat what we wanted, when we wanted. It was not the time to go on a diet. Rama wanted us to enjoy the banquet of life even if it was in a weird coffee shop in the middle of nowhere. He wanted us to enjoy each other's company and form a supportive group. I called him 'The hostess with the mostess.' That's how I perceived him."

There was no sense that Vishnu Systems had "failed." There were no mistakes, only learning experiences.

Upon their return to the West Coast, Rama asked some of the more technical ex-students if they would like to go to Seattle. He hoped many of them would find work at Microsoft to learn more about the ways of large, successful businesses. He also felt that Seattle was a good place to connect with an Asian and Japanese business sensibility. At that time, Japan and its business culture had won international kudos for its management style.

A group of ten intrepid techies set out in their still-packed vehicles to scale the mountains of Microsoft.

Within weeks, many of the stronger software developers found employment at the large software companies. Rama rented a house in Seattle. Brian Dahl recalled that he was the first to get a job at Microsoft. "As a group, we met to go to movies a lot. We sampled lots of restaurants where we talked about new skills, including managing large teams, strategic planning and matrixed organizations. I remember going to a Mexican restaurant and Rama ordering us all shots of tequila. Rama told us a few jokes and got us laughing so hard, we almost slid onto the floor."

Rama founded a new teaching organization, Rama Seminars. For former Lakshmi students, Rama advised, the seminars would not be watered down or a step backwards. But there was no enrollment process.

As Rama began commuting, primarily between Seattle, Boston and Los Angeles, another apartment next door to his top floor Westwood apartment was rented and used as an office. The two-bedroom apartment was minimalistic and overlooked the open green lawns and brick buildings of the UCLA campus. It was a quiet and private spot with Tibetan thangkas on the walls. He chose it for its business energy, very few people visited or worked there.

One of the people who did work there was Kathleen Forge. "There were huge numbers of people coming to Rama Seminars," she said. "We maintained a database of emails and contact information. Rama explained to me that there was a giant mandala of enlightenment. Different people made up parts of the mandala. Before every talk, he would see who was going to show up. He would write down an exact number before the meeting, then look at me and ask, 'What do you think? Does this feel right?' He was teaching me to see, and I would try to feel if the number felt right. He liked to go through that exercise. He was almost always right.

"Working with Rama, we spent tons of time on brochures, ads and rental hall contracts. In terms of Rama's personal preparation for the talks, there was no difference between 20 or one thousand people.

He did not prepare formal notes. Rather, he would scan the attention of all of his (ex) students, looking for the major red flags going on in their attention field. What were their concerns? Where were they placing their attention? What were they struggling with? What is working? What are they succeeding in? What are people dealing with? What are they focusing on? He often spoke with the people he worked with about this. He would scan the dimensions in multiple ways. He would look at major news stories in the world, how one would view that kind of circumstance. He researched what would be in people's attention in order to help them. It was always an occult exercise, and that's how he prepared."

In Los Angeles, the Rama Seminars program took place in an unlikely setting, the upstairs auditorium of the Los Angeles Convention Center (LACC) in downtown L.A. Nestled among freeway off-ramps, the sprawling LACC primarily served as a trade show venue. It was neither intimate nor stylish; it was drab, large, constructed out of concrete slabs. The stage consisted of makeshift risers. The seats were of the metal folding variety. Yet, Rama warmed it up. For over one year, the LACC became home to a mystery school.

Of 1,000 seats in the large, gray auditorium, on any given evening, perhaps 30 were empty. From Hollywood to the furthest corners of Malibu, Los Angelenos came, sat in their folding chairs and became absolutely attentive. The intense stillness that chased thoughts away was pervasive.

As one student commented, "Rama glowed gold upstairs and you'd go downstairs and see a car show."

For the first seminar on January 9–12, "Meditation, Mysticism & Magic, a Four-Evening Intensive in Psychic Development with Rama," everyone who entered the hall received a large, poster-sized four-color brochure. The brochure contained symbols and designs from ancient Egypt, Tibet, Taoism, Atlantis and the modern-day teachings of Carlos Castaneda. It contained poster-sized photos (taken in Lake Tahoe) of Rama as he meditated.

The strategic plan—by opening the massive fold-out and seeing the imagery—ancient memories would be sparked and loosened from deep in the psyche, and Rama would be able to set such souls back on their path.

After the first set of Rama Seminars in Los Angeles, Rama conducted a four-day workshop in Boston. The numbers attending were fewer but he was happy with the new people who came. "There was something different about Boston," software designer James Firgy said. "His dancing in Boston was incomprehensibly amazing. At one point, he just sailed over the couch with total physical perfection. Zazen was playing alongside him. It was not dance as I knew it. It was like multi-dimensional movement. The music and the dance were alive."

"When I saw Rama dance," said Morrell, "I perceived that his alignment to endless existence was what held and moved him. He was like a child, and yet like such a warrior because it took so much courage to just be there and let every step be a dance of eternity."

Rama danced through the seminars of winter. He said he danced with thousands of bodies at one time, going in and out of planes and dimensions. He became the dance, he was not separate from it. Rather than sitting back and passively watching a performance, the instruction was simply to gaze with stillness at Rama as he danced. It was a powerful form of Zen meditation.

The musicians felt it too. Said Lievano, "When we played live while he was dancing, the experience was extremely intense, just off the hook. It felt like he was inside the music and all around it, and of it and making the music with us. When he sat in meditation and we played live on stage, it felt like he was just listening. When he was dancing it was like he was a player in the band. When he was dancing, I felt a lot freer. As a musician, my mind wasn't getting in the way. It was much easier to let go."

In between the seminars, Rama explored. He had disbanded Lakshmi. Vishnu Systems was a non-starter. But still he sought a means of teaching Westerners that would transform the awareness of his current non-students and the people he had yet to meet—and bring them to enlightenment. So far, he had taught forms of yoga and Vedanta and a range of mystic/occult teachings. A software company to employ all his students had not materialized.

In deep meditation, another realization formed regarding how to teach Westerners in a way they might fully grasp and assimilate into their being.

In the first week of April 1986, Rama traveled to Kyoto, Japan with a student friend, Jack Kukulan. Jack, a businessman in his mid-thirties, managed his family's successful grocery operations. He had given generously to Rama's full-page ad campaigns. Rama felt drawn to him because he was deeply kind and unpretentious, which made it very pleasant for Rama to spend time with him. Inviting Jack to Kyoto was Rama's way of appreciating what Jack was doing for him. They would often share ideas on how they would use additional funds to help manifest Rama's vision to bring many people to enlightenment.

After months of formal communications, arrangements were made for Rama and Jack to meet with the abbots of the largest Zen sects. Appointments were set up at the major temples, including Tenryu-ji Temple, Daisen-in Temple, Mt. Hei and Enryakuji Temple. They flew to Kyoto and began their rounds.

Each temple resonated with the history of Zen in Japan. Their first stop was Tenryu-ji, founded in 1345, with its sand gardens and rock waterfalls, designated by the Japanese as a "Special Place of Scenic Beauty." Daisen-in Temple, built between 1509 and 1513, where they met with the Abbot, was even more enchanting, with its classic Zen rock garden and collection of Zen art. As they went from temple to temple, they absorbed the refined, elegant aesthetic of Japanese Zen. When Rama and Kukulan weren't in meetings, they journeyed around Kyoto as tourists, roaming the parks lush with fresh pink cherry blossoms, and sampling the sushi.

"When I visit my brother monks in Japan," Rama said, "and sit down with other Zen masters, and I walk into the monasteries and I meet the Abbot, drink tea with them and have discussions or silence, they look at my long hair and they have their shaved heads, and they look at my crazy clothes and my strange expression—but they feel the power that emanates from my dedication to the practice. So they are comfortable with me, yet they're very uncomfortable. They don't quite know what to do, yet they find they have to accept me because I'm one with the practice. I don't feel at all uncomfortable with them and their austere ways of life because that's what works for them.

"I was honored by the five largest Zen sects in Kyoto. I have been invited by Seiko Hirata, the Zen Master of the Tenryu-ji Temple; Soen Ozeki, the Abbot of the Daisen-in Temple and Mr. Genko Naiyama, the Secretary General of the Nanzen-ji Temple to bring my Zen students to Kyoto to learn some Japanese Zen."

According to Rama, Soen Ozeki asked why Rama wanted to bring his students to Kyoto. Rama responded, "Why not?" The Abbot then gave his consent. Rama mischievously noted that the Abbot promised he would use "the stick" if the students were not meditating well.

> *They invited me, after meeting me and examining me, to come any time to Kyoto and bring all of my students to stay in their monasteries. This is a terrific honor for a Westerner. I had to prove myself to them. And I did. I sat in long interviews with them. They examined me, they examined my knowledge of Buddhism. And every single major order afforded me that. All five said, "Bring your students any time, Dr. Lenz, and come stay in our monasteries. We would be honored.*

When he returned from Japan, Rama prepared for the next phase of teaching. In late April, he sent a mailing to his 400 former students. The message arrived inside a large red envelope with a golden dragon on the front.

The letter explained that since he had closed the Lakshmi teaching center at the end of the previous summer, he had taken almost a year off. During that time, he had reflected upon how he could best serve the needs of the tens of thousands of people around the world who were interested in the study of knowledge and power. As a result, he had formulated a new program called the Zen Seminar Program.

> *Why Zen? Why not? I have spent many lifetimes as a spiritual teacher. During several of these lifetimes I have been a Zen Master. It is my belief that Tantric Zen— which differs quite strongly from the type of Zen that is being taught in most Zen monasteries in Japan today—is a perfect form of Self Discovery for this age. Tantric Zen is essentially formless Zen. It is closely related to Chan— the original Chinese Zen. It is also very similar to Tibetan Vajrayana Buddhism, the early Chinese Taoism and Jnana Yoga.*

When I received the letter from Rama, in spite of reading his explanation, I logged a mental question about why he really was switching from a focus on Vedanta and tantric mysticism to Zen. On the evening of the first Zen seminar in the last week of April 1986, Rama came up to me during a break. Without any preamble, he said, "I'm shifting the focus to Zen because it's the closest to what I teach." And then he walked off to speak with someone else.

That exchange, plus what he had written in his mailing, became my koan. How could Rama go to Japan and become a Zen Master, or a Tantric Zen Master? Why would he want to do that? Why would a Tantric Zen Master be more likely to transform a meditation practitioner's awareness than an "Enlightened Teacher" or a "Tantric Mystic" or "head of software company"?

A koan has no correct answer, but this is what I observed. With the role of Zen Master, Rama introduced a formality into the teaching. The student of a Zen Master does not expect emotional support. A Zen Master is more detached, interacting with students more with the mind than the emotions—like jnana yoga. As a Zen Master, Rama upped the aesthetic of all his teachings. I observed that Rama did not step back from his previous teachings, he just built on them.

The Rama I saw on stage—Zen Master Rama—was more powerful, centered, the life force emanating from him the strongest it had ever been. The detachment and stillness of Zen was his next step or expression of light.

With the emphasis on Zen, his words—"I am your koan"—moved to the forefront of learning. Koans were integral to Rama's Zen teaching. His definition—

A koan is a multi-level structural device that is designed to help a person expand their awareness. Koans can be long or short, verbal or non-verbal.

Koans are particularly effective in Zen study because they work largely through inference. As you concentrate on a koan it becomes a pivotal point of reference between the ever-changing seas of perception and awareness.

Most people are prisoners of their thoughts. They have become so accustomed to thinking about life in specific and repetitive ways that they no longer perceive life directly. Instead of experiencing life in its pure "suchness" and without illusions, they see only shadows of reality. The essential purpose of the koan is to give someone something to concentrate on that will help them to slip out of their conceptual mind-set and enter into Zen mind—the direct perception of existence without shadows.

> *The koan is one of my favorite forms of expression. In fact many of the things I do and say are koans. My brochures, my advertisements and, of course, many of my talks at Zen Seminars are koans.*

A Rama koan:

> *Zen doesn't believe in the reconciliation of opposites because from the point of view of Zen, there is no point of view.*

A Rama koan:

One evening, going to a Zen Seminar at the L.A. Convention Center, I drove behind Rama into the underground garage, a dismal, drab cement labyrinth of poles and signage. I watched Rama pull up to the attendant in the booth and saw that they spoke. The exchange lasted less than a minute. Rama smiled and joked around. I noticed him touching the fellow's hand when he took the parking ticket.

Then it was my turn to drive up and receive a ticket. I rolled my car forward and glanced at this young African-American man whom I normally would have ignored like wallpaper in a doctor's waiting room. Suddenly, I couldn't miss him. He was lit up like a megawatt sunlamp. The kid was floating, radiant, smiling ear to ear. He looked like a rishi in a Himalayan cave. Rama had zapped him with pure light and kundalini energy. He spun him into stillness.

Rama explained his foundational stance on Zen:

> *What I term Tantric Zen, I could also refer to as old Zen, the original face of Zen, or new Zen, contemporary Zen practice—no mind, the mirror of existence. Tantric Zen is Zen in its essence.*

> *Bodhidharma, who brought Zen from India to the Orient, taught a very pure type of Zen. Zen is meditation, the actual experience of life—directly, immediately, with no buffers.*

Over the course of time, different schools of Zen have evolved, principally the Rinzai and Soto orders of Zen. There have been lots of Zen teachers, Zen masters. Books have been written about Zen, commentaries on sutras. A whole hierarchy has developed for the teaching and practice of Zen. And Zen has become, to a certain degree, institutionalized.

Tantric Zen is the original Zen—Zen without rules, Zen without form. Zen can certainly take rules and form. So Tantric Zen might have some rules and form, but it would also remain formless, even though it has rules and form. Tantric Zen is the awareness of the infinitude of all things. To gain that awareness, to be it, is enlightenment. Enlightenment frees you from the pain and suffering of limited states of mind.

Question from the audience: You said that Tantric Zen might have some rules. What would they be?

Tantric Zen is a state of mind. Now let me give you a little classical background here. In most forms of self-discovery—different pathways that lead to knowledge, empowerment, enlightenment and a generally good time—there are lots of do's and don'ts, thou shalt's and thou shalt not's. Those do's and don'ts are there to help persons who want to expand their mind and learn more about the nature of being and be freed from the limitations, the limited states of mind that most persons experience.

Zen is a very quick path to empowerment and enlightenment and knowledge and development of the mind and all of its faculties—creative, analytic and other. But it's not fast for the person who's comfortable with it. It is just fast in comparison to other paths. The mind develops very quickly with the practice of Zen. Zen is for the tantric individual. By that I mean, if you're a real stickler for the rules, I don't think that you'll have much fun with Zen, at least not original Zen.

To ensure that rule sticklers and rule breakers got a taste of original Zen, Rama returned to the Harry Langdon studios to take new photos befitting a late 20th century Zen master. He wore black leather, sunglasses, cool jeans. His hair was coiffed to perfection.

He used the photos in edgy ad spreads throughout Northern and Southern California, in Chicago, New York and Boston. Fees from the seminars paid it forward to buy the next set of ads.

Who would take full page ads in mainstream newspapers like the *Los Angeles Times* and *New York Times* for talks on mystical topics featuring a brand new Zen Master title and chic, gender-bending photos? A tantric Zen master would. The ads and photos served as the first koan.

Several years earlier, Rama had placed Shunryu Suzuki's *Zen Mind, Beginner's Mind* on the short list of his students' must-read books. Suzuki is known for this adage: "In the beginner's mind there are many possibilities, but in the expert's there are few."

The ads filtered out experts and brought thousands of new people to his four-day seminars as well as a new level of notoriety.

A Rama koan:

Old Zen is the reduction of concepts to absurdity.

A Rama koan:

*I'm a Zen master. I'm a teacher but I have no students.
Isn't that Zen?*

The Zen Seminars began in earnest during the summer. All talks were titled "Evening Intensive Seminars in Tantric Zen with Zen Master Rama."

"I went to a Zen Seminar with Rama in 1986, thinking it was going to be the oddest evening of my life," said George Lewis, a long time Oakland resident. "I'd been practicing Zen for many years and was familiar with koan study. Out comes Zen Master Rama wearing all black, with that big mop of hair. On comes the loud electronic music. I was ready to sit back and suppress my laughter. He began to dance and suddenly, my mind became absolutely still. The experience of pure stillness lasted throughout the dance. I had not known this before. Afterwards, a classic koan, one of the best known in Zen, lodged in my mind: What is the sound of one hand clapping? I heard it in that stillness."

Zen Seminar audience member: How come you say different things at different times about the same topic?

Everything I say is just one way of looking at things. Another time I may suggest five other ways to look at the same thing, or the opposite way. You have to feel what your body knows is appropriate for you to do at any given time, not just blindly follow my suggestions.

Zen Seminar audience member: Is the relationship with a Zen master different than with teachers of other traditions?

> *You never devote yourself to a teacher. You devote yourself to the practice. The teacher is there to teach. The way Zen masters teach is not just through talking—they teach in a variety of ways. They interact with you in powerful and often surprising ways, sometimes shocking ways that cause you to shift awareness.*[50]

A Rama koan:

"I attended the Zen Seminars in 1986 but had never spoken to Rama," said Howard Green, a database engineer. "One night, I stood in line, chatting with a friend outside the hall in the L.A. Convention Center. The static electrical discharge suddenly rose about 1,000 percent. Rama was walking along the hallway, passing all the people in line. When I turned around, he was only a few feet away. I said 'Hi,' and I had a big smile on my face. He said, 'Hi, Howard, how are you?' and he got a big grin on his face as he walked past.

"I was thrown. He knows my name! I'm not just hiding out in the audience, slipping by unnoticed. All my hang-ups, vanities and fears are on his radar! I sensed he was glad to see me. If he felt that way, we must have a connection. What, why, how? He asked how I was doing. Did he already know? How was I doing? Who am I? This exchange with the Zen Master didn't stop when he walked past me. It changes as I change."

A Rama koan:

During the Zen Seminar in Los Angeles, Rama read aloud two letters he had received. One was from someone who wrote a sincere, insightful letter about her life and spiritual progress. The writing style was excellent and the report positive.

In the same tone of voice, Rama read the next letter, from someone who had just done a spread in *Penthouse Magazine*. She was excited and proud to be selected as a Penthouse Pet. She said she felt

---

50 Lenz, Frederick (Rama). "Advanced Meditation Practices." *Zen Tapes*. Los Angeles: Lakshmi Inc., 1986.

empowered during the photo session. She sent in photos which he opened up and showed to everybody.

Rama paused. "You're thinking that the person who wrote about her spiritual life is real, and the Penthouse gal is full of shit. But this Penthouse gal is real. She's sincere. You may be judging her based on your own prejudices but she is real. She is more in touch with herself and true to herself than this other person who is wallowing in spiritual b.s.

"*Penthouse* is more real than *Playboy*. If you're going to do something, do it right."

A Rama koan:

After a light dinner in Westwood, Rama, Jack Kukulan and Richard Hammon wandered up Hilgard Avenue, home to dozens of sorority and fraternity houses at UCLA. Crowds of students spilled out the front doors. The night throbbed with the sound of loud music and expensive cars roaring up and down the street. Taking it all in, Rama said, "All the frivolity, all the sex, all the orgasms are like dirt under the fingernail of the Buddha."

A Rama koan:

During a four-evening seminar in Tantric Zen at the L.A. Convention Center, Roger Cantu, who had first encountered Rama at UCLA, recalled, "I was sitting near the front of the auditorium. We'd been waiting for Rama's arrival for at least 30 minutes since the scheduled start of the lecture. Usually the crowd chatted boisterously, but tonight lots of people sat up straight and meditated. The crowd of over 1,000 people was unusually quiet.

"Then Rama walked on stage with his briefcase. After a few steps, he appeared to notice the unusual silence. All eyes were on him. He paused for several beats, soaking in the deep quiet, then yelled at the top of his lungs in a singsong cadence, 'Hi Honey, I'm home!'

"The silence lasted one more moment. Suddenly, the audience exploded in laughter, like a cloudburst. It was as if Rama had multiplied himself 1,000 times and personally punctured each person's spiritual ego."

Slow it down. Relax, be cool, says the Zen Master. Look at how beautiful life is, and just keep looking until you see

it. You don't see what is in front of you because you're so
distracted by your thoughts.

November 1986, third night of a Zen Seminar. People milled around in front of the entrance to the auditorium. Across the sea of people, I saw Rama walking around, stopping to talk with people. He was easy to spot because of his height, made taller by the orb of curly hair around his head. Wherever he headed, a slight parting of the seas phenomenon opened pathways in the clusters of folks intently chatting with each other. As soon as I saw him, I gave myself my 'DON'T try to push yourself into his attention' lecture, which usually had the effect of a robust internal dialogue as to whether or not I in fact WAS pushing myself into his attention. Moments later, Rama strode up to me.

"Hi Beak," he said, his arms crossed. The first time he had said "Hi, Beak" to me, I thought he was referring to my nose and felt highly insulted. Now I knew it was an affectionate term.

"Hi Rama," I responded. He wore a light gray sweater, tailored shirt and dark slacks. Very classy.

"How's the job?" he asked.

I pondered my response. As the year had gone by, I found myself regretting my selection of Tri-Star TV as a next career move. I was not busy enough. The company was so new that almost a year had passed with little production activity requiring publicity. The money was good but I was not challenged and felt drained. I bundled this scenario into my response to Rama—"Not so great. I'm pretty bored."

"Sounds like it's time to change jobs," he said. "You're not looking too frosty."

Now, even though I knew this, I felt my stomach clench. I had received a Criticism. I nodded and felt, well, un-frosty. Rama walked off to talk to the next person. His comment goaded me into fourth gear on circulating my resume.

The Hollywood PR circle is small. I got the word out that I was looking for work and a few weeks later interviewed for a position as Vice President of Publicity and Promotion at Stephen J. Cannell Productions, then one of the busiest TV production studios in L.A. I landed the job, which turned out to be the best position I ever had in my PR career.

December 1, 1986—Rama mailed a letter to his formerly enrolled students.

> *Greetings! The Winter Solstice is the time of ending and beginning. This is a powerful time—a time to contemplate your immortality. A time to forgive, to be forgiven, and to make a fresh start. A time to awaken... The December-January period is the strongest time of the year. It is an easy time to shift states of mind. ...*
>
> *It is Christmas time. An Enlightened Teacher came into the world, taught and died. His message was simple: Forgive. While the human beings of this planet have still not absorbed this simple truth, it remains the truth.*
>
> *It is impossible to move on to new states of mind unless you seek the forgiveness of those you've offended. If there is someone you feel you have offended, injured or not been faithful to, I recommend that you write them a letter and simply tell them that you are sorry. Your letter will enable you to let go of any guilt you may be carrying and will allow you to make a fresh start in the New Year.*
>
> *Advanced teachers always forgive. It is inevitable that anyone who seeks knowledge and power will make many mistakes. It is the teacher's job to point out mistakes so that an individual doesn't continue to hurt themselves or others. Often, in the student's confusion, she or he directs anger at the teacher, blaming them for the pain they are experiencing or for their own mistakes.*
>
> *You only find your teacher once in many lifetimes. Never be afraid to see them and meditate with them. Your teacher always understands and always forgives. Your teacher knows that as long as you keep trying, one day you will succeed. Never be afraid to see your teacher. Never.*

Someone recently asked whom I consider to be students of mine? I consider those persons to be my students who come and meditate with me on a regular basis, who, in spite of the hardships and difficulties on the path of knowledge, still continue to try, and who respect me as I respect them. I will continue to empower, teach, enlighten and love those persons who come to meditate with me.

After the December Zen Seminars in Los Angeles and Boston, Rama began house-hunting for his first home to own. He centered his search on Stony Brook, New York, the college town where he had lived and received his Ph.D. In mid-December, he initiated the purchase of a house on Christianson Avenue in Stony Brook, the kind of house a college professor would buy—a two-story dwelling with conventional rooms, a basement and a modest backyard. While the house itself was quiet, with old, thick walls and high ceilings, it was located in the middle of a vibrant student neighborhood. The sale went through, and Rama was now a home owner.

Rama then journeyed with Vayu the Scottie to a favorite power spot, Big Sur, where he would complete work on a set of public recordings, *Zen Tapes*. He spoke of advanced meditation.

I'm here in Big Sur, renting a little cabin. I was just out for a walk along the beach and the surf is crashing along what must be the most beautiful coastline in the world. The moonlight is playing on the water. The mountains are behind me. I've got a little fire going here in the fireplace. Maybe you can hear it crackling in the background. I'm sitting here with a cup of tea. I came up here to have some conversations with you.

What do I have to say about advanced meditation? It's a feeling. It's beyond the body and beyond the mind. I would classify beginning meditation—beginning, intermediate, whatever you'd like to call it—as meditation with thought. As long as there's thought in the mind while you're sitting, practicing zazen, then you're in an early stage of meditation, from my point of view. When you're sitting and there's no thought at all—no thought, no image, no idea, no feeling, no sense of no thought, no sense of self or non-self—now you have entered into the realm of advanced meditation.

Advanced meditation is not just sitting meditating. It's addressing all the aspects of life:

Becoming aware of the designs of others, the dark side of others that seek to interfere with our evolution and keeping ourselves distant and closed to such beings, recognizing that they're part of the universal process too, but not a part that we need to be open to at this time;

Spending time alone, particularly in areas of low population density, away from people, where we can feel the stillness, where we don't just pick up psychically everybody's thoughts and desires because if you are just picking up everybody's thoughts and desires, after a while you'll think they're just your own;

Going walking in the woods or on the beach;

Taking weekends and going out into the desert or up into the mountains or to the ocean where there aren't too many people;

Going to the beach, not so much in the summer but in the winter;

Taking short walks in the park down a happy trail;

Spending time with people who are also on the pathway to enlightenment and avoiding people who aren't in your free time;

Being happy to deal with anyone in the world of business or whatever is necessary;

Not judging others, always being open to them;

Avoiding the cult mentality, you know, the super-slick, "I'm superior because I meditate, because I'm on the pathway to enlightenment," the subtle ego nonsense, terrible trap;

Just being real even, happy, being you, but finding out that "you" is far different than you have ever imagined;

Going through this process, reaching for it, yearning for it, aching for enlightenment, aching, but at the same time being responsible;

Working at your job and bringing it to perfection;

Keeping your house perfectly clean;

Keeping your bills in order;

Finding a teacher and studying with them and devoting yourself completely to the study, but in a balanced way, not in a fanatical way;

Having a wonderful sense of humor, particularly about yourself and your own situation, yet not simply laughing but working to change and improve things, even though, at times, it seems impossible.

This is advanced meditation.

Eternity is everywhere. It stretches endlessly in all directions, never beginning and never ending. Merge with it. Embrace it. Let go of your ideas and your concepts of what Zen is, what Zen masters are, who you are and what life is and what death is. Be free and disciplined.

"With Rama as the Zen Master," said Howard Green, "you found out that you were judging something by a set of patterns, stuck in a way of thinking. He would shatter that in a brilliant and funny way. It was fun and scary and exciting. The floor was always moving and you didn't know which way gravity was pulling because it was always pulling in a different direction than you expected."

A Rama koan:

*I don't know how much you know about Zen, but you'll
know less when I'm done with you.*

On December 31st, for the "Rama Seminars New Year's Eve Zen
Experience" at the Wilshire Ebell Theater in Los Angeles, I dressed up in
a long, black velvet skirt and a sparkling top. On stage, the band Zazen
played several new compositions. Wearing a tuxedo, Rama danced and
then he spoke, weaving his mix of teaching, stories and humor. I had a
realization/seeing.

Rama frequently spoke about developing yourself psychically.
Sometimes he would start telling a story and then talk more and more
quietly. You had to strain to hear what he was saying. You realized you
were following the story but you couldn't actually hear him.

I saw him at various times set up a joke and then not say the
punch line but transmit it telepathically. When you get the joke, it's
pretty funny. He didactically used joke telling to draw attention to the
fact that you're already psychically capable of knowing the punch line,
not telling it but letting it become a *psychic* punch line. We laughed
about things he didn't say at all. He was so funny, that could easily pass
unnoticed.

On this New Year's Eve, at the end, there was a minute or two
of narrative that was non-spoken. He kept speaking more and more
quietly until he was not talking. I heard him perfectly.

12

1987 - ZEN MASTER RAMA AND PALO ALTO

On the front page of his new *Far Side*[51] calendar for 1987, Rama wrote out a list of New Year's resolutions:

New home
New office
New vacation home
New tape set and video tapes
Books and brochures
Seminars in new cities
Travel seminars

Sail
Swim
Yoga
Karate
Ski
Run
Dance
Hike
Lift

In Boston and Los Angeles, a new, glossy, poster-size leaflet, "Zen Mind and Enlightenment," was handed out to the public. The brochure described Rama's take on Zen.

But what concerned the audience?

Question: What is sexuality about from a spiritual point of view?

We live in an age where sex is seen as a pleasurable experience and that's about it, which is a complete

---

51   *The Far Side* was an offbeat comic strip created by Gary Larson.

misunderstanding of what it is. In other words, people are taking sex on an extremely low level. Our whole culture is inundated with it on a real sleazy level.

Sex is a transmutation of energies, there is a lot of energy released and new beings are sometimes created through it. But it's also liberation of energy. It's as close as most people get to samadhi, as close as they get to the totality. It's their moment of release. It's spiritual in other words, but people don't see it that way, they just want to go out and hump, wear kinky underwear, be sleazy, use it as a control and manipulative device. They're taking it on a very low level. There's not much love connected with it.

Sex is power, it's a very powerful experience. If it's not taken as such or if that power is used in lower ways, it creates a karma. You can always tell by what happens during an era where the weak points in the societal structures are. If we are dealing with a plague that is essentially a sexually transmitted disease, that tells you where the karmic problems are with this world. This world has a total misunderstanding of what sex is all about and what sexual energies are.

People don't get what sex is for or what it can do. As a matter of fact, they use it in abusive ways to get control over others, to denigrate others, to take power from others, so therefore it creates a bad karma.

Sex is a moment of power. For most people it's a loss of power because they don't know how to handle it. They're in states of mind in which they can't see how to handle it. It's only in the higher states of mind that you can see that sex can be used for the transmutation of consciousness to elevate someone, ennoble them and to burn off some bad auric energy. That's what an aspect of tantra is. You have to be in a very high state of mind to do and see that. You have to have an extremely bright aura to even understand that. For most people, sex is a very subsurface experience of power and that's why it creates karma.

Question from a woman in the audience: I've been celibate for many years but I felt recently that a part of that decision might be due to aversion and fear. So I decided to walk through the aversion and I had a sexual experience with a friend of mine. I tried to go into a high, spiritual consciousness, but I found that about an hour later I felt a low grade vortex of energy enter my being and I felt very sick the next couple of months. I had all kinds of viruses, I had a lung infection. I didn't know if it all directly related to that.

> *Of course, yes. You see, I don't advocate celibacy or sexual practice. I think people will do whatever they do, but different things work for different people or they work in different phases of their life. Now as you said, you were celibate for a long time and then you decided to have a sexual encounter and you tried to make it into a higher experience. But whenever you have a sexual encounter with someone, you are blending your aura with theirs, therefore you're picking up their aura. If their aura is vibrating at a rate that is very different than yours, you pull all of that in and then, as you said, afterwards, about an hour later, you felt really sick and you were sick for several months afterwards. That's obviously because you've reached a certain level of purification.*
>
> *If you would have had a sexual encounter with someone whose aura was at the same level as yours, you wouldn't have gotten sick. It wouldn't necessarily take you any higher, it might even take you lower. The problem with sex is that during the act of making love there's a tremendous desire force that's released along with all that sensual feeling. If you get into it and get attached to it, which usually happens to most human beings, since they don't have the dispassion to just watch it like a movie, it then pulls you into the world of desire.*
>
> *In other words, we're up above the clouds and we're up in the sunshine. It's really nice but we get involved with something that takes us down to the earth. Once we're down there, it's not necessarily so easy to get back up*

because it's cloudy down there, it's hard to see, once you enter into that vortex of feelings and emotions. Everything was serene and still and suddenly you're in a stormy sea. It's all crazy and you can't even quite figure out where you were before. Everything is different.

Now for some people, sex is real healthy, it balances them in certain ways, it's not a bad thing at all. Everybody is different, it depends on your evolutionary level. Also, it depends on how high you want to fly. Some people like to meditate, they experience higher ranges of light but they also enjoy some of the human feelings too. They like to be touched, they like to be held, they love, they like to have sex with somebody, whatever it is. That's just a level of mind that they're in.

Other people just want to be purely in the ranges of light. It's very hard just to be in the ranges of light exclusively and have sexual encounters. It's a very, very difficult thing to do and the only people who can do that are enlightened people. I can do that. I can have a sexual encounter and not even notice any more than I notice anything else because my mind is so still and so strong that who cares about the physical feelings? It's no different than anything else. That's because I'm undifferentiated. But human beings can't do that at all. They get pulled into it and it's complicated by the fact that you are also interacting with another human aura and picking up his thoughts, feelings and impressions, and if they're real different than yours that can throw you off balance.

But yeah, that's how come you got sick. So for you, maybe having sex is not such a hot idea. For somebody else, maybe it's a good idea.

Question: Will taking drugs advance my spiritual progress?

No.

Question: Years ago I used to do transcendental meditation. At first it felt good but now, in the meditations that we practice, sometimes I am spaced out and when I go through the process I realize that I'm not doing something correctly. Can you give me any suggestions on how I can alter that so that I can meditate correctly?

> *Don't space out, obviously. You have developed a habit. It's not just when you meditate, it's all the time, you just notice it when you meditate. You have to lead a very different type of life which you've already succeeded in doing partially compared to when we first started working together, right? Definitely, so now you have to continue that process and bring it to higher levels of exactness by interfacing more with very physical things and by being more demanding of yourself, by practicing those concentration exercises every day as described on the introductory and advanced meditation tapes.*

> *You just have to really center yourself and get even more committed to it. Just lock down on the physical even more, use your mind more, demand more exactness and efficiency. When you find yourself moving into the spacey states, you have to will yourself out of it and snap yourself down to the physical. Exercise is good, it brings you right there.*

Question: How is suicide viewed from a Zen Buddhist perspective?

> *A Buddhist suicide is very rare. It will incur bad karma. It will mess up your incarnational pattern because when you die in a low state of mind—angry, despairing, sad, depressed—you are reborn in that same state. There are rare exceptions, for example the self-immolation of the monk in Vietnam who protested the persecution of Buddhists by the government. In his case, it did not incur bad karma; that was a protest staged by an advanced monk.*

Throughout March and April, Rama traveled on his own to scout U.S. locations with growing technology hubs. He visited Palo Alto, California; Boulder, Colorado and Reston, Virginia. He continued to encourage those attending his seminars to check out the technology profession, particularly computer programming, as the strongest career path for the modern seeker.

At the same time, he cut back on the duration of the Zen Seminars.

> *Do you know why I'm not doing four evenings any more in a row? It's too much for people, it's too much energy. If I sit in samadhi for four evenings in a row in these very powerful states of attention I go into, I find that most human beings can't handle it. After two evenings, they're maxed. Three and four are just too much for them, particularly in urban environments. If we were up in the mountains someplace or out in a forest and then all day long, each day you can go and walk around the forest and just absorb, then we can do four but in an urban environment there's no place for you to just get that psychic washing that's essential.*

> *Four evenings is just too much energy for people I find. They don't quite know what to do with it. Around evening three, they start to … gasp … gasp and by evening four they're like GASP … GASP … GASP. (Rama pretended to fall off his chair.) So that's why I'm not doing them anymore, out of respect and deference to the people who come to my seminars.*

That evening, Rama casually mentioned that "the cleanest energy lines" and "the most interesting technology jobs" were found around the Palo Alto area of northern California. Companies like Oracle, Apple, Sun, Intel and Hewlett-Packard were based there. Stanford University served as a hub of creative, new software ideas. Silicon Valley was blooming. Those in the audience who remembered the wind-up to Boston took note. Would Palo Alto be the next move?

In the middle of May, Rama asked all of his former students who had studied with him at any time as well as those who had been regularly attending the Zen Seminars to come to mandatory meetings in either L.A. or Boston. During the mandatory meetings, he said, he would describe a new program starting in the Palo Alto area. The new program would have a technology focus, require higher tuition to attend, and he would individually tell each person who was interested in joining the new program whether or not they could enroll. If the answer was yes, they would once again become a bona fide, enrolled student and would be asked to move to Palo Alto. If no, Rama would ask that person not to attend any of his talks going forward; it was the end of the association.

Davide Khalen attended the Boston meeting at the Unitarian Church in the Back Bay section of Boston.

"I took my seat in one of the wooden pews and relaxed by enjoying the deep, rich wood interior of the chapel," said Khalen. "When Rama arrived, he split up the guys and gals and spoke to the men first while the gals waited outside. When the hall had been sorted, he said, 'I'm going to look at each one of you and decide. How many of you know right now if I'm going to say 'yes?' Only Khalen and one other man raised their hands. 'Optimists,' Rama quipped.

"The men (about 80 in Boston) lined up and each person came up to Rama, one at a time. Rama put his hand on their heart chakra and said 'Yes' or 'No.'

"When he touched my heart," said Khalen, "it was pure love and bliss. He said 'yes.' I had been living and working in New York. The result was that I took a pay cut and moved to San Francisco."

In Los Angeles, with over 500 people present, the West Coast sorting ceremony took place on a sunny Saturday afternoon. Rama announced the new program designed for people involved in information technology and computers. If people were doing well in other professions such as law, music, medicine or public relations, they did not have to move to Northern California but were invited to be part of the program.

I was the only person in that hall who was engaged in "public relations." I felt happily singled out and thanked Rama inwardly. I had already been yes'd.

He said the move was not for everyone, and it was OK to leave. All who decided to leave would receive a karmic blessing, he would clear things for them and set them up. The words were said with love. In six weeks, there would be a final desert Summer Solstice trip that everyone in the room could join, whether they were accepted into the new program or not.

"He gave us the criteria, the specifications we needed to meet in order to move to Palo Alto," said Vera Anderson-Smith, an electronics engineer. "It was all about technology. If we wanted to move, we were to sit on one side of the auditorium. If we did not plan to move to Palo Alto, we were to sit on the other side. I always asked Rama questions. I raised my hand and said, 'Rama, what if I can't make it now? Can I do this in August?' He responded like a cormorant diving for a fish, but in this case, the morsel he was after was my tendency to vacillate and indulge. 'You don't have to do anything,' he shot back. 'You can just go out there and live on your own and never come back.'

"His tone was very stern. Either do it my way or don't. It was very much, you don't have to be here. You're not doing us any favors. I went to sit on the not-going-to-Palo-Alto side of the room. Then, when he asked our side of the room to leave the hall for a while, I went outside. About one third of the people in the room left the hall.

"Once I got outside, I stood in the courtyard of the Ebell Theater and tried to look at what was going on. What did I really want to do? Someone came up to me and made a snide comment about how mean Rama had been in his response to my question. That was not my experience at all, his comments always were buffered with a huge wave of love and with something inner and personal for me. I saw this person as a mirror of my problematic mind-set. I went back into the hall and sat with those who wanted to go to Palo Alto."

Each person came to the front of the hall, one at a time. Rama touched their third eye and said yes or no. Before he did this, he explained that it had nothing to do with whether you were a good person or advanced spiritually. He would simply see if it was a person's dharma to go to Palo Alto or not. He was doing the right thing.

Said Anderson-Smith, "When I went up to the front of the room and he touched my third eye, he said 'yes.' I rearranged my job to work part-time in Palo Alto."

When Lisa Deeh stepped in front of Rama, she recalled, "he touched my third eye and a huge, intense light went off in my mind and heart. I felt infused with light, and out of my peripheral hearing, I heard him say 'no.'

"The light was so effulgent, beautiful and ecstatic, my mind did not get around the 'no,'" Deeh said. "I felt shocked. I walked outside and my mind started in and the emotions rolled in. Then he asked everyone who wanted to, to reenter the hall and meditate. I left after the evening meeting in high alert mode, determined to start my life anew, using the 'no' as a koan."

At the beginning of June, several hundred students began their move to Palo Alto. Rama rented a house there as well. Said Forge, "Every single move had a multi-dimensional impact. He wanted us to stop identifying with our physical circumstances. Transplanting to Palo Alto was a form of self-dissolution. The computer science mystery school was about going constantly beyond yourself and making a jump to something more challenging, pushing yourself to do better, to do more difficult work. All of that sharpened the mind, making the mind disciplined and focused.

"That was the whole methodology of going to Palo Alto. The best people in the industry were located in Silicon Valley. Rama wanted us to go there so we could learn from them. These were occult exercises. He wanted us to use our occult abilities to do something with the energy he gave us that would be positive and happy, that would help make us less solid in terms of how we thought about ourselves, to replace limited images with more positive, expansive images. It was about not sitting around in the same neighborhood where you'd lived for years and you saw everything the same way, so that you'd gotten locked into your seeing.

"The moves to cities with strong technology centers prepared us to get into advanced practice. It was true tantra, using the world to elevate the attention and get the best life."

Rama said he would put out an "energy line" to make it easier to find a job, but, he said, people still had to pound the pavement.

What was an "energy line?" I used to be confused about the concept of an "energy line" because I found the term to be very abstract. Several years later, an incident occurred that defined for me what it meant.

I had taken my dog, Murphy, to a local park to play ball. Suddenly, she ran into the street and was hit by a car. She was alive but her right front paw was limp. The vet told me her leg was broken, but the real danger was internal bleeding. That night, as Murphy stayed at the vet's office for observation, a large group dinner with Rama was held in an elegant setting. I told Rama what happened and he said to me, "She does have internal bleeding, but don't worry, I will put an energy line on it." Of course, I was consumed with worry. The next morning, I went to the vet, and there she was, in good spirits, with a cast on her front leg. I brought her home and watched as she hopped on three legs around my living room.

Suddenly, Murphy disappeared completely and in her place was a Lakeland Terrier-shaped mass of brilliant gold and white sparkling light, exploding at mega speed, like hyper fireworks on the Fourth of July. The sparkling, popping light hopped three-leggedly around the room. After several minutes of witnessing this incredible spectacle—no physical dog, just exploding, exquisitely fizzling gold and white light—I had the thought, 'This is beautiful, but where's Murphy?' Instantly, her physical body returned, the beige curly hair, the floppy ears, white cast, the exuberance—all there, still hopping around. I hugged her.

That's how I learned what an energy line is from an enlightened teacher.

Forge found a job right away. So did Anderson-Smith. Howard Green went to work at Informix. Randy Rochte interviewed at Ford Aerospace in Sunnyvale. "I was talking, presenting myself during the interview," said Rochte. "Suddenly the room turned solid gold, you couldn't see anything but gold light, like butter you could cut with a knife. It was really striking. There was so much gold light in the room that I only could hear the interviewer's voice. Of course, I got the job."

On Saturday, June 20, the group whom Rama had invited to the desert—those going to Palo Alto, those not going to Palo Alto, those applying at the last minute to go to Palo Alto—met at the Casa del Zorro resort in Borrego Springs for a two-day desert journey.

A jewel in the desert, the Casa del Zorro is a luxury hotel in one of the smallest, most backwater desert towns in Southern California. Rama had located and logged it early in his teaching career. His students had met there many times. It was perfect tantra. You'd drive down the quarter-mile-long main street in town, hang a right that shot off of a roundabout, drive another few miles past a few houses and cacti, then suddenly, a resort with a gated entry, fine dining, several swimming pools and an elegant, large conference room appeared like a mirage in the desert.

One hour's drive from La Casa Del Zorro, the desert trip was like a homecoming, but with an edge.

Deeh recalled, "Being in the 'no' group was the bottom. I had studied with him for seven years. I drove out to the desert, parked in the usual spot and walked into the gorge to join the other students. I tried to meditate as deeply as I could. It was starting to get dark. Before the hike began, he said he wanted to meet with the 'no' people. There were eight people, only we came of the hundreds he said 'no' to. It was amazing to us. He talked about the fact that each one of us was a true student. We were right in deciding to come. We had to believe that if he could take us with him, he would. He recalled the scene from the film *Out of Africa* where, at the end, she says, 'You cannot come where I'm going. You would not like it there, you must trust me about this.' He said, 'I wish I could take you with me, but trust me, you would not like it there.' He told us how much he loved us, but it was not right for us."

He then walked over to where Davide Khalen sat on his backpack. "I had confided to one student that I had a hit of LSD in my pocket," said Khalen. "He ratted me out to Rama. Rama, in jeans and sweatshirt, suddenly hovering over me with his arms folded, told me quite firmly that I would not be needing 'substances' that night. After he walked away, I tossed the tablet in the sand."

The group hiked quietly along the wide dirt road. Rama chose a clearing in front of a sloping hill, and people sat in a semi-circle around him as he stood, waiting for all hikers to file in. In the deep desert night, Rama spoke of how important it is to keep your mind sharp and analytical when you aren't meditating. He recommended taking a few minutes every evening to recapitulate what happened during the day to notice how you felt, when and what you learned. Rama said it would help keep your mind sharp and analytical if you make a point of recapitulating your shifts at the end of the day to see what you learned.

One thing we all resist, he said, is WORK. He said when we are struggling we should feel good about it, that the times you are struggling are the times you are most alive. He said it's like when soldiers reminisce about battles. After the battle, it's boring. But when you are in the battle, then you are really living. He said he has to struggle all the time too.

Seated in the sand towards the center of the group, I heard Rama's voice as his physical shape faded in and out. His voice became deeper, more far away. "Be willing to do things yourself, to take responsibility," he said in his deep desert voice. "Eternity is not going to do things for you—whether it be achieving success or gaining enlightenment." He said if he could do it for us, it would already be done.

A sense of unbounded love and commitment filled our tiny enclave, seated together on the sand under 10,000 stars and surrounded by the no time of eternity. "You have no idea what you are capable of."

"During the desert trip," Deeh commented, "I was shedding lifetimes, surrendering my life to the infinite. I saw things that night I had never seen before. That night I could hardly sleep, I put everything in order. The next morning, I went to the Casa's front desk to check out. A few minutes after I got into the line, Rama came over and stood just a few yards in front of me, where several of the guys were holding a place for him. I tried to be composed, trying to hold it together, trying to be calm and silent even though my being was aching. It was probably 10 minutes, finally he got checked out. As he walked past me, he took a rolled up piece of paper and tapped me with it on the top of my head and said, 'See you around.' Looking back, I see he was pushing us through these doorways and helping us to change. He was acting from total love." (Lisa Deeh returned to the study two years later.)

Throughout the summer in Palo Alto, Rama offered "remedial" classes to the group that he now referred as "intermediate students." The focus was on pulling spaced-out lives back together, remembering why you were in the study, and to work. Teching-up the mind and career was an essential part of practice. Rama called the program in Palo Alto his boot camp. He retained his "Zen Master Rama" title for the public, but for the students—his name was always Rama.

For homework, Rama asked his students to watch the film, *Full Metal Jacket,* twice in a movie theater. The film crystallized the experience of the Vietnam War by concentrating on a group of raw, young Marines. The first half of the movie portrayed the volunteers' harrowing boot-camp training under the profane, power-saw guidance of a drill instructor. To survive in a boot camp, you must draw on a deeper level of will power, and you can be energized by that. If the will does not emerge, then success is unlikely. Rama asked the students to achieve that level of focus.

In a meeting at the Cañada College Theater in Redwood City at the end of June, Rama detailed the boot camp requirements:

- Take martial arts classes at least twice a week
- Learn control, discipline and a proper attitude toward the teacher
- Meditate at least 45 minutes twice a day
- Rethink what your intent is
- Decide to be a fighter, a warrior

Rama again said he would help everyone to land jobs in technology. But, he said, you have to be prepared, have the necessary skills, believe, do the things he recommends and pound the pavement. If you were in this remedial group, your lives were strong enough to successfully move into the intermediate study.

He asked everyone to remember how they felt when they began the study—the enthusiasm, the delight, the feeling that anything was possible. The resistance to change was less because no change had really kicked in yet. The mental attitude was positive and upbeat. The point of this remedial time was to bring people back to where they started.

"You have to improve," Rama stated, "because in the aura of enlightenment, which causes you to vibrate faster, if your life isn't tight, you will crash." We had been receiving Rama's empowerments for years. We were a lit up group of humans. Was the energy being used for positive, life-enriching purposes or was it being blown in typical human frailties, including jealousy, anger, selfishness?

On August 25, the group met at Gunn High School in Palo Alto. I had flown up for the evening. When I arrived at the high school auditorium, there was a long line of registration tables manned by a group of women who often worked at Rama's office or were given tasks. Although Rama discouraged cliques of any kind, I felt this group was a kind of "in crowd." I figured Rama was just making sure that no one had to wait in line. I got into the attendance line, and suddenly I "saw" something, like a waking dream when a single image conveys a whole packet of information. In this case, I saw the woman doing registration hand the gal in front of me an admission ticket, and at the same time, I saw that she took life force from that person. It was a straightforward, quick grab, and the person getting the ticket had no idea what happened. It was simple and visible theft.

I was on my guard when I walked up and gave my name to this woman. But actually, I felt pleased that I was able to "see" something—moving into another dimension to understand reality.

When the boot camp session began, Rama asked us what was going on. I raised my hand and he called on me. I wanted to share my "seeing." I said, "I saw someone in the attendance line steal energy from the person at the same time she was handing her a ticket." I sat back, waiting for him to take my seeing, acknowledge it and talk about it as a discussion point. Instead he responded, "You would do the same thing." End of discussion.

That night, Rama asked the group of women taking tickets—people he had worked with closely over the years—to step away from the study and take a break. They had become egotistical, he explained, because he had worked closely with them. Their egotism was harming the other students.

He said he respected these women. They had techy, nimble minds and strong attention fields. But the conditioning of women in the West had hurt them. He didn't blame them, he said, but they had to learn a new way and leaving might be the motivation they needed.

Any sense of superiority on the part of other people in the room, he cautioned, would be completely distorted because these were his best students. The rest of us were nerds with the potential to blow it as well. For this group of women, it was not that they would not see him again, but they had to change before that would happen.

That summer, in preparation for resuming the Zen Seminars in San Francisco, Rama published a new booklet, *The Zen Experience*, featuring color photographs and blocks of prose. Printed on glossy, letter-size paper, the book was understated and elegant, with a motif of rice paper and Japanese calligraphy. It reflected the beautiful, understated Zen art that Rama had encountered in Japan and brought home with him in the form of temple entry tickets, temple brochures and literature. It conveyed a quality about Zen, of something harmonious and unconventional. The most elaborate publication yet, it raised the bar for Rama's public teaching materials.

A Rama koan from *The Zen Experience*:

During the summer in Stony Brook, a realtor brought Rama to an older, rundown, one-story, three-bedroom house on Old Field Road in East Setauket, a neighboring suburb to Stony Brook. The lot was long and narrow, but the back of the ranch-style house faced Long Island Sound and had a long dock that ran out into the water. The location was right. As soon as he saw the home, he decided to purchase it. With the realtor's assistance, he negotiated the sale of the first house and a move into the second house, where he would live for the rest of his life.

In 1987, San Francisco was an established center of Zen teaching. Some great teachers were present, and it may be that Rama hoped the teachers would attend his talks in an open state of mind, along with their students. As he made clear in his handouts, Rama taught old Zen, Zen without rules. A Zen practice in which attainment is measured by one's state of enlightenment, of many, many satoris (realizations). As Rama said in the *Zen Experience,* he was the koan.

In the fall, as the San Francisco Zen Seminars resumed in the massive Masonic Auditorium, Rama took out two-page ads featuring Harry Langdon photos in the *San Francisco Chronicle* and other local print papers. He broke Zen Master perception rules, of course, but he didn't care. He sought seekers who lived in the area, whom he felt would respond to a Tantric Zen approach to enlightenment.

Certainly some of the local student Zennists, the ones who were laboring up the ranks in their Zen groups, staring at walls and not able to stop thought, were annoyed at Rama. How could someone who had not been through the hierarchy claim to be a Zen master? This is arguably an un-Zen train of thought, but nonetheless, Rama's Zen seminars in San Francisco were uniquely challenging. And Rama's innate response was to be more and more truthful. The auditorium was packed with people.

I flew to San Francisco to attend a seminar. When Rama walked out onto the large stage with its smooth, blond, dance-ready hardwood floor, he did not say anything. He wore a black jersey top, black loose pants and black ballet slippers. Recorded Zazen music began to play, and he simply began to dance. He used the whole space, with fluid movements and mudras. I tried to stop thought as he danced. In a meditative state, I saw him shift dimensions and create complex symphonies of awareness that would affect the mind-state of every person in the audience. I also became aware that the people sitting next to me were not getting it at all. They could not believe that a Zen teacher was dancing, wearing gender-neutral clothing, and playing electronic music with a rock and roll beat. They were angry. I felt their Harrumph! This isn't Zen!

Rama was aware of the angry and doubting energy projected at him, but for him, San Francisco was more about the bodhisattva vow. He was doing his job.

Also in mid-September, Rama began offering Zen Seminars in New York City. For the first lecture series, with the help of the students, he purchased two-page ads in the *New York Times*. As on the West Coast, the ads featured a full page Harry Langdon photo and an opposite page of text describing his Zen talks. Rama showed an advance copy of the ad to his Palo Alto students. Said Khalen, "the huge double-truck advert in the *New York Times* was incredible. During the break, I spoke with Rama and said that it was so cool to see his enlightenment in the face of New Yorkers, for all to see. And he said, 'I did that so you could have that experience.'"

The lecture was scheduled for the 2,257-seat City Center Theater on West 55th Street. To operate the New York talks, Rama took several students with him to New York. They sat in front of the hall to distribute tickets. According to one of the students, very few people showed up, and the audience mostly consisted of people working for the hall. "He did not ask why people weren't there. Rama did an amazing meditation.

He was molten gold and the whole hall was liquefied. Afterwards, he took us out to Nirvana, a nearby Indian food restaurant. As we rode up in the elevator, we spoke about technology. He flashed blocks of information to me about artificial intelligence. I've been focused in my career on AI ever since."

In 1987, I became Vice President of Publicity, Advertising and Promotion at Stephen J. Cannell Productions. Stephen Cannell was an independent company that sold content to the three major TV networks and the one upstart, Fox TV. Cable TV and internet TV had not yet emerged as a force; there were four markets and you either made it in those markets or sank.

That year, Cannell had five shows on the air including "Hunter," "21 Jump Street" (launching Johnny Depp's career) and "Wiseguy" (launching Kevin Spacey's career). Cannell had opened a production studio in Vancouver where I spent time on set. It was exciting and fun, and I developed a small swagger for walking on and off sets and sound stages.

I flew to Palo Alto once a month for Rama's classes. In October, Rama approached me at the break and brushed by me—literally touching his shoulder to mine as he walked by. "You're off," he said. In a moment, he was halfway across the floor, talking to another person. I stood there, ears ringing. Koan-like! Terse! The words ricocheted across the spaces in my being. I was "off." What did that mean? Off what? How off? Where off? Why off? I began to look at every aspect of my consciousness, leaving no stone of "offness" unturned. Where was I off? What was "on"?

I did not figure it out that night, nor the next day or the next. But after about four days of reflection, I suddenly realized I was no longer off. Somewhere in the process of self-analysis and meditation, I had toned down my swagger and my blossoming ego. In its place, I felt a tighter connection to Rama's enlightened energy. Through the overgrown woods of offness, I found a clearing that was "on." It was a powerful teaching in three little words, two of which were a contraction.

The Palo Alto group hummed. Jobs had been found in exciting companies, student minds were engaged in new challenges. Contentment slowly emerged.

In early December, having moved into his new Long Island home, Rama announced that going forward, he would only offer classes on the East Coast. He suggested that the students relocate to the

Reston, Virginia, area near Washington, D.C., where there was another new strip of technology companies. He also spoke of the possibility of influencing the elections. He saw that George H. W. Bush would have a negative impact on the well-being of the nation in the years to come. He felt that having proximity to D.C. could help turn the election in favor of Michael Dukakis.

The students, now relocation veterans, made plans to leave Palo Alto at the end of the year. Before the eastern exodus, however, a Winter Solstice two-day desert retreat took place, with its locus the Casa del Zorro.

At the first meeting in the Casa's spacious ballroom, Rama set out six pragmatic tasks for the year ahead. He asked that the students approach them as if they were going to be graded. The tasks—an upgrade and remix from the Boot Camp list—were:

- Practice meditation
- Keep a clean relationship with the teacher
- Achieve career success
- Do martial arts—keep body in shape
- Get out in nature
- Have fun

The night segued into "Name That Tune," a popular TV show from the Sixties and Seventies. Rama and the students took turns humming arcane music, and the students called out their guesses. Soon happy laughter filled the room. The light in the ballroom turned a soft gold. "This is what I was working towards," Rama said. "This feeling in the room is why we went through all the changes." As he spoke, the volume of light rose higher. People had worked hard, taken chances and remembered their excitement about the study. The room was united in sweet camaraderie, no ego dramas. Rama gave everyone an "A" in pragmatic task six.

Several days later, he held a gathering in the neighboring town of Palm Desert for those who had helped with various tasks during the year. The suite had a grand piano and he hung out with the musicians. "In Palo Alto," said Forge, "I made a big jump into a project management position. Rama thought it was a big deal when I got the job. It was a big shift in my career. They gave me my own office. I came in one morning and my entire office was filled with balloons from Rama. It was YAY,

Kathleen got a cool job! Everyone at the office was dying to know who did it. I had to distribute the balloons and flowers just to get into my office.

"Halfway into that job, I hired a brilliant engineer to work for me. I fell in love with him. I started dating him. It was a breakthrough because I had not been in a relationship for a really long time. It was important for me to process that. Then we had the event in Palm Desert. I was doing very little work for Rama. When I showed up at this event, he came up to me and said, 'You are looking really good, what are you up to?' I said I was in a relationship. He said your heart is open, you're glowing, it's obviously a good thing. Do you want to come by and hang out with me and the musicians in my room?

"It was an interesting night because Rama had made a huge transformation. He finally was able to completely cut all of the people who were throwing bad energy at him so they couldn't physically get to him anymore. He made a conscious decision about it. He was tired of being in physical pain all the time. I know that because when I went to his room, I gave him a massage. His shoulders weren't all knotted up. I had never felt that before.

"He said, 'Notice anything different?' I went, 'Yeah, your shoulders are like butter.' He started laughing. 'Isn't it nice? I couldn't handle feeling like that anymore.' I was so impressed. I knew he was about to make another jump. He had to let go of that anchor.

"I stayed the night with him and had an amazing time. We hung out the next day. He was going into samadhi and we were meditating the whole time."

On New Year's Eve, back in San Francisco, I watched Rama dance at the Moscone Center. The hall was filled. He taught as if the entire audience were unanimous in their desire to learn and change.

On New Year's Eve in Palo Alto, thirty miles to the south, cars packed and job/apartment notices given, many students departed for Reston, Virginia and Washington, D.C. Others went straight to New York.

The move east was more than a change of place. Going forward, the "Zen Master Rama" title would no longer be used for the public. A new teaching structure would emerge.

13

1988 - FACING EAST

Washington, D.C.

No man shall be compelled to frequent or support any religious worship or ministry or shall otherwise suffer on account of his religious opinions or belief, but all men shall be free to profess and by argument to maintain, their opinions in matters of religion. - Thomas Jefferson

At the appointed hour on January 17, 1988, several hundred intermediate students garbed in wool, down gloves and puffy coats gathered on the wide, white marble steps of the Jefferson Memorial in Washington, D.C. (or attempted not to gather as armed security guards scanned for linked crowds of any kind). Rama arrived at 4 p.m. In his denims, down jacket and winter-proof boots, he looked like any other tourist bounding up the stairs to the interior of the hall, except that hundreds of people (who had been asked not to look at him) adjusted their formation slightly to be aware of his movements and slowly shuffled in his direction.

Thus he was immediately spotted by the guards who kept a watchful eye on him as he perused Jefferson's writings on religious freedom. His small hand mudras went unnoticed. Ronald Reagan flew overhead in his helicopter.

"I remember a moment at the Jefferson Memorial that was beyond anything I'd ever experienced," said Howard Green. "Prior to visiting the memorial, Rama spoke of the energy lines in D.C. and the occult nature of the placement of the monuments and the memorials. He said the energy patterns in the mall were similar to the structures they used in ancient Egypt.

"I was inside the building. There was a moment when everything shifted. Everything moved into another place. You could tell something monumental happened although you could not see it physically. It was as if Rama grabbed the main trunk line and everything lit up. Everything congealed and crystallized, like when you're bouncing a ball and your hand goes lower and lower and the ball goes faster and faster until it turns into something else. That's what happened there. An energy snapped out of him and something changed. I remember everyone going, what just happened? It was like waking up. It was like being at ground zero, a crazy energy that kept building and building. I was astounded by the nature of the energy, it was so visceral and in your face."

As the clusters of students drew ever closer to where he stood, Rama, sensing the guards' suspicion, turned around and walked back down the stairs towards the parking area, where a car awaited him.

By the third week of January, the move East had been completed.

Why Reston in particular? Said David Silver, "He had gone to D.C. and seen the toll roads and all the new buildings leading to the Dulles Airport. New technology companies were mushrooming up. He was still thinking of a software company that all the students could participate in, and the area resonated. He also said that for many students, it would be a chance to learn about the East Coast business and lifestyle before heading to the final destination, New York City."

"Most of us had the West Coast in our soul," said Anderson-Smith. "I would never have succeeded moving straight from Los Angeles to New York. D.C. was softer, actually a bit Southern in feeling. Along the way, Rama continued the training and inner transformation."

Wherever the location, Rama found new ways to teach. "For one of the meetings," Firgy recalled, "Rama rented a rustic barn. As soon as we entered, he began talking like a redneck hillbilly preacher from down south. 'I reckon you folks are a little angry at me, y'all gotta calm down and let the light of God come into ya.' It was pure improv-style standup, very irreverent, and he made us laugh for hours. If there had been anger in that barn, it was drowned in waves of giggles."

For another meeting in the barn, Rama asked everyone to write a "non-poem," accompanied by a photograph they took, to show and read aloud in front of the group. The poem would be written in one's own style, about anything spiritual that inspired them. The photo would be queued up on a slide projector. When their slide was projected onto a big screen, each person was to stand and recite their non-poem.

"I wrote my poem while driving to the meeting," Anderson-Smith said. "Before I read it, I said to myself, I have to be in a place where it doesn't matter. When I read it aloud to the group, he asked me to read it again. I tried to be neutral as I re-read it, and just did the best I could. He said, 'I like it. You can always tell an ex-nun by their renunciation.' That was the first time I learned that I was one of those female students who had taken the convent route in previous lives." He told Patty Kloor, a former chiropractor, now a database designer, that he particularly liked the feeling of her photo of clouds over the mountains. "For many years," Kloor said, "I mapped back to that picture as a personal pathway and connection between me and Rama."

Initially, because of the lifestyle and culture change, many students struggled to gain a foothold in the D.C. area. Said Mo Hughes, a database engineer, "I recall a meeting in Reston when he told us we were in a lousy consciousness. He announced he was going to fast until he died, unless we corrected our behavior. That freaked me out. We all left and I went out of my way to clean up my act. A few weeks later, when we came back into the room, it was like a different place. It felt cheerful and bright in the hall. Rama came out and acknowledged that we had all raised our energy level and awareness. He said we looked much shinier. 'Oh, and by the way,' he said grinning, pausing to ensure maximum effect, 'right after that meeting I went out and ate a hamburger.'"

Since Rama continued to offer the occasional public lecture in Los Angeles, I flew to Washington only once during the Reston teaching module. I rented a car and stayed in a boutique hotel in Bethesda. I was a D.C. newbie. The day of the seminar, I drove through my nation's capitol. I parked the car to gawk at the White House and nearby agency buildings. Throughout my life in California, any events emanating from the White House or an affiliated agency seemed far away, edicts issued by "those people" in government. Now I was looking across the White House lawn and strolling past the sturdy, serviceable architecture of the Department of Energy, the Department of Defense, the Department of Labor.

Rama stated many times that democracy was the best system of government. That having a strong military was essential to a nation's security. In the heart of D.C., I felt a surprising sense of awe.

During that evening's meeting in Georgetown, at the main auditorium of the Duke Ellington School of the Arts, I raised my hand and described the sense of history and influence I felt in D.C. "That's one of the reasons I brought you here," Rama commented. "In the future, some of you will be selling your software to the government and thc military. The U.S. government needs the best software in the world in order to succeed."

According to Davide Khalen, on another evening at the Duke Ellington School, Rama told the group, "I will meditate and create an opening where you can see a vision of what you must do in this life. It is your vision, not mine." After the meditation, various students shared their perceptions. Said Khalen, "I saw a mental image of the Himalayas and told him about it in front of the group. 'You should go,' he responded. I left for India several weeks later and remained there for several months."

In early May, observing the downwards slope of the Dukakis campaign, its effect on morale in Washington, and the success and mind-states of students who had gone straight to New York, Rama suggested that the whole group begin their move to the Manhattan area. He suggested that working in New York City and living in one of the nicer suburbs of Connecticut or Westchester County would be an ideal combination.

Rama also spoke about Wall Street, that working in the software area in financial services was the sharpest mental game in town. He spoke of DB2, a database management system released several years earlier by IBM. A student asked, why DB2? Rama explained that in the past, data had been stored in a series of long strings called flat files that were very difficult to manipulate. A relational database management system (RDBMS) stored data in tables of rows and columns with connecting relational operators to manipulate the data in tabular form. He said that an RDBMS was much closer to how the mind works. After working in DB2 for a few months, he suggested, the students would notice a big difference in their attention fields.

New York, New York

While the students adjusted to D.C., Rama spent most of his time in New York. One of his first tasks was to remodel his fixer-upper Long Island house. Of the three bedrooms, he designated one bedroom as an exercise room and another as an office. He kept the basement unfinished. He needed to strengthen and refinish the long dock.

Rama lived in his house throughout the makeover, joined by the occasional house guest. Harrison visited for several weeks and reported that Rama had hired a lead contractor and worked with him closely to guide the construction.

"Rama felt that the lead construction person was deliberately delaying," said Harrison. "He used a lot of restraint in dealing with him. I became aware of Rama's profound interactions. He was aware of what happened 250 lifetimes ago. I also got the feeling how challenging it would be when another person is holding your home and personal environment in their hands.

"Rama obtained special marble for the tiles in the kitchen. They felt like power tiles. He really hassled the details of the house. I observed and learned. Everything I did with Rama was always a learning experience.

"The renovations went on for at least nine months and probably longer, but it was still a nice place to live. I loved hearing the lapping of the water."

As a respite from construction, Rama visited some of his old haunts, including a surprise visit to the SUNY Stony Brook office of Paul Dolan, one of the professors who directed his doctorate program.

"I read the Sunday *New York Times* and had opened the magazine section," said Dolan. "There, several pages in, was a picture of Fred announcing a three-day seminar in Carnegie Hall. It was a full double-page spread in the Sunday *Times Magazine*. I thought, wow, that cost a lot of money. The picture of Fred had a nimbus or aura with a halo effect. I put it on my office door and put a cartoon caption on it that said, 'If you get a Ph.D., you don't have to teach English.' About a week later, much to my surprise, Fred came by. He saw the picture and seemed to enjoy the caption. He was very positive and happy. He gave me a tape of one of his talks. I said I was surprised he was back in New York. He said he lived and worked on both coasts.

"The odd thing about the picture was that it was non gender specific. It looked like an angel. One of my students thought it was a woman. Jean-Paul Sartre made a slighting reference to angels, that they don't belong to any gender. The photo had that quality—ethereal and non-earthly." After the surprise visit, Dolan said, he never saw Fred again.

While still in Palo Alto, Rama had approached Corin Robertson during the break period of a student meeting. "I was surprised," said Robertson, "because I'd had very few personal conversations with him before. He suggested that I should not go to D.C. because he saw it was going to melt down. 'Pack, get yourself to New York, go to Westchester County, get a house and I'll meet you there.'" Corin moved directly to New York and found work as a computer programmer. She rented a house in the small, country town of Pound Ridge, a one hour Metro North train ride to and from the city, and home to a large, well-forested state park, Ward Pound Ridge.

Rama enjoyed the occasional two hour drive from his under-construction home to Pound Ridge. Seated together outside the Pound Ridge house on a stone bench, an early spring transforming the backyard into a circle of bright yellow dogwood flowers and lavender tulips, Rama told Corin about the book he planned to write. The working title was *Surfing the Himalayas* and it told of his youthful adventures encountering a teacher in Nepal.

Said Robertson, "His primary focus with me was the lineage of the Rae Chorze Fwaz. We spent many hours talking about Master Fwap, the teacher whom he met and spent time with, and the lineage. Because Rama died at a young age in his previous life in Tibet, there was a broken line. But the lineage was never broken in the inner world. It is a real lineage and the line is already there. Rama did go to Tibet when he was 19. He did run into an old teacher, who was his teacher's teacher. He missed his teacher because of the incarnation sequence, but the next best person to reawaken him was Master Fwap. He told me he had been asked not to divulge his experiences until he knew the time was ready.

"All of *Surfing the Himalayas* is true. The only part that was fictionalized was the use of snowboarding as a teaching metaphor and a means of reaching young people. When he first arrived in Kathmandu, he said he did try a form of snowboarding with a makeshift board. That was how he met Master Fwap. But back then, snowboarding was not his focus. Rama saw that snowboarding was going to get big, and that by the time the book came out it would be a raging sport. He felt many young people would pick up the book because of the snowboarding sub-plot.

"Rama had the book outlined already. One evening as we spoke of the lineage teachings, he said to me, 'We only have ten years left.' I thought he meant that I only had ten years left to study with him and I'd be over it by then. It never occurred to me that that the 'we' referred to him."

For Robertson and others, New York proved to be all that Rama had promised and more. Walking down Fifth Avenue in Manhattan was a whole new ballgame. The pace, the style, the rapid thought process, the old elegance and sophistication, the real streetwise life—a person had to be grounded and alert in order to succeed. New York City was perfect tantra—using everything in your life to grow.

Rama asked Forge to research venues for meetings where the snap and pace of the New York area could be leveraged. While Forge sought and set up high-end meeting places that could retain luminous awareness, Rama held the first meeting of the New York-based teaching on May 23 at a more modest but functional setting—a Unitarian Church in Mount Kisco, Westchester County. Only 50 people were present for the first meeting.

"How are you doing out there?" Rama asked.

As people raised their hands to answer, the light in the room grew stronger. "I had three offers at one investment bank from different departments." "The beauty of Westchester blows my mind." "I walked around Manhattan for three hours and loved it." "I'm earning twice the rate I got in California." "It's so cool to take the train instead of drive." "I feel like I found the right place." Every person spoke. Rama logged the excitement. "New York City is going to force me to change." "It's overwhelming in a good way." "I feel energized and smarter." "The New York business energy is no-nonsense and I'm going to learn from it."

Then, perhaps in response to New York City's total crime rate—73% above the national average—Rama for the first time demonstrated enlightened martial arts. He asked the two members of his newly formed security team—Mo Hughes and Sanford Knaff, both black belts—to step onto the church's stage.

"That night," said Knaff, "when I stood in front of him, he held my wrist and talked for a long time. I was familiar with the concept of ki or life force from Aikido. I was trained to feel other people's ki. As I stood there, I tried to feel his ki. It was not there. Then he did just a little wrist twist and I was on my back on the floor. I was shocked.

"When I stood up, he asked me, 'what did you feel?' I said, 'I kind of felt nothing.' 'Exactly!' he responded. 'Because the movement comes from samadhi, it's not the normal technique.' As he spoke, I realized I did feel something. You know how you go to a very pristine place and you see the landscape and it's like an absence? The energy is so pure that you are almost weightless. I was standing one foot away from Rama. I felt nothing—a pervasive emptiness."

When Hughes came up on the stage, Rama put the palm of his hand in the center of Mo's forehead and said, "Don't let me push you over."

"He gave me a shove and I took a couple of steps back," said Hughes. "Rama said, 'No, you're not fighting.' It was traumatic for me because I was such a heart warrior for him. When he asked me to fight against him, it was the last thing I would ever expect or want to do. We did this four or five times. He kept saying, you're not fighting back. I knew if I really resisted, he could not push me.

"Finally I crossed the line and locked down. Rama blasted me with energy and I went into a full body spasm, like five feet in the air. I hit the ground and backed up about 20 feet. I experienced complete loss of control of my body for at least 10 seconds for no apparent reason. My personal will popped like a circuit breaker, like a spring being pulled. This was not even in my world of possibilities. I had a second degree black belt in karate. I instantly tried to understand what had just frikking happened. I remember it as multiple streams of awareness all happening at once from many points of view. Afterwards, I felt clear and still."

Let the Software Games Begin

When the students did well, Rama responded with more meetings and new interactive tasks to maintain and accelerate the momentum. "Jumps" was his term for the teaching he offered—not a slow, gradual, step by cautious step up the staircase but a constant reaching for the sky, challenging oneself, making positive changes in awareness and self-image that would be supported by his enlightened energy.

Many students seemed to have made a jump by moving to New York. Rama's response was the creation of teams to work together on graphical software games that would push the edge of the technology and engage their minds in complex mental, fun tasks.

To support the program, he formed a new company, Advanced Systems, Inc. (ASI). The first ASI meeting took place on the 101st floor of the World Trade Center in a large meeting room of the restaurant, Windows on the World. The fabled Manhattan skyline, the confluence of the Hudson River and the East River at the tip of Manhattan and the Statue of Liberty served as a breathtaking backdrop.

Perched on a bar chair in a corner of the glass and steel-rimmed space, Rama announced the creation of four software games—Temple of Atlantis, Ancient Egypt, Scottie Spelling (to assist children with spelling), and College (to help college students manage their time and life). Each game would be graphically rich and developed based on "seeing." Each game would have an alpha and beta team; the alphas were more lighthearted, the betas more technically advanced.

Rama then assigned people to the various games. He meditated for a second on each person and gave them their team—alpha or beta. People rearranged their chairs to sit together with their teams. Rama surveyed the group. "I put you together," he said, "because I want you to learn how to work together and create a real team spirit."

Rama shared a high level vision of the four games. He said he also would work with the team members in dreams, and they should follow their intuition. As each set of deliverables was completed, he would provide feedback and refine the story line.

Howard Green was assigned to the beta Egypt team. "In our first meeting, Rama told us about ancient Egypt and what it was like at that time. The high priests led mystery schools. On public occasions, they would come out through a door in the pyramid's wall and set a tone or vibration. All the acolyte priests would then try to match the tone or frequency and broadcast it out. This image made me think of an inner vibrational tone, like meditating with Rama. It felt like there also could be a real auditory tone that would sound, then the priests and the acolyte priests on the platform would reverberate the sound out to everyone in the courtyards below. From there it would translate to everyone else and out to the world. It was a method of translating and transmuting enlightened energy to the world.

"Visually, I imaged the priests coming out of a doorway in the pyramid into a desert that was very rich, not as arid as it is today. I visualized an oasis. The software was built around displaying images of what that whole area would be like and the path of a student learning or navigating from being a novice to taking spiritual lessons at different levels. It was a true adventure game that simulated all the experiences of the student as he or she went through the mystery school.

"As we worked on our own, I had a vision of the pyramids as painted a shiny gold. At one of the first meetings, we showed Rama an image of a shiny gold pyramid. He said yes, that is exactly right, that is how they looked at that time. They were actually painted a gold color. He also confirmed the lush, oasis-like landscape around the pyramids.

"Each time we met with him, whether at a general student meeting or at someone's house, he would look at the Egypt images we came up with. It was not just about the game. He went into great detail, trying to transmit a feeling. I remember him at one point saying, 'That's it, you've nailed it. This is exactly right.' At a subsequent meeting, he initially liked our team's presentation. Then he said, 'This isn't right. You've tapped into something a little dark that isn't supposed to be here. This is making me a bit nauseous.'

"As he described what he was seeing, you were in the hot seat, waiting to get his reaction. It was one-on-one even if others were in the room."

Others in the room received teachings as well. Said Shelly Sheinberg, former guitarist turned software entrepreneur and a member of Atlantis beta, "I learned a lot by watching how Rama reacted to the work produced by the different teams. I compared my reactions to his and realized that because I liked something, it did not make it 'better' than something I did not like. Rama's ideas made me rethink how I saw things in terms of color and shape. I had to reevaluate my judgment."

"Rama assigned the College group the task of coming up with a calendar that students could use to type in their schedules," Mary Gilbart, a member of the alpha team, related. "One of our team members knew about astrology. So as we worked on a design, she suggested we create round calendars, like an astrological chart. We did that and showed our work to Rama at the next meeting at Windows on the World. He chewed us out, he didn't like anything we had. Even so, we felt higher than a kite. At the end of his critique, he said, 'I think everyone's heart is in the right place. I don't know where their heads are, I think their heads are up their asses. You guys just need to get real calendars.' We all laughed so hard."

Another meeting at Windows on the World was scheduled for the following evening. "Our team spent all the next day redoing our graphics," said Gilbart. "Rama's energy was so much in it that we came up with wonderful artwork in one day, including a beautiful, refined college classroom building and kids with backpacks. We showed our work again and Rama was pleased with the art and the teamwork."

"We had a blast in ASI," said Sheinberg. "It wasn't easy because no one had ever created a game with sophisticated graphics and animation that would run on the standard hardware of the day. It was new turf. Computers were slow, graphics cards were primitive, and the large amount of storage needed to support somewhat high resolution graphics was not generally available. It was an uphill battle, but we had talent in our group. Five out of seven students in our team were experts in computer science and mathematics. Two people wrote code to push the VGA card to the limit. I bought special hardware that would run 3D modeling software so we could design with 16 million colors, and the programmers on the team wrote a series of programs to map and transform the graphics file to get us where we needed to go. It worked!

"All these exercises were not to create great software but to learn how to work in teams. Rama kept reminding us, 'I put you together because I want you to learn how to work together.' Still, our Atlantis beta team was not very collaborative—we fought a lot.

"One day, I complained to him about the guys on my team. He said, here's what you have to do. He came right into my face and started yelling. I didn't feel a thing, nothing came out of him at all, no emotion even though he was yelling. It was an amazing demonstration of how not to give it everything you've got and it helped me tremendously.

"Rama was an educator who taught a multi-dimensional curriculum employing task-based learning," said Sheinberg. "For me, there is not a day that goes by that I don't use the skills I developed in that program. By the end, I'd gained such a rich background on the way things work together that I was super prepared for the future directions in software. The breadth of understanding, the ability to figure out how things work to best advantage, I got in the ASI software game training."

After several months, Rama added more games and more teams to the mix. He added another spelling game and asked the group to create scenes of Tibetan monasteries in the Himalayas. The team's graphic artists were professional and experienced designers. "They did gorgeous artwork," Gilbart recalled. "We'd sit in the large meetings and all go, WOW. Rama remarked at one point, 'You know, that's real reverence when you see that stuff. How come you don't express that when you see me?'"

Rama assigned another task to his students—to double their incomes. After making the announcement, he measured the fear and disbelief in the room. His advice—the money would be necessary to live comfortably in New York. Be bold and ask for it. "If you want more money, make more money."

"I thought this assignment was especially important for women," said Sheinberg. "Rama provided what we needed to break down barriers to success. He provided the impetus for getting higher rates. He said, you need to do this. You are not asking for yourself, you are asking for me as an assignment. He provided that push to advance our careers while providing the additional information and energy we needed to be successful. That was his program for students."

"Rama wanted his students to be exposed to the best of New York," Forge explained. "I booked meetings in The Pierre Hotel across from Central Park, and at Tappan Hill in Tarrytown, north of New York City. We used the nicest auditoriums at SUNY Purchase. In order to make that happen, his students needed to up their income levels. It all worked together. He was into developing his students, knowing full well it would help their overall practice.

"This was a big part of his teachings. Money is energy. That's really important. That was made so clear. Our tantric practice at that time was to understand that energy. We had to bring our energy up to make more money. As past life nuns and monks, we had to overcome our aversion to money. Money is the power line of these times. As a Rama student, you could really measure where you were at based on how much money you were making. As Rama frequently summarized, 'Cash flow equals energy flow.'"

Sheinberg worked at a startup financial services firm earning $40 per hour as a contractor. To fulfill Rama's assignment, she went into her boss's office and asked for $80 per hour. She was highly valued at her workplace and got the raise. Several months later, she interviewed for and got a job at $100 per hour, where she worked as a respected consultant. She, along with other Rama students, continued to increase their earnings throughout their consulting careers.

Power Base

In late 1988, Forge was among the first to see Rama's completed home. "The end result was beautiful but surprising, very different from what I expected," she said.

"The house had a Danish, clean feel. The wood and the lines were very precise. The space was open and bright with lots of pastel colors. There was an entryway, then to the right was the living room.

On the left end of the living room were bedrooms. It was not extremely big. It was one story.

"There was a beautiful, subtle peach colored leather couch in the living room and beautiful pastel Asian carpets. It was decorated in subtle, pastel desert colors—sandy with peach and little touches of red here and there, some pale greens and soft aquas. Everything was wide, airy and open. At the back of the living room, a solid row of windows looked out over the water. It was my favorite room. It had that clean Danish look. Light blond hardwood floor, very rich and lovely; ceilings not super high, but higher than normal. Exquisite Tibetan thangkas hung on the wall. There was also a big black grand piano in the living room. Everything sparkled, it was impeccably clean and unlived-in looking.

"Rama's bedroom also had Danish architecture, light colors everywhere. His bedroom was super simple. There was a plain, wood box-style bed frame attached to the wall with a big shelf headboard of pretty wood. That was in the center of the room. He had put in skylights. The bathrooms were relatively small, which is typical of older houses. They had elegant hardware, everything architected high-end and crisp.

"The kitchen was pretty simple since he hardly did any cooking. It had a uniquely styled, big island in the center, and the island faced an open area that also had a view of the water. That island allowed you to use it like a table, sitting around in tall chairs. Everything was so cleanly designed that nothing stood out.

"It surprised me how he did it. You never know what to expect when you're in an enlightened person's house. It was designed to be undistracting to him. It was very simple, with very little to stand out other than the color scheme. It was very consistent with who he is. Lots of transcendence. Not a lot of ego representation. It looked like no one lived there."

14

1989 - VAJRAYANA BUDDHISM

With the software game teams in place, Rama now introduced another level of complexity—the teaching of relational databases. This was precise knowledge—how to parse and represent data (knowledge) in an efficient structural manner that created more rapid responses to queries for information as well as a more natural approach to store data. The topic was the relational database management system (RDBMS) but the subject was the mind. How to make the mind sharper, more nimble, more sophisticated—the ground state for advanced meditation.

In early 1989, five major vendors—IBM's DB2, Oracle, Ingres, Informix and Sybase—competed in the RDBMS space, each with their own representations and approach to accessing and managing VLDBs (very large databases). These databases were used by the major corporations and banks based all over New York City.

At the first meeting of the New Year, held in the large theater of the Performing Arts Center at SUNY Purchase, Rama asked Sanford Knaff to come to the front of the room. He announced that Knaff would be offering a course in DB2 and asked him to organize it. Standing before the group, Knaff agreed.

"I put together a small team," said Knaff, "and we worked to put together a presentation that ran for three nights in a row. We worked hard to pull together our materials, and it went well. At the end of the third evening, Rama came into the classroom. He put us in the front row and praised us. We all felt really high, and I felt especially happy. Lots of students came up to me and thanked me for the course.

"One week later, we met with Rama in one of the beautiful small auditoriums in Carnegie Hall. Rama spent the first half of the meeting talking about how people become egotistical and he cited me in particular. He lambasted me. I was the worst person on earth. I had been so high during the week and now I felt ashamed.

I could feel all my admirers from the week before starting to look at me in horror. During the break, Rama came up to me, winked and said, 'That's my shortcut to enlightenment—public embarrassment.' I thought, 'My God, he was not mad at me at all.' That was the start of my real education."

Also presenting during the first DB2 course was Patti Kloor. "Every single night after work for a week prior to teaching the class, we'd stay up until 2 a.m. putting workbooks together, making it fun. During the three-day class, the teaching really did go well. At the end, Rama had all the teachers sit in the front row and he asked us what was the experience, what did we learn? I said that whenever you have to teach, you end up learning more. While we sat there, I realized that was why he was doing it. As we tried to teach, we ended up absorbing more knowledge and that was the whole point. My teaching topic was modeling relational databases. I would dream about data modeling and saw how the mind and the model are networked. The teaching experience was so charged—I would never have gotten there on my own.

"I did well at work, I knew things about data modeling that I never learned from a book. After teaching the ASI class, I joined a team of people at my job with way more technical experience than I had, and I taught the whole team how to data model. We came up with some innovative ideas. Later, one of the guys from IBM audited our data model. He confirmed that everything we did was right. In fact, some of our design decisions were incorporated into the next version of DB2."

Over the next few months, each of the major databases was taught several times by different people in different ways. An all-girl group taught Oracle. An all-guy group taught Ingres. For the second Ingres class, Gilbart recalled, "The guys came in one by one. They were all in drag. They all wore low cut women's evening gowns with body suit camisoles up to their chests. We became hysterical with laughter, and I learned a lot about Ingres.

"In the second DB2 class, one guy wanted to let you know he was an expert in DB2 and one gal seemed terrified to speak. But I saw both of them transform when they gave their talks. He turned into a nice, humble person. She got courage and confidence. There was a magical amount of transformative energy. As I sat there I observed beautiful examples of what Rama's energy did to people in the context of teaching about technology—whatever ailed them got fixed."

Under Rama's guidance, classes expanded to programming languages and mathematics. It was mind training, emulating the discipline of Tibetan monastic training. It was career training, introducing the hottest technologies in the most concise and practical manner. The classes provided an opening, an introduction and a core set of understandings, a mental challenge and a career path, a social gathering and a chance for fun and laughter, a time to sit in Rama's energy field in the most pure and advantageous way. It was understood that people interested in a particular technology or skill would then go out on their own and read more books and/or get vendor certifications in that skill set.

The classes created a fertile ground for transformation in his students' awareness. And that was Rama's strategy—edging his students towards a place where the level of teaching complexity could increase.

Vajradharma Initiation

During the student meeting of January 23, 1989, Rama advised the students that the next evening would be unique. He asked everyone to meditate perfectly in the morning and to perform some aerobic exercise. He asked everyone to wear their best clothes to the meeting and to arrive on time. He asked the women not to wear makeup on their foreheads. He said he would be giving a life-changing empowerment. I flew from L.A. to attend.

On Saturday, January 24, the large Tarrytown Marriott Ballroom was transformed. Hundreds of balloons and pastel roses lined the stage. For the first time, a collection of 20 Tibetan thangkas encircled the room on walls and easels. The room throbbed with the ground zero, effulgent, cell-stirring energy that Rama sent into the hall prior to a meeting. On this night, we did not have to wait long. Rama took his seat on the raised stage soon after the meeting start time of 8 p.m.

He explained that, although it was early in the incarnation to be doing so, he had decided to initiate us as American Buddhist monks. A monk, as he defined it, was not related to celibacy. A monk was a seeker of enlightenment. Tonight all of the Buddhas and bodhisattvas that came before us welcomed us into the order. Now we were all in a thangka with Rama in the middle. That was all he said before beginning the empowerment. For further explanation, he quipped with a Yiddish accent, "Better not to know."

The initiation began. He explained that he would call people up in groups, according to age, with the youngest first, and each group should form a single file line in the center aisle. When we stood in front of him, he would place his thumb on our third eye and meditate for a few moments. While standing there, we should try to clear our minds. He added that if we couldn't stop our thoughts, even if it was the grossest thought in the world, he would understand. He said he would give us a taste of samadhi. When he finished, he would hand each of us a rose. We should then place the rose on our chair and leave the room.

He called out "18 years and younger." Several people came to the center of the room and got in a line.

Since I was older than most of the students by at least one decade, I watched respectfully as each student came up to him. But for me, the initiation had already happened.

As soon as I heard Rama's words, that I was about to be initiated as an American Buddhist monk, something happened. I became an American Buddhist monk. I felt the sealing of holes in my being. I felt past and future lifetimes condensing, converging and becoming more and more compact into this moment. The "me" observing my fellow students walk up to Rama one at a time was an American Buddhist monk and I knew, to my extreme relief and gratitude, that it was an enduring benediction.

As the students walked up to Rama, I also kept an eye on the thangkas—including Avalokiteshvara, White Tara, Padmasambhava, Padmasambhava's primary disciple Yeshe Tsogyal, Milarepa and his teacher Marpa. As time passed and the ceremony deepened, I felt I was at a Tibetan theme park, where the paintings come alive and watch as you go by. The living presence of these great teachers filled the room, honoring the initiation and the teacher. My chair resided in a monastic hall where initiations of the disciples were witnessed and celebrated by what Rama called "the company of the enlightened." They were partying. It was an initiation jam!

When Vera Anderson-Smith received her initiation, she said, "He touched my third eye. I went somewhere else, out of my body. It was dark, cool, beautiful, peaceful, silent. He spoke to me from far away. It shocked me and I felt myself coming back to consciousness. I hadn't felt him at all. He was compassionate but laughing. 'How sad, how depressed you are,' he said. 'Don't be. Be happy, your life has just begun.' During the break, I could feel myself spinning."

When it was Forge's turn to receive the empowerment, Rama said in a loud voice, "AH YES, it's Kathleen. She was Genghis Khan in her previous life." They both laughed.

"My experience was so strong that Rama had to call a security guy to escort me out of the room, as I almost collapsed to the floor when Rama touched my third eye," said Steve Diehl. "I was completely out of my body and out of 'who I believed myself to be.' So much so that I was holding onto a pillar (after being escorted outside the room) to try to keep from, what seemed to me, literally floating away."

"Age 40 to 43." That was my group. I stood up and got in line in the center of the ballroom.

When I stood before Rama, I kept my eyes open as he touched my third eye. The feeling was cool, liquid and still. And then he handed me a rose.

Soon the ceremony was over and we took a break. Afterwards, when all the American Buddhist monks were seated back in the room, Rama explained that there are many types of initiations. Each one has a certain power. A teacher gives them to a student at a very specific time—sometimes because the student has earned it, sometimes because the student needs it, sometimes both. An initiation leaves an indelible mark on the student's multi-life being.

On this night, Rama explained, he gave us two initiations: Vajra and Dharma. The Vajra initiation was the initiation of power. It bestowed the ability to defeat any opponent and to break through the ultimate opponent, which is thought. We were given the power to break through conditioning and past life tendencies, which was particularly important for women, who had to overcome centuries of repression and misogyny.

He said he had cut our karmic ties for us because otherwise we would not do it for years and we could not afford the time.

The second empowerment was Dharma: the power to teach. It endowed the capacity and the gift of teaching about the dharma and meditation. He advised us that we were not ready to begin teaching yet, but when we did, we would have the support of all those who had taught before us. Now we carried the imprint of this initiation, and our lives should reflect and serve as examples of the holy dharma.

Finally, he said that we were all American Buddhist monks and if we traveled to any monastery in the world, we would be able to state that and be welcomed. When he dies, it will be our duty to carry on the teachings of the American Buddhist Society. While he is alive, we should talk about meditation to anyone who genuinely asks.

Rama said we students had no idea what just happened to us and wouldn't for a long time. It was something that would unfold and express itself as life presented the necessary circumstances. Suddenly we would simply find ourselves doing things we never could do before. Now we would be able to conquer things that held us up in the past.

He added that while we as a group were not necessarily ready to receive these advanced initiations, he couldn't wait any longer; he wanted to be assured that the line of initiated Buddhists would continue. When we needed it, when it was the dharma, we would be able to access the power of this initiation.

With the Vajradharma initiation, Rama established a new teaching direction. He called it "cycling" his past lives. This was his lineage, Vajrayana Tantric Buddhism, and the vajra master performing the initiation—Rama—had reached a different stage as a Buddhist. This initiation was the beginning—over the next nine years, the complex mandala of Vajrayana (Tibetan) Buddhism would be translated into a new way for the West.

Several weeks later, at the end of February, as I listened to the East Coast students describe their breakthroughs and felt the high energy in the technical classes, I found myself doing something I could never do before. I left public relations. I left Hollywood and moved to New York to begin my career in technology. On February 28, when I arrived late for my first New York student meeting as a Westchester resident, Rama saw me come in the auditorium door at the back of the hall. He paused and looked at me across the sea of people in the room. "Whenever you've been successful at one profession," he said, "you'll be successful in another."

March, 1989—Rama spoke about "intentions" and asked the students to write down their intention to develop their careers or business. This was to be like a contract that was placed on the meditation table. Davide Khalen recalled writing a $1 million dollar check as a gift to Rama and putting it on his small table, thinking he had to be nuts to believe he could ever do such a thing. But in six years' time, after the sale of his financial trading system for several million dollars, he was able to do just that.

The Lineage

The March 31 evening meeting at the Marriott White Plains ballroom drew to a close. The software game teams had demonstrated their latest graphic creations. During the group meditation, golden light barreled through the hall. Before leaving for the night for their respective houses and apartments across the tri-state area, Rama asked the students to form a circle around the room. He went around the circle, briefly touching each person in the center of the forehead, saying "yes" or "no." He did not explain why he was doing this. He then asked those people (approximately 45 out of 300) who received a "yes" to remain in the room and move to the front of the hall after the others had gone.

As she looked at the occupants of the first few rows of seats, said Corin Robertson, it seemed like the people there were not those with whom Rama had spent a lot of time in this incarnation. "Most of us thought we were the dregs of the group," she said. Rama spoke in a quiet tone about the Rae Chorze Fwaz lineage, that he was spinning the lineage to the West in this lifetime. He said that the origins of the lineage could be traced back to Tibet, Japan, China, India and ancient Egypt to the place where the lineage had first been founded—Atlantis. He said that the people remaining in the room had all been teaching on his behalf in other lifetimes. He emphasized that we were teachers.

"He laid out how it was all going to happen. He talked about bringing in the new, young students. We had all done it before. He said there was a virtual teaching thangka and we were part of that thangka. 'There is a painting and you are in it. You are my thangka.'

"I think most of us were somewhat stunned. I almost felt a heavy responsibility come over me that I was not prepared for. Because I did not think I would be in the thangka. It was for real. You could feel the ancient agreements in the room. He had told me this individually about one year earlier, but I did not take it to heart. I did not believe it. It was only sitting in that room that I believed it."

"He lifted everyone's energy and purified it," said James Firgy, who was also in the room. "He had to lift everyone high. He told us, 'You are going to teach now, and this is the most amazing energy I can give you.'"

For me, the meeting put everything into context. I realized that the software and games, the classes, the moves, the empowerments, running the technical businesses—all were about virtual monastic cooperation.

We had a group task as well as individual goals. To accomplish the group task—to revive and maintain an ancient lineage—we had to honor each other, Rama, and his body of teachings. This is the core of Buddhism, the Three Jewels—the teacher, the teachings and the sangha (the community).

I sensed that everything Rama had done so far was providing his students with the multi-dimensional arts and skills they would need to keep the lineage going long after he was gone.

Within two years of this meeting at the White Plains Marriott, Rama opened the lineage teaching to any of his enrolled students who were inspired to teach others and soon, a new group of "wild-eyed seekers" joined the virtual thangka.

15

GAZING FORWARD

This chapter summarizes Rama's life and key teachings for the remainder of 1989 through 1998, when he dropped the physical teaching body. Details of these years—Book Two of Rama's biography—are, at the time of this writing, a gleam in the biographer's eye.

Rama picked what he taught his students very carefully. It is fascinating how accurately; he did a very thorough job. He multi-tasked in many dimensions as he restated a number of the great traditions.

In 1989, many elements of his teaching came together. By formulating a way to teach technology, asking the people who were advanced in a particular discipline to pull together curricula that opened new possibilities for others and became self-generating, the Advanced Systems model flourished. The next five years focused on instruction in a vast range of emerging technologies as well as business skills such as sales and marketing. This culminated in the forming of student businesses under the banner of Infinity Plus Consulting, Inc.

At the same time, Rama took his students through refinement school at many levels—venues, dress, travel, film, literature, and of course, meditation practice. His teaching that money is energy and critical to success in the American Buddhist monk world built confidence and set the students up for greater adventures in the years to come.

Towards the end of 1989, as Rama looked at iterations of the software games, he pulled the plug on many of the games. He said he knew what his students really wanted—to become successful in business. The groups were re-formed and by the summer of 1990, teams that had been working, for example, on calendars for college students became engaged in projects such as encryption software, reusable architectures for complex business computer networks or technologically advanced scheduling systems.

During 1989 and 1990, Rama recorded the *Tantric Buddhism* talk series of 27 key tenets of American Tantric Buddhism.

Also in 1990, Rama announced, "I'm going to do something that will cause the biggest transition of your whole lives. I'm going to raise the tuition." The fee had been $600 per month and went up to $1,000 per month. It caused everyone to take their career to another level. The tuition, while remaining affordable, continued to rise over the next eight years as Rama raised the bar.

In the early nineties, Rama cut back on his public teaching activities. Instead he prepared a precise new set of public teaching materials—a CD talk set called *The Enlightenment Cycle*,[52] a one hour video titled *Tantric Buddhism with Rama*[53] as well as special Zazen meditation music—*Enlightenment*[54] and *Canyons of Light*[55]—and he encouraged his students to teach and to continue to look for the past life souls he was meant to encounter and help. Students formed teams and established teaching bases around the country, where they worked their careers by day and offered meditation classes several times a week by night. As handouts, they gave out Rama's new teaching materials. Their target audience was young people age 18 to 29. After teaching the classes, Rama's students would invite those who were interested to attend a lecture by Rama on the East or West Coast.

Starting in 1992, as the new students came to meet with Rama in elegant settings—The Four Seasons in Beverly Hills on the West Coast, The Pierre in New York on the East—they experienced the same mind-bending experiences as the first wave of students. Rama designated the original enrolled students as "ST1" and the new students who enrolled as "ST2." Star Trek 1 and Star Trek 2.

Leah Morrell described her guests' reaction to first meeting Rama. "Rama put out such beautiful light for the new kids and he would

---

52 Lenz, Frederick (Rama). *The Enlightenment Cycle*. CD talk set.
    www.ramameditationsociety.org/enlightenment-cycle-talkset
53 Lenz, Frederick (Rama). *Tantric Buddhism with Rama*. DVD.
    www.ramameditationsociety.org/tantric-buddhism-rama
54 Zazen. *Enlightenment*. CD.
    www.ramatalks.com/meditation-music/zazen.html
55 Zazen. *Canyons of Light*. CD.
    www.ramatalks.com/meditation-music/zazen.html

talk to them like someone who was very with it, but speaking about all those amazing things. It was the best ever. It was the highest level I had ever seen. Now you're bringing other people in, the highest of all highs.

"I had kids in jeans and T-shirts from Berkeley and they were so excited about dressing up in beautiful formal wear. The first time I took a group of them hiking and I told them about it and what it meant to see an enlightened teacher, they were all up for it. It was so much fun sprucing up the students. Girls in gowns and boys in tuxes. Black tie attire. We drove down together to Beverly Hills from the San Francisco Bay Area.

"At the first meeting, Rama came out wearing black leather. They were just blown away. The break came and he met the kids and shook their hands. They were sitting there with their mouths gaping open. One of my guests said, 'It feels like I took ten hits of acid.' The next time, we drove down south again for a four-night seminar at the Westin in Beverly Hills. We were all in the elevator, glowing. This man walks in and he looks at all of us all dressed up and he said, 'You must be going to a great event.' Javier goes, 'Yah, God's in town and you're invited.'

"Rama used to let us bring all the students up to meet him. He would sit there and they would introduce themselves. Rama would say something to each one. Then, if they were interested, they got to apply to be a student. They had to get professional photos taken for their applications. Rama met with them on the West Coast as students until June of '93, then most of them started heading to New York."

The new students went directly into computer science and software. Rama met with them for talks, hikes in Ward Pound Ridge in northern Westchester County, for Rave parties at hip gathering spots in Manhattan, for career success seminars. For several years, he met with them separately from the older students who by then had fanned out across the country.

Concurrent to teaching the new students, he worked more closely with the senior students on developing an array of technical products. Many products used artificial intelligence—expert systems, neural networks, genetic algorithms and various combinations thereof. Rama enjoyed applying neural nets and expert systems to commercial problems and encouraged his students to take these complex technologies and make them available to the corporate world or to governments and the military. He worked with teams on educational software. He was fascinated by networking and how to build computer networks correctly. He worked closely with a group of students who developed a networking product.

Several students developed a new way of finding hidden patterns in large amounts of data, a.k.a. "data mining." Still other students worked on products for medical forecasting and unbreakable encryption. Each student team would interact with Rama to perfect or kaizen their offerings. As with every think tank entrepreneurial venture, not all of the businesses succeeded. But some of them did and were purchased by large software companies for seven figure amounts.

Behind all the activity: increasingly powerful stillness, emanations of pure white light, a ground zero connection to pulsating being and a consistent, ineffable love.

In the beginning of 1992, Rama initiated all his senior students into the American Buddhist Society. At the end of 1992, the students were initiated into the Order of the Rae Chorze Fwaz School of Tantric Buddhism.

The first edition of *Surfing the Himalayas* was published in 1993. Rama stated that it contained all the teachings he wanted everyone in the world to know. In 1994, the book was circulated to commercial book agents and was picked up immediately. It was published by St. Martin's Press in 1995 and hit best-seller lists across the country. The sequel, *Snowboarding to Nirvana*, also published by St. Martin's, came out in 1996.

Rama discovered technical scuba diving in the early 90s. He loved the beauty and stillness of the sea and eventually took the PADI training to become a divemaster. He enjoyed diving to depths of 300 feet or more and encouraged his students to take up diving and get their first PADI diving certification.

Learning from new locations expanded. Rama began offering special trips to Europe and Australasia. Students traveled in small groups with Rama to Zermatt, Munich, Paris, London, Amsterdam and Rome. Other travel destinations included Fiji, Hawaii and Bali. Scuba diving trips were held at five-star hotels in the Cayman Islands, Nevis, St. Bart's and other Caribbean destinations. Why five-star? The locations and the refinement supported light.

In Bermuda, in September, 1997, Rama gave all students who had read a list of over 30 traditional Buddhist texts and answered a series of written questions (which he read and graded) a teaching empowerment. At this point, after many ups and downs in their progress, many students were towards the bottom of the undulating bell curve of consciousness—meaning not meditating well and not all that happy. Also, Rama told the students, "You are riding my energy." That meant people were relying on Rama to take them up to high states and not doing the work themselves.

After the Bermuda teaching empowerment, Rama said that the group was now set up to teach, and they could say that Rama was their teacher, but they were not to say they were teaching on his behalf. They did not represent him.

Starting in 1997, instead of regular meetings, Rama only saw his students quarterly, on "Power Trips." These outrageous trips to five-star hotels in the Caribbean brought ST1s and ST2s together. Everyone played on their own all day and met with Rama at night for evenings of lectures, dance, food and drink. Rama stuffed everyone's awareness with luminosity and stillness as each person dropped their guard, had fun and relaxed. If Rama saw there was a need to spend more time with a student, he did. But for the most part, his students were not drawing that level of interaction. And he knew his time was limited.

Over three nights in December, 1997, Rama gave the Kalachakra empowerment to all his current and former students. "The Kalachakra empowerment causes a complete break with your karma," he said. "How else could enlightenment be possible?" When asked by someone in the audience why he didn't do it sooner, Rama replied, "Because I couldn't."

During 1997 and 1998, Rama worked with his attorney, Norman Oberstein, his accountant, Norm Marcus, and an estate planning attorney to set up the Frederick P. Lenz Foundation for American Buddhism. (As of this writing, the Lenz Foundation[56] has made grants totaling close to $6,000,000 to over 80 U.S.-based non-profit Buddhist organizations.)

Beginning in January, 1998, Rama meticulously and precisely wrapped down his life as a teacher. Most students were completely unaware of his intent. He held three student meetings during 1998. In the first, he spoke at length against committing suicide. Don't do it. He said that whatever state of mind you are in at the moment of death will carry over into your next life.

---

56 www.FrederickLenzFoundation.org

In the next meeting, he said that everyone in the room (about 500 people consisting of ST1s and ST2s) was now entering the Advanced Program. He said we would soon be undergoing a "Zen test of loyalty."

In the final meeting, he held a golf contest where people dressed in their best golf attire (he had recommended golf as a fine sport to learn) participated in a golf clothing contest. The winners received a set of Buddhist books. He shared his thoughts on the key to successful relationships and marriages. On an individual basis, he cleaned up every open issue. He asked an assistant to phone every student and provide final guidance and feedback.

During the last month of his life, Rama and his companion for this period, Savitri Lacey, spoke at length about his decision to leave the physical body. Rama was a non-returner. He had merged with nirvana in his early thirties. After that, everything he did was a courtesy, done out of love and service. He was a teacher to the core of his being. He could have chosen any exit he wanted.

"Rama saw his choice of when and how to drop the physical body as a protest against how enlightenment is treated in America," said Lacey. "He said his action would be like that of the Vietnamese monk, Thich Quang Duc, who self-immolated in 1963 to protest the South Vietnamese government's persecution of Buddhists." (The photograph of the monk's peaceful countenance and erect posture as flames engulfed him had been flashed all over the world and graced the cover of *Time Magazine*.) Lacey said she tried to talk Rama out of it, but he was firm in his decision and seeing.

His physical pain level had reached new heights because of negative, one-sided media coverage that started in 1987 but became increasingly twisted. In 1998, there was no social media where different views could be shared. The concept of organized haters was not well known.

As the years of depraved media outbursts continued, Rama stated he had been "crucified in the media." For a being of compassion, to know that other people, strangers, would hate him based on viewing or reading falsehoods was doubly problematic—such people would earn bad karma because they were hating innocence. They were hating their own essence, light.

"I am not angry at the former students who lied about me to the media," Rama said in his final gathering. "They just fell into very low states of mind. But they went too far, and now I can't help them."

Rama had spent one-third of 1997 in bed battling various illnesses. His students were not making the jumps in awareness that they had done at the start of the decade. They were not going through the inner doorways he held open for them. He was up against human nature—no more change! Many students were in push-back mode. He no longer had the physical strength to flip the situation around, as he had done so many times before.

What radical thing could he do to cause the students to finally wake up and change? With his exit, Rama multi-tasked.

The day before Rama left us in the physical, I visited North Tarrytown's Rockefeller Park with my dogs. After completing the loop around Swan Lake, I perched on a large, flat rock to enjoy the open fields and early spring greenery. As I sat in stillness, I felt a turning in the center of my chest, as if a knob were being adjusted. Because of the love that accompanied this sensation, I knew it was Rama and that my entire incarnational pattern and sequencing had just changed forever.

Rama's mahasamadhi on April 12 produced a different effect on all who knew him. Forge described it as like a nuclear, ground zero explosion. "It was the most amazing moment in time when I learned about it. He went to a new level of being—the nirvana, infinite, void part of his being, the void side of Rama. It was a shock but it was so planned. He could have exited in so many different ways. He was a teacher; he was still teaching."

Another response:

> When I found out he was gone
> what I thought about was his heart,
> how he loved with a palpable intensity,
> the way he smiled at us at the end
> of a shattering night of silent fireworks.
>
> I also thought of his love of oblivion,
> the way his eyes would sink into the sky
> and you could just see the depths,
> the spaces, the spheres, the vast windy heights
> that drenched his skin with ecstasy.
>
> We all basked in the reflected radiance
> of his presence, the bright forms of oblivion

that swirled around his body,
the gleaming trails of sweet stardust
that fed our lives and our hunger.

Now he's gone: there are so many questions
that I was too timid or vain to ask
and so many thoughts to keep at bay,
dark insects trying to swarm into the spaces
that he cleared out inside me.

It took some time for me to understand
but now I know that despite my fears
nothing can possibly undo or even damage
the hidden passageways he already built
with sturdy beams of light.

Now I see how he grabbed hold of
a lucent edge of my mind,
then bounded laughing into the sky,
still holding me fiercely, danced on stars,
stretched me to the quivering edge

Then he leaped off,
smiling at us at the end
of a shattering night of silent fireworks.

> Michael Chang
> New York City, April 1998 [57]

---

57 Chang, Michael. "Grappling With His Departure"
    www.RamaTribute.org > Gratitude

OTHER NOTES

Zazen Music

The Zazen story continues in 1986, after Rama asked the band to take a break and work on their own music.

1986

> *I should start a rock 'n roll band and play at exclusive clubs throughout the lokas. That wouldn't be a bad thing to do, make music. The audiences would never know why when they listened to the music they were going out of time.*

> - Rama

After their six month hiatus in late 1985, during which Lievano produced a solo album, *One Mind*, the three musicians—Andy West, Steve Kaplan and Joaquin Lievano—rejoined forces. In early January, they played a public concert at the L.A. Convention Center. "Rama was looking to see what we would come up with," said Lievano. "We had each changed. We made it a point to try to work together beyond our pettiness for the sake of the music and to do the best possible job we could for our teacher."

"I realized that working with Rama altered the way I thought about playing, almost like starting over. I had a way that worked for me, and I felt that wouldn't work for Rama. I had to take a new approach and be open to his suggestions. I had to restart from point A over and over again."

After the January concert, Rama encouraged the musicians to write new compositions that would be played at the public Rama Seminars. They were rechristened by Rama with the band name of Zazen. Over the next six months, working out of Kaplan's house in the Hollywood Hills, they composed 26 songs.

In early summer of 1986, they performed *Samsara*—two albums worth of the music they had been writing (and that Rama had been dancing to) since the beginning. "He came up to me at one of the seminars prior to the live recording of *Samsara*, said Lievano. "He said, 'I've been waiting for you to be ready.' He grabbed my shoulder and a surge of energy went through my body. 'You're finally ready, now it's time.' We'd been working with him, sharing the music as it evolved via cassette recordings that he would listen to and comment on. Now he was ready to get *Samsara* out of the way so we could go on to new things."

For the next project, Rama asked the band to do an album based on his past lives in Japan. "He gave us the album title *Samurai*," said Lievano. "When we first met with him, he asked us for the names of the songs. We had working titles that didn't mean anything. There was a song called, 'What? You Have Furniture?' He told us, obviously you need help with the titles!

"Rama worked with us on the song titles and described what he wanted each song to represent. To help us, as we worked on *Samurai*, he took us out to the chic hangouts in L.A. He loved being around where successful people were. At the same time he wanted to give us a sense of places where people like that would go. We went to expensive restaurants where he was able to take our awareness to really high levels. As working musicians, we never would have gone to most of those places, we would have rejected it. It was a great education.

"We talked a lot about the most popular pop artists of the day including Madonna and Michael Jackson. The context was that the music business can be harsh. He mentioned that Michael Jackson was a very sensitive guy and would not be living long. Madonna was tough and did not have any problem with fame. He said that being in the limelight and stardom was really not all it's cracked up to be. It was a warning, he was trying to tell us that that was really not what we were going for, we were just going for the music.

"One evening, during one of these outings, Rama said to us, 'I want you to make a commitment because this is going to go on for a long time.' He said it would be like nothing we had experienced before. We had to be open to a new experience in the way we thought about music and wrote music. Because he was going to start to get a little bit more involved. There would be things we would feel pulled to do and we could choose to go that way or go with him. He asked, are you ready to make that commitment? I wasn't sure if I was ready for that because I had lots of dreams and goals I wanted to achieve. I wasn't sure if I could make a commitment, but I said yes, I was ready to do it."

"Rama was totally jazzed about what we came up with for *Samurai*," Lievano said. "He got more and more excited with what we did. Starting with *Samurai*, we came out with a new album every two months. In 1986, we completed *Samsara*, *Samurai* and *Urban Destruction*. We were still working at day jobs and not living together. Andy had just started to go to computer school. Finding the time to create and rehearse was tough but we managed to do it.

"Rama told us not to worry about the creative process. He said, 'I'm going to work with you in the dream plane. Just keep writing, I'll be right there with you.'"

The band continued their work in Kaplan's home in an upstairs room with some recording equipment, composing the music that was performed live at the seminars. They often stayed up for 24 hours at a stretch but didn't get tired. Rama would let the band know if things didn't go right and the trio would go back to the drawing board.

"He liked the live music because he felt he could do his magic as it was going down on the tape. After the live performance, we went into the studio to mix the music. Rama made it clear that during the live performance, he placed enlightened energy in between the notes. That energy would then be imparted to anyone listening to the music."

As a gesture and teaching tool, Rama invited the Zazen band members to travel with him to places of power such as Santa Fe or the Grand Canyon.

"The music was so challenging and what he wanted us to do with it was such a leap for us that we really needed to go to new places and get away from everything," Lievano explained. "Every time we went on a trip with him it was mind blowing. These were working trips. We'd queue up to a certain section of a song and Rama would say, 'Right here. You could do a different sound.' We would go in detail through every line of the music with Rama making suggestions. Being in that aura all day long was life changing. When we got home, we'd have all this immense energy and the insight to do something with it. The ideas came much more readily after a trip."

In every album, Rama asked the band to make music that would take the listener to another world, a beautiful world. On *Urban Destruction*, which tapped into the mind-set of Los Angeles, Rama's favorite piece was "LA Digital Mindscapes." It was close to 30 minutes of jazz and rock music. Rama told the band that he wanted to do it someday with an orchestra because he felt the music was that good.

"It was hard," said Lievano, "but what made it easier for us was that Rama loved music and so did we. It was our lives, it was what we did."

1987

The German band, Tangerine Dream, toured the U.S. in early 1987. Tangerine Dream created vibrant and varied electronic music that Rama had used for years in group meditations, prior to the forming of Zazen. Rama and the Zazen trio bought third row seats and saw Tangerine Dream perform live at Irvine Meadows in Orange County, California. They sat together and watched closely. When the concert ended, Rama and the three musicians remained in their seats. "What those guys just did is similar to what I want you to do, but I want you to take it much further," Rama said. "Tangerine Dream created a whole new world, like Jimi Hendrix, something never heard before in music. Just complete innovation. I want every album we do to be a complete new innovation and open up a new world for people."

Lievano recalled that he again said, in order to do that, "We needed to really clean up our lives, clean up the holes in our beings, cut the lines to people who drain us, start new relationships and end old ones. Every time he had a talk with us like that, I would go home and clean my inner and outer house, I would go through my being and look for ways to close up the openings and start fresh. I did that over and over again."

Rama and Zazen were on fire. They came out with a new album every three months during 1987. The first was *Light Saber*, music inspired by Tolkien's *Lord of the Rings* trilogy. Rama had assigned the books as student reading, and as the songs were produced, they were played for all the students. Rama often danced to the musical themes of Middle Earth—evoking elves and hobbits and dwarves.

After *Light Saber*, Rama told the band, "The next one is an important one. It will be your birthday gift to me. I want you to write an album about me." He gave them the song titles.

"He asked if we were familiar with the Zen paintings, 'Searching for the Ox' or '10 Bulls,'" said Lievano. "I was not. So Rama suggested we read about it. He said it was one of the ways that you represent the enlightenment process, through a cycle of drawings or paintings."

The *Zen Master* album was divided into three sections, "The Celestial Suite," "The Desert Suite," and the third section called "Searching for the Ox." He asked the band to make it as beautiful as they could, and that is what they did.

"We worked together at Steve's house, and as the music evolved, it became more and more lush and beautiful. We knew that he was working with us inwardly. He knew if things were going right and he had a lot of faith in us. We could tell when we logged onto something truthful and high. We'd all been playing live in the seminars with Rama for over a year, and we knew the high, clear mind that we could log into—Rama's awareness.

"Of course, it wasn't always like that. Sometimes we stayed up without sleep for too long. Once, we showed up after a seminar started, looking disheveled having been up for days. We handed him an audio cassette. He put it in his tape player, played it and flung it across the stage. It was a hard balance, and he expected us to figure it out. Because if you stay up too many nights you start to lose it, you have no perspective."

The first time Rama heard *Zen Master* was at a live performance held at a public seminar on February 9, Rama's birthday. After the performance, said Lievano, Rama was ecstatic. "He really loved *Zen Master*. All I remember him telling us is that we did well, we did it right. Those words were accompanied by a majestic inner empowerment.

"He told us he was really pleased with the fact that every album seemed to be getting better and better."

The next album, *Occult Dancer* was about the worlds that Rama goes into in his dancing. It has the energy of the desert, a musical rendering of the changing energies of the desert at different times of day—Sunrise, Noon, Sunset, Midnight, and 4 AM. Rama wanted it to be a very deep album that captured the mystery and magic of the desert. At his direction, the music starts out simply. With each track, the complexity increases.

Said Lievano, "*Occult Dancer* was recorded live. Side two had a technical problem with buzz. We booked the studio to fix it and set up the studio to form a circle around him. He sat in the center and meditated while we played.

"By contrast, he wanted *Mandala of Light* to be more meditative and New Age, more for the masses. It was lighter and melodic but still, from our viewpoint, a breakthrough in melody and arrangements. We cut *Mandala of Light* in the studio. He again sat in the middle of the band and meditated as we recorded it. We did it in just one take from beginning to end. We were well rehearsed.

"Over the next years from *Samsara* to *Samurai*, he would give basic instructions and we would go for it. With each album he became more and more involved. He was waiting for us to get to a certain level of awareness so we could really work together."

In all of the music, whether recorded live or in a studio, Rama said that he placed enlightened energy in between the notes.

1988

> *I am mainly in the music. I show Zazen my mind, and from it they structure the music. Then I patch it to the planes of light. The further you push into the music, the closer you'll get to my mind.* - Rama

After taking a break in the second half of 1987 (Rama's "boot camp" period), the band returned to their multi-album release schedule in 1988. They first created *Atlantis Rising*, working out of a studio with Rama. Elements of the next album, *Mystery School*, began during the creation of *Atlantis Rising*.

With the album *Mystery School*, Rama first became fully engaged in the writing, recording and producing of Zazen music. He revealed his idea for a new album during the recording of *Atlantis Rising*. He planted the seed for the feeling he wanted by talking of new music that would be about contrasts. Rama showed the band what he meant by playing his ideas on the studio piano between takes of *Atlantis*. His prowess on the keyboard shocked the musicians as he first played simple melodies that were soft and childlike, and then radically changed the mood by playing crashing, colliding chords and rhythms. He spoke of multiple worlds, one hidden behind another.

"Together," said Lievano, "the band would reach into these worlds, starting with slow, sweet melodies that would then be 'sliced' through by a pyramidal shaft, an obelisk of energy coming from another world, overpowering with its intensity. The music was to reflect the power and beauty of the mystery schools of ancient Egypt."

Rama liked *Atlantis Rising* and *Mystery School* so much that he released them on CD as well as tape. *Mystery School* was the first album in which he played an active role in the production.

Rama explained that midway through each song he would introduce a transition from something simple - that the three Zazen musicians were comfortable with - into something much more complex that would challenge them.

He then said that midway in each incarnation his teaching would go through a similar transition, and that this was being reflected in his music.

Zazen next began work on *Retrograde Planet*, a musical sonic tour of the solar system, one song for each of the nine planets. Rama shared an early version of the album for the students in Palo Alto, but the actual tape was not released for over a year.

Initially Rama talked to the band about the significance of the planets and their symbolism but after the first version of the album was completed, he focused completely on the music itself and the direction he wanted it to evolve. The second version fused long themes with intricate mood and tempo changes. Ultimately, six versions of the album were completed before it was released.

Also in the summer of 1988, Rama began work with Zazen on *Tantra*. The project began as a separate album called *India*. Then Rama decided he wanted to make it in four parts so Zazen went back to the beginning. It took seven months and was finished in the spring of 1989. In order to write *Tantra*, Zazen journeyed with Rama to the desert, to Santa Fe, to Hawaii, to Vermont.

The inspiration was pulled from past lives in India, China, Tibet and the current life in America. At the power places they visited, the Zazen band members meditated and gathered together bits and pieces of songs, just enough material for approximately one minute sections. New melodies were then written and these sections were added as if coming from a completely different world. These new parts "sliced" into the original melodies with a different, unrelated theme but still somehow remained cohesive with the first melodies. Once the musicians had done this, a third, wholly new underlying section was added. Finally, Rama added a fourth section with a fugal motif of intertwining themes being played simultaneously. This was to be a combination of the first melody, the melody from the second section and the third underlying section.

"This is the way in which Rama built the masterpiece he carried in his mind," said Lievano, "putting the band through their paces to get the music out. For him, music was a refuge. He said there was nothing more beautiful to him than the music.

"When we were working on *Tantra*, said Lievano, "he told us that he wanted us to listen to Beethoven's string quartets. Rama loved Beethoven's string quartets. He admired these as some of the greatest works ever written, although they are less popular than Beethoven's other works. The string quartets are intense, angular and complex. He played them for us as a musical model. He told us he wanted this kind of energy on *Tantra* because it was like him—intense and complex."

1989+

Throughout 1989, Rama and the band logged many hours in a music studio, creating, reviewing and producing the albums that contained Rama's energy between the notes. The albums released that year were *Atlantis Rising, Mystery School* (first rendition), *Retrograde Planet* (first rendition), *Samurai* (second rendition), and *Tantra*.

Over the next seven years, 16 more albums were released, both original work and remakes of earlier albums (which were so different than the original that they were, in effect, new work.) The styles ranged from hard rock to lyrical and poignant.

On the final night that he met with the students in March, 1998, Rama asked Lievano (Bodhi) to improvise some music, giving him no special instructions. Bodhi improvised all the evening's music on the spot. As the evening drew to an end, Rama said good night and goodbye to the people he loved. "Just play one more song and I will dance," Rama told Bodhi.

Rama danced, and when they left the stage, he said, "We're going to do a new album starting with the last song you just played. This last song will be the first song of the new album." He said the piece was like a meditation, thus giving the song its original working °title, "Meditation." "Himalayan Sunset" is this song today on Lievano's *Ecologie* album, played very much as it was for the first time, on that highly charged evening.

Any of the musical works released by Zazen from 1986 to 1997 can be used for meditation.

FURTHER INFORMATION

Rama Meditation Society
www.ramameditationsociety.org

The Frederick P. Lenz Foundation for American Buddhism
www.fredericklenzfoundation.org

Surfing the Himalayas: A Spiritual Adventure
by Frederick Lenz

Snowboarding to Nirvana: A Spiritual Journey
by Frederick Lenz

91138566R00177